No Votes for Women

No Votes for Women

*The New York State
Anti-Suffrage Movement*

SUSAN GOODIER

University of Illinois Press

URBANA, CHICAGO, AND SPRINGFIELD

Library of Congress Cataloging-in-Publication Data
Goodier, Susan.
No votes for women : the New York state
anti-suffrage movement / Susan Goodier.
p. cm. — (Women in American history)
Includes bibliographical references and index.
ISBN 978-0-252-03747-4 (alk. paper) —
ISBN 978-0-252-07898-9 (pbk. : alk. paper) —
ISBN 978-0-252-09467-5 (e-book)
1. Women—Suffrage—New York (State)—History.
2. Sex role—New York (State)—History.
3. New York (State)—Politics and government—1865–1950.
I. Title.
JK1911.N7G66   2012 3
324.6'2309747—dc23   2012028167

Contents

Acknowledgments

This project began several years ago at the University at Albany. Richard F. Hamm, Iris Berger, Amy Murrell Taylor, all of the University at Albany History Department, and Sally Roesch Wagner, Executive Director of the Matilda Joslyn Gage Center in Fayetteville, New York, offered encouragement and support as well as professional vigilance over my work. They all continued to support my work in one way or another during the process of revising the material as a book. Other readers who have influenced me and helped me to clarify my ideas include Kristi Andersen of the Maxwell School of Syracuse University, Elisabeth Israels Perry of St. Louis University, Nancy Campbell of Rensselaer Polytechnic Institute, and Crista DeLuzio of Southern Methodist University.

I am especially grateful to Richard Hamm of the University at Albany, who read and critiqued every single rewritten chapter, and to Nancy Unger of Santa Clara University, who also read every chapter at least once. I am still amazed at the generous spirits of these two people. My writing group, the Rochester area United States History working-papers draft group (RUSH) critiqued one of the chapters, and I have benefited greatly from the input of members, including Alison Parker, John Daly, Jon-Paul Dyson, Peter Eisenstadt, Jennifer Lloyd, Megan Obourn, Dorinda Outram, and Diane Palmer. I am also especially grateful to my readers at the University of Illinois Press, Judy Wellman and Melanie Gustafson, for their constructive criticism. Each reader was diligent over my work, asking probing questions, challenging me to think more deeply and to ask myself bigger questions. I am well aware of how deeply I am in their collective debt. None of these people are responsible for any of my errors or omissions, of course, but the book is far better for having had their attention.

People at several academic institutions have been remarkably supportive in any number of ways. During a teaching appointment at Cazenovia College I benefited from the support of Judy Azzoto, Diane Carpenter, Stephanie Leeds, Grazyna Kozaczka, and Maryrose Eannace. Tim Hickey of Utica College helped in the search for obscure resources. I am particularly indebted to the staff at Burke Library at Hamilton College in Clinton, New York. I have benefitted from years of assistance from reference librarians such as Anne Nassar, Kristin Strohmeyer, Lynn Mayo, and Glynis Asu, as well as staff members Philip Gisondi and Cynthia McKelvey. Toward the end of my revising period, I received scholar-in-residence status at Hamilton College, which was just the encouragement and support I needed.

I have had the pleasure of working with some very fine assistance and support at various archives and historical societies. At Vassar College, Dean M. Rogers of Special Collections was very helpful, as was Colleen Mallet, Associate Registrar, and Eileen Witte of the Alumnae and Alumni Department. Mary Huth of the Department of Rare Books and Special Collections at the University of Rochester assisted me on several occasions. Sarah Katherine Gordon at the Kroch Library of Cornell University went out of her way to be helpful to me during and following my several days of research there. On two research trips to the Library of Congress, I was ably assisted by several very helpful and enthusiastic people, including Abby Yochelson, Sheridan Harvey (who admitted she is descended from the anti-suffragist Henry Stimson), and Janice Ruth. Rosemary Fry Plakas, then involved in the project to digitize the Miller suffrage scrapbooks, sent me digitized images she thought I should see. Diana Carey and Sarah Hutcheon assisted me at the Schlesinger Library. Sharon Cooney at the New York State Historic Site at Lorenzo in Cazenovia was a researcher's dream. She let me know whenever she discovered yet another pile of anti-suffrage materials, let me read them before they were accessioned, and then made copies of all the pages I asked for. Sue Shutte at Ringwood State Park was extremely helpful in compiling materials on Sarah Amelia Hewitt. I would also like to thank Enid Mastrianni for generously sharing her extensive files and notes on Prestonia Mann Martin; Pat Blackler, the village historian at the Skaneateles Historical Society; the staffs of the New

York State Library and Manuscripts and Special Collections division, and W. Douglas McCombs of the Albany Museum of History and Art. Volunteers at the Clinton Historical Society, Coline Jenkins of the Elizabeth Cady Stanton Trust, the staffs of the Cazenovia Public Library and the Guilford Free Library, as well as Erin Crissman, then at Historic Cherry Hill, all accommodated my requests for information.

My research was supported with several travel and research grants over the years as I studied the topic of women's anti-suffrage activity. The Gilder Lehrman Institute of American History supported a week of research at the New York Public Library. I was thrilled to be the recipient of a four-week fellowship at the Jacob Rader Marcus Center of the American Jewish Archives at Hebrew Union College in Cincinnati, Ohio, to research the extensive papers of Annie Nathan Meyer. Gary Zola, executive director, encouraged me to apply for the fellowship, and Kevin Proffitt was especially helpful to me. I also appreciated the excellent support of research assistants Camille Servizzi, Elise Nienaber, and Vicki Lipski. The Lilly Library of Indiana University at Bloomington gave me a two-week Helm Fellowship research grant to support me as I worked through the Gilder Collection. The staff there is excellent and very accommodating. I also received a travel grant to visit the Lou Henry Hoover papers at the Hoover Presidential Library in Long Branch, Iowa, where I was assisted by a friendly and helpful staff. In the summer of 2009 I had the distinct pleasure of a six-week Margaret Storrs Grierson Scholar-in-Residence Fellowship at the Sophia Smith Collection at Smith College. Sherrill Redmon, Amy Hague, Susan Barker, Karen Kukil, and other members of the staff encouraged my work, suggested additional sources, and applauded my progress. I am extremely grateful to Laurie Matheson, Editor-in-Chief at the University of Illinois Press, for encouraging me and believing in my work right from the beginning.

Anyone working on such an intense and time-consuming project must rely on friends and family to help get her through. I am especially grateful to Kerry Daly, Lauren Kozakiewicz, and Laura Wittern-Keller. My family offered support in the myriad ways families always support one of their own, sometimes listening for hours as I talked about anti-suffragists and their movement. Chris Anderson, knowing absolutely nothing about anti-suffrage when we met, is now nearly an expert on the topic. Most impressive of all, never having read Virginia Woolf, he consistently makes sure I have the best room in the house in which to write.

Introduction

As the founders of the United States debated the role of government and its relationship to the people, as they composed their documents establishing a unique and enduring nation, they gave virtually no thought to the rights and position of women in the polity. The Constitution never directly mentioned women. Women's participation in citizenship was not even implied, and voting rights, left to individual states to determine, usually related to property ownership at a time when most property belonged to men.[1] The core ideas of democracy, heavily influenced by policymakers' understanding of English common law, kept married women from a legal right to own property, and, by extension, from a right to vote. Women could not and did not participate in the polity. When some women began agitating for the right to vote in the 1840s, most observers expressed revulsion, contempt, or disbelief.

As historian Paula Baker explains, most Americans associated political participation with a specific definition of masculinity. The attributes of character associated with manhood—courage, loyalty, industry, and independence—were those attributes described as most worthy of public reward. Participation in politics, especially the right to vote, therefore, was a powerful symbol of manhood and, in essence, helped to keep the spheres of women and men separate. Because politics meant voting and office holding, most men considered changing public policies to include women in the electorate to be emasculating or "nonpolitical."[2] As state legislators lifted property restrictions over the course of the nineteenth century, all men ostensibly shared the ability to exercise the franchise, despite the class and ethnic differences that separated them. Furthermore, according to Ellen Carol DuBois, because of a deep reverence for the vote, and its limitation by sex, women expected that if they ever possessed the vote, it would signify "a total transformation of their lives."[3] To leading woman suffragists, as those who would agitate for the vote were called, access to the ballot was not just a political right. It was the means by which women could change the world, counter the undesirable effects of industrialization, improve women's wages, and combat corruption and wrongdoing.[4] Yet, for women to make use of this extraordinarily powerful instrument was once inconceivable to most observers.

Because property restrictions no longer applied to voting rights as the nineteenth century drew to a close, race and gender became the defining factors for who was eligible for the franchise.[5] Suffrage demands and organizations provided those who opposed the vote with targets for their arguments. Calls for woman suffrage reflected an escalating national debate about the purpose of women's higher education, women's right to full citizenship, and the development of women's political awareness. Whether articulated by women or by men, reactions to calls for women's right to vote related to fears that altering deeply revered gender roles would irreparably disrupt society. Most nineteenth-century commentators saw strict differentiation between the roles of women and men as crucial to the proper functioning of the nation. The growth of industry in the United States intensified the apparent differences between the roles of women and men, encouraging deeper consideration of the spheres occupied by each gender.[6] Much of the impetus for promoting gender role separation stemmed from the "insistence on the separation of home and family from market and state" that dominated the thinking of the time.[7] Women, responsible for the oversight of private homes, served the nation-state as wives and mothers. Their attention to the needs of the family and the home was seen as critical; the home was the "bulwark against social disorder." Conservative men and women argued that the family structure, necessitating the "subordination of women," was critical to the preservation of social order.[8] Conservatives put the family and an ordered society before the needs of individual women.

This book demonstrates the resilience of the "separate spheres" ideology for a specific class of white New York women and men, making it useful as an analytical framework. Although today we interpret a whole-hearted commitment to domesticity as a weakening of women's power, during the nineteenth century it appeared to be the best alternative for women to do their duty for the state. Women's role was clearly defined and held in high regard, offered an "arena for self-development," and at the time was in their best interests, albeit within the "framework of male dominance."[9] Women were encouraged to understand their selflessness, even self-sacrifice, as the "female equivalent to self-fulfillment," as Kathryn Kish Sklar attests.[10] According to the separate spheres ideology, women had power as significant as that of men to influence the greater good of the nation-state.

Stephanie Coontz argues that the last decade of the nineteenth century represented the "apex of the doctrine of separate spheres—between morality and business, between laissez-faire justifications of capitalism and the cult of domesticity." The separate spheres doctrine was explicit in daily life as well as in ideology, and it would not be challenged easily.[11] Around the turn of the century, new concepts of women's place and role necessarily adapted to be more in line with Progressive Era changes. Women were morally responsible for protecting the private sphere and their families from the consequences of industrialization.[12] Women needed to protect men and their families from ravages arising from the "competition, conflicts, and insecurities of an expanding capitalist democracy."[13] A well-functioning society depended on women to perform their function in the separate sphere of the home.[14] Their role in the home defined women; increasingly, a role outside the home defined men. Most significantly, the male head of household held the responsibility for maintaining the relationship of the family to the government.[15] Clearly the ideas of what constituted "true womanhood" decreed that women were not political beings.[16] Accordingly, the proposal to enfranchise women, to legitimate their place in the polity as individuals rather than as part of a family unit, was a "direct attack upon the doctrine of separate spheres."[17]

From the end of the Civil War to the turn of the twentieth century, factors that produced innovations in industry, commerce, finance, and social services led to immense wealth for some and new jobs for working and middle-class people. While New York State was still torn by the class conflicts and immigration problems that had plagued it before the Civil War, the working-class strengthened their activist organizations, and the middle-class and elites expanded their reform efforts.[18] The political situation in the state was complicated by bossism and political machines, as well as by distinct differences in thinking between those who lived near or in New York City and those who lived in the predominantly rural areas of the rest of the state. New York women who opposed their enfranchisement became gradually more concerned about protecting what they saw as women's right not to be men, although until early in 1894 there was no organizational activity on their part. The advent of the New York State Constitutional Convention that year provided the impetus for anti-suffrage women to create what they thought would be temporary organizations to protest their enfranchisement and protect what they perceived as women's proper place in the polity.

Particularly in the years between 1890 and 1920, the rapid social changes related to industrialization and immigration challenged the basically conservative beliefs of white, middle class, "native-born" Americans.[19] One writer expressed a dominant attitude of those years, lamenting that civilization was "sick with the pollution of selfishness, of gold thirst, of ignorance, and of crime. It is groaning and raging in the throes of its disease, and nations hold their breath in fearful suspense of what the crisis will be."[20] It was a period when the intersection of traditional and modern ideas, combined with an idealistic "faith in the perfectibility of mankind, optimism and a sense of progress, and a belief in general moral standards" led to the development of a modern state.[21] It was a time of unparalleled change; according to Glenda Gilmore, the changes wrought by advances in industry and technology, compounded by the mass movement of people into urban areas for jobs "threatened to overthrow tradition everywhere."[22] Allowing women to vote seemed to be an idea more drastic than the other changes that had been taking place in areas of women's expanding privileges, such as improved educational opportunities and the greater range of professions employing women. Many anti-suffragists also benefited from increased education and professionalism for women, often citing success in these areas as evidence of women's progress. Unlike suffragists, antis did not advocate progress for women as individuals; for conservative anti-suffragists, education meant women would be better wives and mothers.

One anti-suffragist wrote that "the Anti-Suffragist stands in the very front rank of progress for she is a *preventive philanthropist.*" Antis saw suffragists as "retarding the truest progress" exemplified by the "supremacy of law, order and morality."[23] Woman suffrage challenged more than arguments about power and democracy; it challenged ideas about women and their proper place in society. Theories relating to social Darwinism and scientific motherhood influenced conventions about the accepted roles of women in the polity; sexual difference was considered to be the "driving force of progressive evolution."[24] These theories ultimately created a "crisis" in determining appropriate gender roles, for more women and men became aware of the "inherent contradictions and inevitable exceptions" to ideal womanhood. The imaginary boundary between the public, male sphere and the private, female sphere as it had existed in the nineteenth century was continually being breached.[25]

Members of newly formed anti-suffrage organizations actively resisted changes and sought order as they adhered to their conservative outlook on the world.[26] Conservatives believed that the woman suffrage movement reflected dangers to society in general. Business and politics represented a world fraught with trouble. To counter this, home—the traditional sphere of women—should be a refuge, a place safe from the necessary evils of a progressive, outside world. That progress would be useless without the "ennobled" and "conservative influence of the home." Antis considered the home to be the "bulwark against social disorder," critically important for the stability of the nation.[27] Although conservative women have been an important feature of the American political landscape since the nineteenth century, they are generally overlooked in historical studies.

Organized anti-suffrage women—the conservative women of their time—sought to preserve what they perceived as the special and unique place of women in the polity. Rather than seeing this preservation as limiting women, they believed they were encouraging women to use the best of their gender's inherent talents. They also argued that political enfranchisement, and the partisan membership that necessarily followed, would stifle women's advancement. In their view the only way society could advance was for women to maintain their own sphere of influence and remain distinctly different from men. Therefore, anti-suffragists contended that they were fighting to preserve women's rights by establishing organizations to resist their political enfranchisement.

As her role had expanded, even the "true woman" of the nineteenth century was encouraged to join organizations as an extension of her domestic duties and part of her responsibilities to the state. Baker refers to this kind of women's activism as "municipal housekeeping," reflecting the anxiety Progressive Era middle-class women felt about being criticized for their work in public affairs.[28] As historian Estelle Freedman shows, women's volunteer and reform organizations benefited society yet simultaneously offered women "a degree of public authority."[29] Anti-suffragists subscribed to the belief that women's power base, the private home, was equivalent to the masculine power base in the public realm. Anti-suffragists believed that progress was dependent on a clear separation of women's work from men's work. They believed that women, participating in reform and philanthropy as a natural extension of their domesticity, already had all the power they needed, particularly in areas thought to be of special interest to women. Recognizing that there were many people who suffered with problems that women's special talents could alleviate, women who opposed the vote argued that women would lose their exceptional and altruistic power to solve those problems and reform the polity if the vote circumscribed their talents. Anti-suffragists had no disagreement with establishing reform organizations as an extension of women's influence and power and joined them at rates on a par with suffragists.

Anti-suffragists additionally established their own organizations in response to the suffrage organizations' increasingly insistent calls for women's enfranchisement. Antis obviously feared the spread of suffragist ideas, but, more than that, they feared the loss of women's power to influence the nation-state by using their uniquely feminine techniques. For suffragists, obtaining the vote meant having authentic power to influence the state. Most anti-suffragist women argued that obtaining the vote would reduce women to simply holding political power on the same level as men. To anti-suffragist leaders, such equality invalidated the power to reform the nation-state that women derived from their special sphere.[30]

The rationale suffragists used to argue for the right to vote throughout the seventy-two-year campaign developed and changed partly because of the success of the arguments that anti-suffragists presented. Anti-suffragists argued that women had other opportunities to wield power and influence than through enfranchisement. Therefore a study of anti-suffragism expands our understanding of women's political activism and behavior of the past, and it heightens our awareness of the radicalism of the woman suffrage movement.[31] We need to accept the sincerity of the female antis who developed organizations to oppose suffragists, not condemn them for being on the "wrong" side of a movement that ultimately succeeded. The majority of women who were leaders in the anti-suffrage movement were earnest, intelligent, often educated and professional women who sincerely believed that women, and the nation-state, would suffer when women achieved political equality with men. They held onto that belief even as they expressed a growing anti-socialism and patriotic rhetoric during the era of the First World War.

This study of New York State anti-suffrage organizations facilitates an understanding of the conservatism prevalent in the wealthy class of women from which its membership was drawn, heightening our awareness of the courage of the suffragists—women who faced adversity and public censure to agitate for women's rights. In order to organize effectively, groups have to constitute themselves as capable of collective action. Susan Marshall, for one, clearly shows that anti-suffragists' "access to money, leisure, and extensive social networks facilitated the growth of the countermovement to suffrage."[32] Anti-suffragists sought to preserve what they perceived as traditional family and political values, values they were convinced suffragists wanted to destroy. The cross-fertilization and counter appropriation of the other side's arguments was a critical component of both the suffrage and anti-suffrage movements. By recognizing the political activism of anti-suffragists, this study also adds to the increasing historiography of conservative women's politics.[33] The anti-suffrage movement, with its political activism, represents an important stage in conceptualizing and consolidating the appropriate role of women in a democracy.

The primary goal of this study is to understand the movement for women's rights from the point of view of the women who opposed their enfranchisement in New York State. Recovering a clearer understanding of attitudes regarding women's power, as well as the meaning of the vote to women of the time, more accurately illuminates any study of women's rights movements of the nineteenth and twentieth centuries. Whether for or against women's suffrage, each group wholeheartedly believed in some form of women's rights. I analyze activities at the local and state levels, and those that connected New York State to the national perspective, in an effort to clarify the importance of anti-suffragism for the suffrage movement, as well as for the movement for women's rights. I do not treat anti-suffragism in isolation, however, and address the convergence in New York State between the two movements.

What is generally understood about the anti-suffrage movement is overshadowed by two basic misconceptions. The first is that the rhetoric of men who opposed women's suffrage is synonymous with the rhetoric of all anti-suffrage, a misconception that has often silenced the women who opposed enfranchisement. Men articulated only some of the anti-suffrage arguments, and they were far less involved than women in public anti-suffrage activity. In the New York State anti-suffrage movement, especially between 1895 and 1914, anti-suffrage leaders considered men to be antagonistic or at least unhelpful to women's anti-suffrage activism. While anti-suffragists fully supported the patriarchy and all it stood for, they insisted that their movement was independent of the influence of men. The second misconception is that the period of the most virulent organized anti-suffragism—after New York voters enfranchised women and until the mid-1920s—defines the entire anti-suffrage movement. Prewar anti-suffragism was very different from the anti-suffragism following the granting of woman suffrage in New York. In actuality, the type of woman who joined the anti-suffrage movement, while remaining conservative and acquiescent to the patriarchal system, changed during the course of the movement's existence.

A few feminist studies of suffrage denigrate and underestimate anti-suffragists. Perhaps some of this attitude derives from the fact that most historians of suffrage have relied almost exclusively on the writing of suffragists when they discuss anti-suffragists and their organizations. Anti-suffragists did not write books about their experiences in the movement, so they took no opportunity to justify their beliefs or actions. Suffrage leader Carrie Chapman Catt, in *Woman Suffrage and Politics: The Inner Story of the Suffrage Movement,* contended that the speeches of the anti-suffragists "indicated at times an anxious disturbance of mind lest the privileges they enjoyed might be lost in the rights to be gained." Catt wrote that the manager of New York State anti-suffrage activities was a "paid outsider" and that many of the women officers were workers in name only. She also argued that many women converted to suffragism after attending the parlor meetings of the antis.[34] While there is some truth in what Catt wrote, her comments suggest that suffragist leaders developed the habit of belittling socially prominent anti-suffragists to make them less threatening to timid or reluctant suffragists. The attitudes of Catt and others like her have been echoed in much of the literature on the suffrage movement written ever since.

The women of New York State stood at the forefront of the critical discussions surrounding voting rights that took place in the years between the end of the Civil War and the beginning of the New Deal era. New York was the logical place for dynamic political activity, for it was an economic, political, and cultural leader during the period.[35] Geographically a large state, New York ranges in diversity from New York City, its huge metropolitan center, to several industrialized upstate cities, to sprawling rural farmlands, to the environmentally protected Adirondack Park. By 1900 the state had a population of 7,268,012 people, many of whom were immigrants.[36] The heavily populated state had more representatives in Congress (thirty-four) and more electoral votes (thirty-six) than any other state in the union, making it critical to electoral politics. In terms of culture and ideas, New York City was (and remains) the publishing capital of the nation and the source for a number of leading periodicals and opinion journals. Elsewhere, the tremendously popular and influential Chautauqua lecture circuit disseminated ideas throughout upstate and rural areas.[37] From the 1890s New York City reformers led campaigns for social and economic justice that sparked similar campaigns in other regions of the nation.

Calls for women's right to vote sounded in the Jefferson County legislature and at Wesleyan Chapel in Seneca Falls in the 1840s, and by 1869 the state hosted a strong and effective state suffrage organization. Suffrage groups, often called political equality clubs in the rural areas, developed in towns and villages all over the state, many well before the 1890s. Many of the most dynamic and influential suffrage leaders, including Elizabeth Cady Stanton, Matilda Joslyn Gage, Susan B. Anthony, Lillie Devereux Blake, and Mariana Chapman lived in the state and focused much of their energy there. Suffragists considered New York the "stronghold of opposition" and the state most important to win in the eastern United States.[38] In the chapter she contributed to *Victory: How Women Won It*, Gertrude Foster Brown declared that the state was "at once the hope and the despair of the suffragists."[39]

For much of the time woman suffrage was in contention, Tammany Hall Democrats and upstate Republicans, although at odds with each other on virtually every political issue, were united in their opposition to woman suffrage. Those who opposed woman suffrage included men in the liquor business, politicians, textile interests, party machines, and bureaucrats at every governmental level.[40] While differences in their reasons for opposition existed, each group, wrongly assuming that all women agreed on major political issues, feared that women's power would increase with the vote. A women's bloc would assuredly curtail the oppositional groups' profits or other interests. The women who organized to oppose woman suffrage were separate and distinct from these male-dominated groups, and as anti-suffrage historian Thomas Jablonsky contends, did not need men to tell them what to do to carry on political activities, nor were they the "puppets" of other interests.[41]

The female leadership of the New York State anti-suffrage movement constituted the most dynamic and influential group of all the organized anti-suffragists in the country. While there were women all over the United States who worked against women's voting rights, the anti-suffrage leaders in New York State were more politicized than the organized anti-suffrage women of other states. It took until 1895 to launch, but New York female anti-suffragists established a state organization with branches in cities and towns all over the state. By 1911 they had established and headquartered the National Association Opposed to Woman Suffrage. All of the national anti-suffrage leaders hailed from New York State, and New York anti-suffrage speakers, like suffrage speakers, traveled all over the country to influence women and men on the issue of women voting. Representatives of the anti-suffrage organizations attended state and federal legislative meetings. New York antis wrote many of the influential articles and books that disseminated their arguments across the nation. The New York State campaign, with its suffrage and anti-suffrage confrontations, was critical to winning the campaign for the federal amendment.

An important reason for New York anti-suffragists' assertiveness lay in their close relationships to reform efforts throughout the period. Already deeply committed to philanthropy and often members of the very same organizations to which suffragists belonged, New York's antis emulated the suffragists more than anti-suffragists in any other state. Michael McGerr discusses the "period of stunning political experimentation" when women focused on education and advertising and on drawing politics off the public streets and into private homes.[42] New York City anti-suffragists in particular, but other urban anti-suffragists as well, were influenced by and appropriated for their own use the exciting mass-marketing techniques first employed by the suffragists to encourage support. They lobbied legislators at the state and national levels to support their views, and they studied politics in an effort to counter suffrage contentions. Antis in other states deliberately strove to be different from the suffragists; as Susan Marshall observes, Massachusetts anti-suffragists were very reluctant to use suffragist techniques to fight enfranchisement.[43] According to Elna Green, members of southern anti-suffrage organizations in Virginia and Maryland were proud of avoiding public and newspaper debates.[44] In contrast, New York State antis looked at the techniques suffragists used and did their best to emulate them for their own gain.

While the focus of this study is on New York State anti-suffragism, a state-based movement that has only been peripheral in earlier studies, the influence of New York anti-suffrage leadership was national in scope, for they confidently believed they represented the majority of the nation's population.[45] Many of the national anti-suffrage leaders came from the state, and all the national-level presidents did so. New York anti-suffragists represented all those who accepted the social, cultural, religious, and legal mandates that claimed that women were bound to rights, privileges, and responsibilities different from those of men. Like suffragists, they argued that women were just as important to the nation-state as men, and just as necessary to its efficient functioning.

The women of the anti-suffrage movement responded in various ways to the activities of the suffrage movement throughout its existence, adjusting their behavior as the need for attention increased. Members of the New York organization traveled to assist with anti-suffrage campaigns around the country, spreading their influence widely. An analysis of New York State leadership reveals the process of women's politicization as women educated themselves about their political responsibilities for the purposes of opposing woman suffrage. The New York State anti-suffragist leadership promoted a strict division of responsibilities along gender lines as the solution to many problems facing the nation-state. Some of those who thought seriously about the meaning of women's rights continued to believe that the nation-state functioned far more effectively if each sex maintained separate responsibilities.

Anti-suffragists and suffragists were involved in a fascinating battle of wits. They invited each other to debate, attended—even crashed—each other's meetings, and vied for the public's attention at virtually every kind of social function. Furthermore, while members of anti-suffrage organizations believed that women reigned in the private realm, they found it necessary to enter the public domain to argue against enfranchisement for women. To do so, anti-suffragists frequently engaged in political behavior, whether or not they recognized it as such. Simultaneously, anti-suffragists eagerly acknowledged the women who remained in the private realm. In fact, anti-suffragists hailed the very inactivity and silence of women as indicative of their opposition to suffrage.[46]

Women's anti-suffrage organizations represented the most challenging group for suffragists to convince of their arguments. Suffragists consciously strove to find arguments to refute anti-suffragists' objections.[47] To a great degree, anti-suffrage opposition served to hone suffrage arguments, providing the impetus for increasingly persuasive suffrage platforms. For example, suffragists returned to the celebration and preservation of the separate spheres ideology consistently used by anti-suffragists for their own arguments. Indeed, suffragists portrayed women's voting as a panacea; by enfranchising the pure and moral woman, the nation's political ills would be solved. From this point of view female anti-suffragists ironically provided much of the impetus for the ultimate success of the woman suffrage movement. Although initially anti-suffragists organized to protect their special sphere of influence, drawing on the same mass-media techniques suffragists utilized so well to influence their supporters, many anti-suffragists gradually came to accept various ideas the suffragists promoted. In the process of campaigning against woman suffrage, most anti-suffragists came to see, perhaps reluctantly, or possibly with some relief, the advantages of their enfranchisement. As we will discover, understanding the attitudes of the opposing movement, as well as the rather reluctant reciprocity between the two groups, will therefore serve to further illuminate the suffrage movement itself.

Chapter 1 explores the earliest attempts by conservative women to organize anti-suffrage activity. It was not until Susan B. Anthony and other suffragists conducted state tours in preparation for the New York State Constitutional Convention that anti-suffragists surprised suffragists by establishing temporary organizations to prevent the removal of the word "male" from the state constitution, and presented their views in opposition to enfranchisement and the protection of their existing rights. Their rhetoric developed out of the tradition of male anti-suffrage rhetoric, but the women articulated their own views of opposition to enfranchisement. Women who established these short-lived organizations laid the foundation for the women who established organizations in the next period of anti-suffrage.

Chapter 2 illustrates the nascent attempts of anti-suffragists to prevent their enfranchisement. The most prominent and effective anti-suffrage organizations that developed in New York State between 1895 and 1911 deliberately excluded men. Certainly, anti-suffragists were married to or related to some of the most politically powerful men in state and national government. However, a significant portion of college-educated, professional, and self-supporting women opposed suffrage. Once the antis established their organizations, they became a force powerful enough to help prolong the battle for woman suffrage in the state. The New York State organization provided speakers for lectures at clubs and social events in and outside the state, spreading their influence broadly. By the end of the period, New York antis had established a national organization.

Activities of the anti-suffrage movement ebbed and flowed with those of the suffrage movement, suggesting the responsive nature of both movements. This process forms the subject of chapter 3. The leadership of Alice Hill Chittenden, elected in the fall of 1912 to serve as president of the New York State Association Opposed to Woman Suffrage, accounts for the increased politicization of the anti-suffrage movement. Anti-suffragists won this battle, apparent in the results of the November 1915 referendum. However, it is also apparent by 1915 that anti-suffrage leaders faced serious challenges to their campaign to prevent enfranchisement, leading to a far different campaign for the 1917 referendum.

The second campaign for woman suffrage in New York State was entirely different from the first and is the subject of chapter 4. Following the advent of the Great War, Alice Hill Chittenden, although continuing to serve as president of the state anti-suffrage association, focused her reform energy on war preparedness and the American Red Cross more than on suffrage. Historians have long posited that women won the right to vote as a reward for their war efforts. However, anti-suffragists, individually and as a group, committed their resources earlier and far more fully to the war effort than did suffragists. The Great War so distracted the anti-suffragists that they essentially dropped out of the battle, allowing the suffragists to win sooner than they otherwise would have. This subtle but important detail has been overshadowed by Tammany's famous reversal on the question in 1917. Once women won suffrage in New York State, the federal amendment would soon enfranchise all women in the United States.

After women in New York State won enfranchisement, there was a noteworthy split in the anti-suffrage movement. Chapter 5 tells of the expected end of the anti-suffrage movement, highlighting much of the public and residual animosity toward women's enfranchisement. The women antis restructured the New York State Association Opposed to Woman Suffrage as the Women Voters' Anti-Suffrage Party and worked against a federal amendment. The Woman Patriot Publishing Company absorbed the National Association Opposed to Woman Suffrage. Although New York State anti-suffragists had always been influential in national level work, in 1917, with a change in leadership, they moved the national headquarters to Washington, D.C., and continued their efforts to prevent the passage of the federal amendment. Men increasingly dominated the movement, and the anti-suffrage tone became desperate-sounding and even venomous. The national movement operated in a far different mode from the previous women's anti-suffrage movement under its second president, Alice Hay Wadsworth, and her successor, Mary G. Kilbreth. The anti-suffrage movement fades in the late 1920s, and the *Woman Patriot* ceased publication in 1932.

While chapter 5 tells the expected story of anti-suffrage, chapter 6 offers an alternative—but far more logical—end to the story of anti-suffrage. In the process of preventing their enfranchisement, many former anti-suffrage women came to see the value of political involvement and power. This represents the experience of most New York anti-suffrage leaders and their supporters after enfranchisement. Quite a few former anti-suffragists, including, in particular, Alice Hill Chittenden, appeared to welcome the new political role for women and became involved in party politics with the specific goal of educating women to make good use of the franchise. This chapter tells of the politicization of former anti-suffragists and the ways they chose to play their role as enfranchised members of the polity. Many of these women became active members of the Republican Party, carrying on their political activity in much the same way as they had for anti-suffragism, this time voting and loyal to a political party.

New York State was the site of exciting anti-suffrage activity during the movement for woman suffrage. Anti-suffrage women represented a significant portion of the population that feared that the tremendous changes of the Progressive Era would reduce or eliminate women's political and social power. But they also represent a growing sophistication and understanding of expanded possibilities for women as politicized citizens of the United States. The New York State anti-suffrage women themselves, the groups they organized, and their political behavior warrant a more specific focus than has previously been given them. Their victories and defeats tell us much about how woman suffrage came to be won and further illuminate the politicization process for women during the Progressive Era. Rather than condemning those women for accepting or even trying to preserve the status quo, this study is an attempt to understand them, to acknowledge the views of the women who represented them, to value their position on suffrage, and to acknowledge their political activism. In the process we better understand an important aspect of the quest for women's equality.

1. Anti-Suffragists at the 1894 New York State Constitutional Convention

The *New York World* called it an "insurrection." In anticipation of the New York constitutional convention to be held in the summer of 1894, women all over the state responded to the call for the enfranchisement of women. For months, Susan B. Anthony, Elizabeth Cady Stanton, Carrie Chapman Catt, Dr. Mary Walker, Anna Howard Shaw, Lillie Devereux Blake, Mariana W. Chapman, Harriet May Mills, and other prominent state and national suffrage leaders toured the state, urging support for their cause in parlors and public places. During an address given in Albany, someone asked Anthony if the women of New York actually desired the vote. She answered rather equivocally, "They do not oppose it." It was the truth as far as she knew. Certainly, no organization of women existed in the state to counter suffragist claims. Ida Husted Harper, Anthony's friend and biographer as well as one of the editors of the *History of Woman Suffrage*, admitted that suffragists had long struggled with the complete indifference of many of the women they were working so hard to enfranchise.[1]

To suffragists' great surprise, then, committees of women suddenly "aroused all along the line" to publicly resist their enfranchisement.[2] Until this time, it had been mostly men who had openly articulated opposition to woman suffrage, usually relying on the Bible for supportive evidence. As the convention date neared, New York State women opposed to enfranchisement realized that by remaining silent, they were in effect supporting woman suffrage. If they did not resist, it seemed that there was a real chance that the legislature of New

York would "impose" the ballot upon them. To many of the women who had been silent up to that point, it was time to formally express their opposition.[3] Like-minded women organized committees in Brooklyn, New York City, Albany, Utica, and elsewhere in the state to prevent members of the convention from changing the wording of the state constitution. Susan B. Anthony, like many other female suffragists, found it inconceivable that so many women were resistant to their enfranchisement, and she blamed husbands for influencing their wives to oppose the vote.[4] Whether motivated by pressure from family members or for other reasons, the organized female anti-suffragists of New York would become the most challenging of the opponents the suffragists faced in their long campaign.

The convention had drawn attention from as early as 1887, when voters approved the need to revise the state constitution. Democrats prevented the election of delegates until 1893 in the hopes that their party would be in the majority, but of the 168 total delegates, only sixty-five were Democrats.[5] At issue was the elimination of the word "male" from Article II, Section I of the state constitution. Governors David Hill in 1887 and Roswell Flower in 1892 agreed that women could be represented at the convention. Not surprisingly, however, no women were nominated. No one seriously considered nominating Susan B. Anthony, well known to the Republicans in her district, although she was widely respected for her familiarity with constitutional law. Ida Husted Harper denounced the spoils-dominated political culture, pointing out that the ten dollars the delegates drew each day for five months made the positions too precious to give to anyone who was outside of the electorate. In spite of their exclusion from official delegation, suffragists determined to educate the public, distribute petitions, and promote a strong "public sentiment" for woman suffrage before the convention.[6]

Although woman suffrage did not see much progress during the last decade of the nineteenth century, it was not a period of "doldrums," as some historians have called it. The 1894 convention provided an opportunity for a reinvigorated, albeit more conservative, group of suffragists to work together for the cause. The two main suffrage organizations, the National Woman Suffrage Association and the American Woman Suffrage Association, had rejoined forces in February 1890 as the National American Woman Suffrage Association. Fears of increased immigration caused a rethinking of the earlier natural rights arguments of woman suffrage, and suffragists "began to put less emphasis on the common humanity of men and women."[7] This joining resulted in a focus on state campaigns rather than on the federal campaigns the National Woman Suffrage Association had long advocated.[8] A shift occurred, too, in the arguments women used to advocate for the vote, a point first noted by scholar Aileen Kraditor. Suffragists contended that the vote would "enlarge women's interests and intellect" as they participated in running government. They would become better mothers who could teach their children about the experience of citizenship, and they would be better wives as they became their husbands' equals. The arguments that dominated to the end of the suffrage movement encompassed the idea that women's political equality would be as good for the government as it would be for women.[9] The 1890s saw a gathering of momentum and energy in preparation for the intensity of the battle after 1900.[10]

In the half-century of woman suffrage agitation, much of it taking place in the Empire State, advocates had faced either an apathetic (on the part of women) or a hostile (on the part of men) reception. Male commentators initially articulated the primary arguments, emerging from patriarchal and Christian ideologies, against women's enfranchisement. Apparently content to let men to speak for them, few anti-suffragist women published their views or expressed them publicly. By the late 1860s and early 1870s, when some women began to present their own anti-suffrage arguments in print, they often reflected arguments of male writers. Key ideas included a strict gender-based division of duties to the nation-state, a need for increased education for women, and the articulation of dutifulness to the patriarchal family and the mandates of institutionalized Christianity. Women who deviated from these norms by showing interest or participating in politics or by resisting domestic responsibilities were "manly" or "unsexed." One newspaper described the 1853 national woman suffrage convention, held in New York, as "a gathering of unsexed women, unsexed in mind, all of them publicly propounding the doctrine that they be allowed to step out of their appropriate sphere to the neglect of those duties which both human and divine law have assigned them."[11] Ignoring the directives of true womanhood evoked hostility in the press and probably dissuaded some potential supporters of woman suffrage from joining the movement. Public attention to woman suffrage nevertheless increased, compelling some women to respond. Nineteenth-century women's arguments opposed to woman suffrage reached their fullest articulation in the writings of Catharine Esther Beecher and Susan Fenimore Cooper. Although neither woman ever married, thereby failing to live out the creed that women best served society as wives and mothers, both adamantly supported the ideology of separate spheres.

In 1870, Susan Fenimore Cooper, daughter and amanuensis of author James Fenimore Cooper, wrote "A Letter to the Christian Women of America" for *Harper's New Monthly Magazine*. She was widely acknowledged as a writer and naturalist, having published the popular *Rural Hours*, a book about the seasons in upstate New York, in 1868. According to Cooper, a devout Episcopalian, a woman was historically and logically subordinate to a man for three main reasons. First, she was his physical inferior, making her "entirely in his power, quite incapable of self-defense, trusting to his generosity for protection." Second, "though in a very much less degree," woman was "inferior to man in intellect," although Cooper acknowledged that intellectual inferiority probably resulted from physical inferiority. Finally, the directives of Christianity made it very clear that woman necessarily held a subordinate position relative to man. No woman could call herself a Christian if she denied her subordinate role. Her role, as decreed by God, was meant to be distinctly different from that of man.[12]

Society, in Cooper's view, was soundest where "each sex conscientiously discharges its own duties, without intruding on those of the other," echoing a view similar to male anti-suffrage writers of the time and advocates of the doctrine of separate spheres. She methodically refuted every argument presented by what she termed the "emancipation movement of women." While Cooper acknowledged that there were areas of law where women suffered abuses, she believed that those laws could be changed without resorting to suffrage for women. As for women's right to the ballot, she was adamant that it was not "an absolutely inalienable right universal in its application."[13] Enfranchising women would distract them from their more important duties at home, which would be injurious to themselves, their families, and the nation-state.

Cooper believed most women were not politically astute enough to make informed and beneficent decisions. As far as Cooper was concerned, enfranchising women would lead to the "perilous convulsions of a revolution more truly formidable than any yet attempted on earth." Gender roles must remain distinctly different for the nation to survive intact, for the home was equal in importance to the nation-state. Women should keep "aloof from all public personal action in the political field." No legislation could improve the moral civilization of the country nor eliminate the evils society faced; that was women's special and worthwhile work.[14]

Anti-suffragists and conservatives agreed that expanded education was far more important for women than enfranchisement. Catharine Esther Beecher, daughter of Lyman Beecher, the preacher and revivalist, feared that woman suffrage heralded an imminent national crisis challenging the "most sacred interests of woman and of the family state." Higher education for women, as articulated by Beecher, was an extension of women's domestic role and would allow a woman an independent living. To help meet her goals, in 1852 she founded the American Woman's Educational Association.[15] It sought, according to its constitution, to establish permanent, endowed educational institutions in order to provide women a "liberal education, honorable position, and remunerative employment *in their appropriate profession*." The "distinctive profession" of women related to caring for and educating children and the "conservation of the family state."[16] Beecher's particular goal was economic independence for women.

In 1869 Beecher argued that any "wrongs" involving women would be solved by promoting and supporting education for women on a par with men, fully negating any need for the ballot.[17] According to Beecher's biographer, Kathryn Kish Sklar, the impetus for Beecher's life task stemmed from the need to contradict any possible influence by Angelina and Sarah Grimké, the Quaker abolitionists and women's rights activists, on women's collective consciousness. Beecher and the Grimkés were in agreement that women were important to the "forces shaping American life," but they vehemently disagreed about the ways "female influence should be exerted."[18] Beecher accepted the idea that woman's sphere should be expanded, but only in ways compatible with the separate spheres ideology. To disseminate her views further, she delivered addresses in New York City, Hartford, and Boston to discuss women's position in society and woman suffrage.

In December 1870, in what may have been the first public debate between women on the topic, Beecher took the podium at the Boston Music Hall to argue against woman suffrage. Mary Livermore responded with arguments in support of votes for women. Livermore had not supported rights, public speaking, or activism for women until her transformative experience working with the Sanitary Commission during the Civil War. Extremely successful at fundraising and charitable benevolence, she had struggled against men who subverted her contributions. It ultimately convinced her of the need for women's rights.[19] Beecher asserted that no emergency existed that required the whole sex to take on the responsibilities of civil government demanded by the few women who wanted suffrage. An intelligent woman would refuse to be "dragged from her appropriate sphere to bear the burdens of the state."[20] The ballot was, at best, an indirect method for solving problems. She pointed out that under New York State law women had more advantages than men had. A woman had unlimited and independent control of her property but regardless of how rich a wife was, the husband had to support her and the children. It had also become easier for a woman than for a man to obtain a divorce.[21] She contended that further professionalization of women's work would only add to their advantages.

For Beecher, economic independence and equality of opportunity in education for the professions, not political equality, were vital needs for women. The nation-state needed women's education and training far more than it needed the votes of unwilling women. Professional education and training, through the formal schooling advocated by Beecher, should result in an extension of women's rights. She, like Cooper and a number of male writers, argued that the "doctrine of woman's subjection" posited by John Stuart Mill and his followers was both illogical and anti-Christian. She saw women's enfranchisement as an act of oppression; conscientious women would have to take on additional duties if the state granted them suffrage. Passionately and painstakingly arguing against suffrage in public forums and in several books, Beecher represented many of the professional, educated women who opposed their own enfranchisement into the twentieth century. She also predicted that if the woman suffrage party came closer to achieving its aim, anti-suffragists, with the support of "both the pulpit and the press" would create their own organizations.[22]

One short-lived anti-suffrage organization of prominent women had been founded following the 1869 introduction of an amendment to enfranchise women.[23] Under the leadership of Madeleine Vinton Dahlgren, widow of the Civil War admiral, the Anti-Sixteenth Amendment Society prepared a petition to send to Congress. The society included Mrs. William Tecumseh Sherman, wife of the Civil War general, Catharine Beecher, and Almira Lincoln Phelps, the sister of Emma Willard, founder of the female seminary in Troy, New York.[24] To encourage broad support for their views, they reprinted the petition in *Godey's Lady's Book and Magazine*.[25] Although the popular periodical generally excluded politics from its pages, the editor encouraged readers to copy the petition and collect signatures. At least five thousand signatures supported the petition by the time the society presented it to Congress in February 1871.[26]

"The Protest," as the women titled their petition, claimed that "a higher sphere, apart from public life" demanded the "full measure of duties and responsibilities" of women and declared their unwillingness to "bear other and heavier burdens." It further argued that woman suffrage would harm children by increasing the potential for "discord" in marriages and families, increasing the "already alarming prevalence" of divorce in the country.[27] They believed that "no general law, affecting the condition of all women, should be framed to meet exceptional discontent." Women all over the country signed the petitions.[28] In response, New Yorker Matilda Joslyn Gage, chair of the committee on arrangements for the National Woman Suffrage Association, invited Dahlgren and other anti-suffragists to attend the association's convention in 1872. According to the *Syracuse Journal*, Dahlgren declined the invitation by writing "that by even asking them to debate, Gage had entirely ignored the principle which they sought to defend: 'the preservation of female modesty.'"[29] Dahlgren nevertheless remained ready to confront the suffrage issue if it made it to the floor of Congress.

Not until January of 1878 did Dahlgren have a chance to present her views to a committee of Congress. Early that month, the Committee on Privileges and Elections heard arguments on both sides for the proposed sixteenth amendment. Suffragists, including Elizabeth Cady Stanton, Matilda Joslyn Gage, and ten other National Woman Suffrage Association members all spoke. Dahlgren, on "behalf of silent women"—those reluctant to present their views in public—kept her "female modesty" intact and did not herself appear. Instead, she submitted to the committee a written statement, the "Protest against Woman Suffrage." Invoking the so-called immutable laws of Christianity, she argued that women already had distinct duties and that enfranchisement would endanger women's special privileges. Women, in her view, were already well represented by the heads of their families. Although Dahlgren herself no longer had any representative male family members, she believed it was her patriotic duty to trust to the intelligence of the masculine electorate as the "greatest good for the greatest number." No record exists of how Congressmen responded to her plea not to open "a Pandora's Box by way of experiment" with universal suffrage, but the discussion of a woman suffrage amendment did not make it to the debate floor that year.[30]

Nascent efforts on the part of women who opposed woman suffrage to publicly present their views did not immediately lead to the development of viable political organizations, although, like many nineteenth-century women, they belonged to benevolent and church-related clubs and organizations. Membership in these reform organizations had long been touted as a logical extension of women's role as guardians of morality.[31] In fact, many of the women who would come out as anti-suffragists had a long history of involvement in public reform activities, particularly those most compatible with the ideology of true womanhood and separate spheres. Kate Gannett Wells, a wealthy Bostonian who opposed woman suffrage, wrote in 1880 that organizations served as the ideal way for women who were seeking "concerted action" to work together without the "cooperation of men."[32] Specific areas of proper women's work—domestic, educational, charitable, and religious and moral—did not include politics. Their organizational activity was touted as the ideal way for the "true woman" to achieve political or social change; the more closely their reform work resembled the work women did in the home, the more readily women and society accepted it.[33] The success of women's clubs in reform efforts provided plenty of evidence for the view that women could solve societal problems without political enfranchisement. To anti-suffragists, the woman suffrage movement was the "antithesis of the glorification of separate spheres," and implied that there was nothing particularly special about either gender. Not only would woman's enfranchisement weaken women's distinctive reforming power, it endangered the clear division between male political rituals and female charitable work.[34]

When pressed by the progress of suffrage preparations for the constitutional convention, "true" women, armed with a legacy of membership in women's benevolent societies and clubs, responded by creating oppositional committees. These small groups of anti-suffrage women, or remonstrants, as they were often called at first, gathered in parlor meetings around the state. It was "purely a local and spontaneous movement . . . expressing the convictions of a large body of women who have hitherto kept silent," claimed the announcement of the new movement in the *Outlook*. Anti-suffragists had no intention of entering into a "political struggle for their rights," although they expressed awareness that they might be forced to do so.[35] While many of the women who participated had husbands who probably did influence their public behavior, these early groups presented themselves as independent of male anti-suffrage influence.[36] Compatible with each other and with the men who supported them, at this stage the anti-suffragists seemed confident of broad support and quick success. The committees composed of the most active anti-suffrage women in the state came from New York City and Brooklyn. On April 18 and again on April 21, 1894, twenty-one women meeting at the Willow Street home of Mrs.

William A. Putnam in Brooklyn signed the original "Preamble and Protest," which reiterated the ideological arguments of Susan Fenimore Cooper and Catharine Beecher.[37]

The women who gathered at Putnam's lovely Greek revival townhouse had long known each other socially and through their club and reform activities. Virtually all of the women who attended these first meetings, and who dominated the women's anti-suffrage movement throughout, were elite, often very wealthy, white women who personally adhered to the separate spheres ideology. Members of this first contingent of anti-suffragists were between the ages of thirty-nine and fifty-seven at the time of the convention; virtually all were married with several children. They were conservative in their thinking and had the leisure and financial security to be prominently involved in any number of social reform causes and philanthropy. Many of them saw suffragists as "making trouble"[38] for womanhood and determined to use their organizational ability and social status to prevent women's enfranchisement.

At the same time, it seems clear that these women were essentially prisoners of their class, oblivious to how insulated they were by financial security. They personally enjoyed all of the privileges and protections of their prescribed sphere yet suffered virtually none of its crippling limitations. They could not comprehend the desperate straits of many powerless, resourceless, working-class women (especially married ones with children), for whom their prescriptions of education and professions were naïve. Their unconscious elitism profoundly affected their perspective on the political needs of women.

The committee meeting at the Putnam townhouse drew members primarily from the exclusive Brooklyn Heights area.[39] Carolyn R. R. Haines Putnam (1854–1940), hostess for the meeting, was the wife of a wealthy banker and philanthropist. A lover of music and literature, she held membership in the Colonial Dames of America and in the Daughters of the American Revolution. She and her husband were ardent supporters of the Brooklyn Museum of Arts and Sciences, donating paintings, china, lace, and other objects as well as money to the museum.[40] Her reform work included service as chair of the finance committee for St. Christopher's Hospital for Babies and as manager of the Female Employment Society.[41] She also supported the Hampton Institute of Virginia, Pundita Ramabai's school for child widows in India, and a variety of other causes.[42] Putnam would serve the anti-suffrage movement most often as president of the Brooklyn Auxiliary to the New York State Association Opposed to Woman Suffrage, but when called upon, she consented to hold office in the state association. She did not publish her views on anti-suffrage, instead serving the anti-suffrage movement as a patron, attending and hosting meetings, just as she served the other causes important to her.

A woman who would play a more dominant role in anti-suffrage at this early stage was Abby Hamlin Abbott (1840–1907). She was well known as the supportive helpmate of her husband, Lyman Abbott, who, in addition to editing the *Outlook*, was the pastor who succeeded the popular Henry Ward Beecher at Plymouth Congregational Church in Brooklyn.[43] Abby Abbott had raised two daughters and four sons; her family, home, husband, and religion made up the most important aspects of her life. She personified the ideal of true womanhood, which influenced her writings and actions as a member of the anti-suffrage contingent.[44] Abbott was widely known for her advice columns, first as "Aunt Patience" in the *Christian Union* (which preceded the *Outlook* and was also edited by Lyman Abbott), then as Mrs. Lyman Abbott for the very popular *Ladies' Home Journal*. Under the editorship of Edward Bok, the magazine was written for the "modern" women who "learned new things to improve their domestic sphere" and entered the "public sphere only as their moral influence was required." The connection to the magazine and its editor suited the unassuming Abbott perfectly, convinced as she was that Bok knew what women wanted.[45] A member of the Daughters of the American Revolution, she was heavily involved in reform, particularly in the Brooklyn and New York City Indian Associations, the Young Women's Christian Association, the City Mission and Tract Society, the Brooklyn Women's Club, and kindergartens and missionary work.[46] She had reportedly converted her husband from his budding support of woman suffrage during the early years of their marriage.[47] While Abby Abbott feared that too much discussion between those who supported woman suffrage and those who opposed it might devolve into arguments, she acknowledged that she had friends on both sides of the issue.[48]

Anyone in New York City who was anybody knew the Gilders. Helena de Kay Gilder (1847–1916) was the wife of Richard Watson Gilder, poet and editor of *Century* magazine. Although not as wealthy as most of the other anti-suffrage leaders, the Gilders moved in the best circles and entertained the most notable people in art, literature, politics, and reform at their home in New York or at Four Brooks Farm, their summer house in Tyringham, Massachusetts. Helena and her husband were very close friends of Grover Cleveland and his wife, and often visited the White House. They later became friends of Theodore Roosevelt.[49] For years the Gilders conducted informal

Both Helena de Kay Gilder and Richard Watson Gilder earnestly supported the anti-suffrage movement, as did many of their friends. Photo courtesy of the Lilly Library, Indiana University, Bloomington, Ind.

Friday evening receptions at their home, "The Studio," at 103 East 15th Street. The most important people of the literary and art worlds gathered for light refreshments, fascinating talk, and music. On any given week visitors included Walt Whitman, Henry James, Cecilia Beaux, Mark Twain, Madame Helena Modjeska, William Dean Howells, Adele Aus der Ohe, and anyone drawn to the Gilders and their set.[50]

As a young woman, Helena de Kay had shown great promise as a still-life and figure painter, studying from 1866 to 1869 in the new women's program at the Free School of Art for Women at the Cooper Union for the Advancement of Science and Art. De Kay also studied at the Ladies' Art Association and the Antique School of the National Academy of Design, and with other artists, including John LaFarge and Winslow Homer; from 1872 until 1873 she shared a studio with artist Maria Oakley.[51] For two years she resisted pressure from Richard to marry him, even writing frankly that she "hated the domestic thing." Yet, once she agreed to their marriage, she put aside her dreams of an independent artistic career and accepted the self-sacrifice required of a nineteenth-century "true woman."[52]

She remained interested in the art world for some years after her marriage. Dissatisfied with the inconsistent teaching hours and policies at the National Academy of Art, Helena helped to found the Art Students League of New York to enable students to study art more systematically. Complete equality between women and men, students and instructors, was mandated at the league.[53] In 1877, still discontented with the conservative and limiting exhibition policies of the National Academy of Art, Helena founded, with artists Wyatt Eaton, Augustus St. Gaudens, and Walter Shirlaw, the Society of American Artists, which encouraged "diversity in the arts" as well as the "individuality of the creator."[54] She even served on a committee to raise money for the Johns Hopkins Hospital Post-Graduate Course to admit women on the same basis as it did men.[55] Until 1886 she continued to exhibit some of her artwork, but after the birth of her fifth child and the exhibition of one more painting, she gave up the idea of an art career entirely.[56] In spite of her personal innovativeness and the courage to challenge prevailing views on women in art and the professions, she wholeheartedly supported a traditional role for women as wives and mothers, adamantly opposing any political role for women.

Almost immediately after the April committee meetings, Helena Gilder detailed the reasons she opposed woman suffrage in a long letter to her dearest friend, Mary Hallock Foote. Foote, also an artist, enjoyed a great deal of success both as an illustrator and as an author of stories about the western United States.[57] Gilder focused on the difference between women and men in her letter, writing that "all education, all philanthropy, all society are her demesne, and it seems to me it is wide enough without a pretense of governing, when she could only drop a ballot, and could not enforce the law which that ballot is meant to stand for."[58] She, like many other anti-suffragists, believed in an inextricable link between military service and voting; only a person able to sacrifice himself on the battlefield earned the right to vote. Before she could mail it, Richard took the letter to the offices of the *Critic*, a weekly publication of literary criticism edited by his sister, Jeannette Gilder, and their brother, Joseph B. Gilder (although Richard opposed woman suffrage, he did not use the *Century* to air his views). In spite of its being unusual for the publication, the letter appeared as the lead article in the August 4, 1894, issue. It was also printed and distributed as a pamphlet, then reprinted in 1909. Apparently, Helena was widely praised for the letter, and Richard remarked that the antis "seem to think that they have therein found a voice."[59]

Not all of the Gilders' friends agreed with Helena's views, however. Sarah Blake Sturgis Shaw (1815–1902; mother of both Colonel Robert Gould Shaw, commander of the all-black 54th Massachusetts regiment during the Civil War, and Josephine Lowell Shaw, social justice reformer and founder of the New York Consumers' League) was upset by Helena's letter and its publication, and expressed disappointment that Helena would do what she could to prevent other women from getting the vote. As Sarah Shaw, who claimed she had wanted the vote for forty years put it, "Now, may I ask, my dear child, why in the world if I want to vote, & you don't, you should try to prevent me?" Still, Shaw professed her love for Helena and hoped they could continue their friendship and correspondence, not an unusual reaction between friends at odds on their views of woman suffrage.[60]

Helena's sister-in-law, Jeannette Gilder (1849–1916), was also a member of these early committees. A single woman, taller than average, she was slightly masculine in appearance and could intimidate people with her "forbidding manner and quick temper."[61] Rebellious even as a child, she began earning a living at age fifteen when her father died; she disdained jobs traditionally open for women. After working as a researcher for a historian writing about New Jersey troops during the Civil War, she wrote for various newspapers before finding her niche as a literary editor for *Scribner's Monthly*, then as a dramatic and musical critic for the *New York Herald*. She and her brother founded the *Critic*, where she served as an editor from January 1881 to September 1906, when it merged with *Putnam's Monthly*. After the merger, she continued to write "The Lounger," one of the most popular columns in the *Critic*. She also worked as a correspondent for a number of newspapers in London, Boston, Chicago, as well as New York. She wrote articles and plays, edited several books, including eight volumes of *Masterpieces of the World's Best Literature*, and wrote books, including novels and *The Autobiography of a Tom-boy* in 1900 and *The Tom-boy at Work* in 1904. At one time she took in another brother's four motherless children, hiring other women to care for them while she went to her office.[62]

In May 1894 *Harper's Bazar* published Gilder's article, "Why I Am Opposed to Woman Suffrage." Although she had early entered a field once considered to be exclusively a male profession, she did not think women strong enough to participate in a political life. As far as she was concerned, it would be "too public, too wearing, and too unfitted to the nature of women." She contended that the vote was much more than putting a slip of paper in a ballot box. It meant holding office, attending primaries, and sitting on juries. Not only would women voting not bring about the "earthly paradise" suffragists seemed to expect, a political life would destroy home life. She had tried raising children and knew that women who were mothers had enough to do without adding politics to their responsibilities. Gilder argued that a woman could find a "sufficiently engrossing 'sphere' in the very important work of training her children." A mother should be more pleased to be the mother of an important man than to be a member of Congress. Gilder wanted all avenues of learning and industry open to women, but the ballot was a "bomb" and could only do harm to women.[63]

The Gilder's friend and an important champion of the Society of American Artists and other Gilder projects, Mariana Griswold Van Rensselaer (1851–1934) also opposed woman suffrage.[64] Extraordinary as the first female professional art critic, she was born into a family with wealth, status, and powerful political connections. She was educated first at home and later in Dresden where the family relocated when Mariana was seventeen. After touring Europe, she married Schuyler Van Rensselaer, a mining engineer (who died of lung disease in 1884), and eventually bore one son (who died of tuberculosis in 1894). She published books, articles, and reviews on art, architecture, biography, landscape gardening, history, and other topics. As prolific and worldly as she was, Van Rensselaer "believed it was woman's role to influence and educate."[65] In view of the privileges they already had women did not need political rights.

Mariana Van Rensselaer articulated her particular views about women in articles for the *New York World* in May and June 1894; later, the New York State Association Opposed to Woman Suffrage published the series in a booklet and distributed it broadly. Point by point she dissected the arguments presented by advocates of woman suffrage, although clearly from an elitist perspective. She admonished the women who did not want the vote, or who were at least unsure of its advisability, to make their views known. She considered the enfranchisement of millions of women a risk not worth taking. Women already held more privileges than men under the law. Specifically, Van Rensselaer wrote, a woman had control of her earnings, her personal property, and any real estate she owned. She could carry on a business or profession, she had no responsibility for her husband's debts, and she was not required to support him. She could sue and be sued, and she could make contracts. She had no obligation to serve on juries. With her husband she had equal rights to their children and, yet, he was obligated to support her and her children. Women were entitled to alimony in the event of a divorce, while a man could not ask for alimony. She was entitled to one third of her husband's real estate upon his death, but he was not entitled to her property after death if there were no children. Van Rensselaer concluded that the distribution of labor and privileges between women and men seemed fair, that the different roles of women and men were critically important, and that it was "slander" to claim that men did not already take good care of women.[66] Van Rensselaer's name would often appear as an officer of an anti-suffrage organization, but she rarely attended anti-suffrage functions.

In contrast, Lucy Parkman Scott (1854–1937), another good friend of Helena Gilder, seemed to be a driving force of the anti-suffrage movement. Married to Francis Markoe Scott, a lawyer who would be elected to the New York Supreme Court for the 1898 to 1911 term, she had three daughters.[67] She would spend a number of years serving as president of the New York State Association Opposed to Woman Suffrage, and she hosted many of the anti-suffrage executive board meetings at her Park Avenue home.[68] She often wrote editorials that appeared in the *Brooklyn Daily Eagle* and the *New York Times*. The *Critic* praised Lucy Scott's "convincing" address before the judiciary committee of the senate of New York in May of 1897. Her article, "The Legal Status of Women," was a reply to an editorial in the *New York Times* by Harriette M. Johnston-Wood, and she wrote "The Militant and the Child" in response to a *Century* article by Edna Kenton, the well known feminist. Scott was a strong advocate for women's separate sphere, telling the *New York Times* that "nothing could be more disastrous to the Nation's life than a general devotion of women to affairs outside the home."[69] She also seemed especially comfortable discussing the legal aspects of the woman suffrage controversy, not surprising for the wife of a lawyer and judge. From her conservative perspective, any legal wrongs that women bore could be ameliorated without resorting to the ballot.[70]

Widely known for her support of working-class children, Josephine Jewell Dodge (1855–1928) was clearly influenced by her sense of the rightness of the separate spheres ideology. She was the daughter of Marshall Jewell, a wealthy merchant who was also a two-term Connecticut governor, a U.S. minister to Russia, and postmaster-general in Ulysses S. Grant's cabinet. Josephine was educated at Hartford public schools. She attended Vassar College from 1870 to 1873, ending her formal education to accompany her family to St. Petersburg. In 1875 she married Arthur Murray Dodge in one of the "most brilliant and important social event[s]" of Hartford.[71] The youngest son of one of the richest men in New York, he managed his family's Great Lakes timber business. He also founded the New York Charity Organization Society and would serve on the boards of a number of large businesses. The couple had six sons, one of whom died at age three. Described by friends as "bird like," Josephine was diminutive in stature. She loved music, embroidery, and the dramatic arts, and often lent or donated important artifacts to New York museums. She was a member of both the New York Drama League and the Colony Club. A Presbyterian who was widowed in 1896, Josephine Dodge was deeply committed to philanthropy and good works.[72]

Dodge's interest in children's charities began soon after the birth of her first son. By 1878 she sponsored the Virginia Day Nursery in the slums of the East Side of New York. In 1888 she founded the Jewell Day Nursery; in addition to concerns for the health and well-being of working-class children, the broader goal was to instill middle-class "American" values in immigrant and lower-class children. She also supported the Hope Day Nursery for Colored Children in East Harlem. A member of the board of directors for an exhibit of the state of New York, she demonstrated a day care center model at the 1893 Columbian Exposition in Chicago. By 1895, with her exposition committee, she founded the Association of Day Nurseries in New York City, and in 1898 became the founder and director of the National Federation of Day Nurseries to centralize day nurseries. The federation could boast seven hundred affiliates within two decades. Other children's charities, including the Children's Charitable Union and the New York Kindergarten Association, also benefited from her patronage.[73] Her interest in philanthropy extended to the Legal Aid Society of New York, the Welfare Council of New York, the National Civic Federation, the National Florence Crittenden Association, and the Public Education Association.[74]

Josephine Dodge is assessed by the author of an article on the Federation of Day Nurseries for *Harper's Bazar* as having "admirable executive ability, unusual tact, and a remarkably clear, practical, discriminating judgment."[75] These same qualities would serve her well as she represented anti-suffragists at most of their social functions and legislative meetings from 1894 to 1917. She was often interviewed for her anti-suffrage views and wrote a number of articles for the organization. Eventually she would edit the *Woman Protest*, the national publication of the anti-suffragists. Dodge became president of the National Association Opposed to Woman Suffrage in 1911, serving until 1917.

In addition to an executive committee that included Josephine Jewell Dodge and Helena de Kay Gilder, with Lucy Parkman Scott as chair, the names of other prominent women of Brooklyn and New York City peppered the newspaper reports of anti-suffrage meetings and activities. Caroline A. Keith Greer (1845–1919) was the wife of David H. Greer, rector of St. Bartholomew's Protestant Episcopal Church. Because of his career, they had moved from Kentucky (where they met) and Rhode Island, coming to New York City in 1888. Her husband would succeed to the bishopric in 1908.[76] The couple had two sons and two daughters. Her name was often in the society pages, and the couple vacationed with the Vanderbilts in Newport or with other friends in the Berkshires. In addition to holding teas with some regularity and attending musical functions, Caroline Greer supported causes such as the Playground Association of America, the Children's Aid Society, the Home for the Friendless, the Five Points Mission, the King's Daughters, the Church Hospital and Dispensary, St. Luke's Home for Aged Women, and the Young Women's Christian Association. She was even one of the patrons of Wellesley College. A member of the Colonial Dames of America, she frequently attended anti-suffrage functions, and served on the nominating committee in 1910.[77]

Caroline McPhail Bergen (1859–1930) warranted her own entry in the 1908 edition of *Who's Who in New York City and State*. In January 1881, she married Tunis Bergen, a lawyer who served on the boards of railroads and business enterprises and opposed woman suffrage. The couple belonged to the Dutch Reformed Church. A Willow Street neighbor of Carolyn Putnam, Bergen was particularly active in the American Association for Promoting Hygiene and Public Baths. She also supported the Playgrounds Association of New York, the Brooklyn Free Kindergarten Society, and served as an officer of the New York City Visiting Committee of the State Charities Aid Association, as well as on

other committees that saw to the needs of children. Bergen lent her name to
the anti-suffrage cause, serving on committees and attending meetings, where
she would speak, but she did not publish her views. Suffragists expressed some
surprise that Caroline Bergen joined the anti-suffrage movement, considering
her a "very thoughtful woman" who should be on the suffrage side.[78]

Names like Florence Lockwood, Mrs. Clarence E. Beebe, Mrs. George
White Field, Mrs. Thomas S. Moore, and Mrs. Thomas E. Stillman mean little
to us today, but those who published their names in the society pages and on
the lists of anti-suffragists expected readers to know them. Other names are a
little more recognizable because of the men to whom they were related. Elizabeth Ruff Stetson (d. 1917) married Francis Lynde Stetson in 1873. He was legal
counsel for J. Pierpont Morgan and general counsel for U.S. Steel Corporation,
Northern Pacific Railway Company, U.S. Rubber Company, United States
Express Company, and similar companies. The couple, apparently childless,
belonged to the Episcopal Church of the Incarnation on Madison Avenue.
They supported causes such as the State Charities Aid Association, Education
in the Industrial and Fine Arts, the Prison Association, the Woman's Hospital, the Lincoln Hospital and Home (for poor people of color), the New
York Babies' Hospital, and the Legal Aid Society. Her husband was often a
speaker at anti-suffrage meetings (and would be one of the male advisors to
anti-suffrage organizations), but while she attended—and hosted—meetings
and served on committees, she rarely spoke or wrote about her anti-suffrage
views.[79] Observers considered the participation of these women behind the
lines to be significant to the movement.

Anti-suffragists belonged to the economic class that Sven Beckert describes
in *The Monied Metropolis*. Their families "owned and invested capital, employed wage workers (or, at the very least, servants), did not work for wages
themselves, and did not work manually."[80] Of those anti-suffrage women in
New York State who had a profession, typically they worked as authors, editors, or journalists of the "gentle correspondent" type. These women were
quick to say that they did not oppose higher education and professional advancements for women, an argument that was conspicuous throughout their
movement. Determined to behave in ways they believed appropriate for their
sex, they were just as determined to prove that women were not ready to participate in politics. They believed that advancement for women should be a
slow and steady process that began with professionalism through education.

Perhaps, but not certainly, educational advancement would eventually lead to political responsibilities.[81]

With the convention approaching, women with anti-suffrage views gathered more signatures for their petitions, while Carolyn Putnam suggested additional activities to prevent their enfranchisement.[82] Reflecting the privileged status of the early organizers on both sides of the suffrage issue, anti-suffragists set up temporary headquarters in the ladies' reception room at the Waldorf Astoria, while suffragists established theirs at Sherry's.[83] Supporters could sign copies of the "Protest" at the Waldorf, the Cooper Union, and at Brancard's, and they could also take copies of the petition to obtain additional signatures. The *New York Times* listed the names of many of the women from the city who signed the petitions, noting that most were heavily involved in philanthropic work and already well-aware of civic and governmental responsibilities. By the time the antis finished their signature drive, more than five thousand women from ninety-four cities, towns, and villages in thirty-five counties across the state had signed.[84]

Press reports revealed exciting details of the new, formal rivalry, especially during April 1894, when frantic preparations for the convention were underway. Both anti-suffragists and suffragists held more meetings and gathered more petitions. There was some rather unusual excitement too, as when Josephine Dodge created "a little diversion." She brazenly marched into a suffrage meeting and read aloud the official anti-suffrage protest. She breezed out after informing the audience that the petition was available for signing at the Waldorf.[85] Other New York anti-suffrage women were also confrontational, even at this early stage. Abby Abbott invited Mariana W. Chapman, a leading Brooklyn suffragist, to speak at a parlor meeting. Abbott believed that the audience should hear both sides of the question.[86] These confrontations foreshadowed the behavior of New York anti-suffragists in the next decades.

Anti-suffragists held other meetings in both New York City and Brooklyn. New York City anti-suffrage women met on April 25, 1894, at the home of Elizabeth Stetson, whose husband was a delegate to the constitutional convention. The *New York Times* posted reminders that this group, too, would receive signatures of support at the Hotel Waldorf. On May 3, 1894, another meeting of the Brooklyn women was called to order by Abby Abbott at the home of Mrs. Joseph C. Hoagland. Several speakers addressed the assembly, including Rev. Theodore L. Cuyler of the Presbyterian Church. He argued that "the Creator made man and woman to govern, but in totally different spheres and methods." He feared men would "degenerate into domestic and social barbarism" if women "snatch[ed] after the ballot, the juryman's seat, and the police baton of civil authority." Clearly, thoughtful people would not want such disruption in their lives. Based on the numbers of women signing the petitions, he said, more women opposed suffrage than supported it. Cuyler insisted, however, that more men were in favor of the vote for women than against it.[87] Meanwhile, elsewhere in the state other groups of anti-suffrage women were also gathering in preparation for the constitutional convention.

On April 27, 1894, Anna Parker [Mrs. John V. L.] Pruyn, of the Pruyn Paper Company family, presided over a meeting of Albany women who opposed the enfranchisement of women. The women of the capital city determined to obtain signatures for their own protest against removing the word "male" from the state constitution. Although they held another meeting, highlighting several male speakers, the Albany group did not declare itself to be an official organization.[88] Neither did the Brooklyn antis intend to found a permanent organization. Their final meeting was held at the home of a Mrs. Wadsworth on St. Mark's Avenue, and the last act of the twenty-one members was to prepare their formal pamphlet for the constitutional convention, including "a list of names calculated to strike terror to the hearts of the opposing forces." Antis believed their names alone illustrated the power of their influence.[89] Proud that they had "carried on without organization, systematic canvassing, or public meetings," the women were certain that they had made their political sentiments clear. Dodge announced that their work had been brought to a "successful conclusion."[90] These anti-suffrage women naively believed they could put the entire matter to rest with one determined effort.

Public interest in the suffrage question increased. The May 12, 1894, issue of *Harper's Bazar* featured a series of articles for and against woman suffrage, including Abby Abbott's "Why We Protest." Abbott contended that there were no assurances that women's enfranchisement would rectify society's problems. In addition, she pointed out that woman had not proved herself so perfect in her "smaller realm"—the home—that she was ready to "assume the more extended obligations of statecraft." Here, she criticized lower-class women, the class from whom elite women drew their servants, for not keeping up with their work at home while they worked outside it.[91] The *Outlook* reported on the increased activity in New York relating to woman suffrage and the convention. Contending that the movement "could not be laughed down," Lyman Abbott pointed out that "American democracy cannot refuse the ballot to woman on the ground of her incompetence."[92] He pledged his support to the many thoughtful, intelligent, educated women who did not want to increase the electorate.[93] A debate published in May 1894 indicates the confrontational nature of the relationship between anti-suffrage and suffrage women. Abbott asked Mary Putnam Jacobi, M.D. to contribute her views. Jacobi argued that since the nature of representative government had changed in the previous fifty years, the nature of the relationship of women to the government also had to change. Political equality logically followed the "industrial equality" women had already gained. The constitutional convention would simply be an opportunity to air the views of those who wanted suffrage for women; it was not disrespectful of the views of those who protested the request for woman suffrage, or those who were not interested in the question. Writing for the opposition, novelist and historian Maud Wilder Goodwin cautioned that not enough was known about the social and political changes that would come from enfranchising women to make it worth the risk. She believed that woman suffrage would "encumber" an already overly complicated government. She pleaded that more time should be granted to hear the broad range of opinions on the topic.[94]

The *Outlook* published another pair of articles addressing the duty and right of suffrage. Abbott pointed out that his periodical had always been "in favor of reform——liberal, progressive, fearless of changes, in politics, industry, society, even in religious thought." The publication even advocated the enfranchisement of all "subject races"—"the Indian, the negro, the Chinese." Aware that the expressed opposition of the *Outlook* to woman suffrage might appear to be "inconsistent with its general position," he detailed why he did not support women's enfranchisement. Contending that his publication represented the "silent majority" of women who did not want the vote, he argued that the vote was not a voice, but was "the force behind all forces," it was "authority." Because women naturally shrank from the "bearing of rule and the exercising of compulsion over the community," the ballot was not their duty.[95] The following week he addressed the question of the ballot as a right, arguing that it was not a natural right; the vote was an acquired right. The right to vote was not the same as the life, liberty, and property rights conferred and protected by the Constitution of the United States. The government was under no obligation to confer voting rights on anyone, and certainly not on everyone. The New York constitutional convention must assure that extending suffrage would not inflict on women a "burden" they did not want, one men did not need them to share, nor should it inflict on society an "unknown, if not an unknowable, element to the political forces of the State."[96]

As authors published debates on the merits of women's enfranchisement, the time had come for the constitutional convention. Anna Pruyn opened the "convention summer" with a dinner party in honor of Joseph Choate and Elihu Root.[97] Clearly, the anti-suffragists had the elite influence necessary to make their views known to the men who would make the decisions related to women's enfranchisement. When the convention assembled on May 15, 1894, Choate, a Republican attorney, presided. Choate was well known for his involvement with the Committee of Seventy, which had been instrumental in breaking up the Tweed ring. He apparently viewed women's suffrage differently than did his wife, who had signed a pro-suffrage petition and held meetings in New York City to educate others on the topic.[98]

Elihu Root, district attorney, political speaker, and also a Republican, was quickly rising in eminence in the state. He served as chairman of the judiciary committee, one of twenty-seven regular committees. Not only was he responsible for the general management of the convention, he addressed it on virtually every issue.[99] To the delegates, their most important business was the readjustment of legislative apportionment; but to women on both sides of the suffrage debate, woman's right to vote was the only significant issue.[100] The members of the convention allowed Susan B. Anthony to present her views concerning woman suffrage on May 24; other suffragists spoke on May 31, and suffragists of the senatorial districts addressed the body on June 7. The "Remonstrants" were given time a week later, on June 14, to present their views. The petitions submitted by the remonstrants held the signatures of no men, only those of women of age twenty-one years or older. The names of working women were included, as well as "those more fortunately situated."[101] In keeping with their perception of the proper place of women, they had asked a man to present their views to the delegates. That man was Francis Markoe Scott, a Democrat, husband of Lucy Parkman Scott. Francis Scott pointed out that although few could remember a time when some women were not asking for the right to vote, it had never before seemed sufficiently viable to force any women to actively oppose suffragists. As far as he was concerned, the changes proposed by suffragists were "revolutionary"; they would "sap the foundation and overthrow the structure of existing society." Furthermore, based on the fundamental differences between men and women, the "ultimate and immutable" argument against women voting was "simply because men can fight and women cannot." He reminded the delegates that the extension of suffrage to "those who lack the power to enforce respect for their authority" would "destroy the interdependence of men and women . . . which alone makes social development and progress possible."[102] Although he purported to speak for the women, Scott presented arguments rather different from those in the petition. Whereas the women focused on their right and need to be protected from the public realm, he was primarily concerned with women's inability to function in that realm.[103] A number of other convention delegates also spoke for the anti-suffrage view, in essentially the same vein as Scott.[104] One delegate contended that women's participation in politics would be as destructive in the home as a civil war was to the state. Paraphrasing Lincoln, he expressed the fear that "the house would become inevitably and forever divided against itself."[105] In spite of differences in the specific arguments against woman suffrage, anti-suffrage women—perhaps intimidated by their first foray into politics—were, for the time being, content to let men speak for them. At the same time, they wanted to make the point that anti-suffragists, unlike suffragists, knew how to behave like "proper" women in public.

In August the committee submitted its report, recommending that the word "male" remain in the state constitution and that the issue not be submitted to the people of the state for a vote. But the idea of a plebiscite did not die easily. The delegates who spoke the evening of August 8 argued that regardless of the opinion of the suffrage committee, the question should be submitted to the voters.[106] Some, while supporting the decision to keep the word "male" in the state constitution, were willing to submit the question to the voters. Conversely, Henry J. Cookinham of Utica, an anti-suffragist member of the suffrage committee, contended that the people, through their petitions, had already made it clear that the majority did not support woman suffrage.[107] The meeting adjourned without the members reaching a final decision.

The next day Cookinham finally proposed that the Committee on Rules set a time limit for the debate on woman suffrage, scheduled to end on the evening of August 15. Several more members spoke similarly to those who argued the previous day, and Elihu Root added his own views.[108] He believed that granting suffrage to women not only represented a loss to women, it would be "an injury to the State, and to every man and every woman in the State."

Reflecting his elitism, he further contended that "in politics there is struggle, strife, contention, bitterness, heart-burning, excitement, agitation, everything which is adverse to the true character of woman.... Woman in strife becomes hard, harsh, unlovable, repulsive; as far removed from that gentle creature to whom we all owe allegiance and to whom we confess submission, as the heaven is removed from the earth."[109] The final vote at the convention was fifty-eight in favor of submission of the suffrage issue to the people, and ninety-eight against, in agreement with the recommendation of the committee.[110] Relieved by the decision, the New York, Brooklyn, and Albany anti-suffrage ladies returned to their usual philanthropic and domestic duties, eager to "divest themselves of the publicity and notoriety so objectionably thrust upon them," as the *New York Times* would later write about the short-lived committees.[111]

From this point until the end of the campaign, which, in spite of their protestations, these women would have to enter, female anti-suffragists expounded their claims. Suffrage was a duty they did not want imposed on them; it was not a privilege, and it was incompatible with the many duties women already bore. They would argue that the private household was an important unit of the nation-state and that gaining the vote would alleviate no "practical injustice." The women who would serve the anti-suffrage movement believed that the roles of men and women were "divinely ordered" to be different both in the home and in the wider world of the state. Increasing the electorate would not improve the quality of the vote, and the majority of women were content to remain in their current state of representation: members of "household suffrage." Rather than being required to hold public office, which they perceived to be a natural consequence of voting and inconsistent with their present duties, women's energies would be better spent in the more "efficient performance" of their prescribed duties. Perhaps one of the most compelling arguments to their adherents was their contention that woman would be deprived of the "special privileges hitherto accorded to her by law."[112] To these women, suffrage seemed like a selfish, individualistic demand, incompatible with the role of the selfless, "true" woman who would preserve the sanctity of her home and family.[113]

The conservative women who opposed woman suffrage enough to form organizations did so in an effort to preserve the separate spheres ideology. Realizing that suffragists intended the utter destruction of the ideological separation between the sexes, anti-suffragists rallied to protect it.[114] They knew women would otherwise lose the justification for their authority in the home and their reform work outside of it. They professed pride in being unorganized, in using few resources, in being supported by volunteers, and in not pushing anyone to convert to anti-suffrage.[115] Although reluctant to organize to oppose woman suffrage, the response of anti-suffrage women to the 1894 New York State constitutional convention with the submission of the "Protest" to the delegates represents a distinct change in the behavior of women who subscribed to the mandates of "true womanhood." With enough provocation, women who opposed woman suffrage would leave their separate sphere to ensure that they would be protected from the burden of the ballot.

2. Establishing New York State Anti-Suffrage Organizations, 1895–1911

Within the year following the 1894 constitutional convention in New York, the colors of the suffrage and anti-suffrage factions again "streamed from Camp Sherry and Camp Waldorf." Male observers, "to whom it is all very incomprehensible, though very amusing," awaited the coming struggle between antis and suffragists "from such safe points of view as they may be able to secure," according to the *New York Times*.[1] The reporter's view illustrates the public perception of the escalating tensions between anti-suffrage and suffrage women in the waning years of the century. Soon, some would claim that "women hate each other," although admitting that not all women agreed with that assessment.[2] Women on both sides of the suffrage issue continued the nineteenth-century practice of working together in philanthropic groups and women's clubs to promote a variety of reforms. What changed in the 1890s—and elicited bewildered commentary—was that suddenly women organized clubs with the primary purpose of *opposing* their enfranchisement. Developing and coordinating the activities of anti-suffrage organizations ultimately politicized many of these women, in spite of their resistance to voting.

Although anti-suffrage women continued to be strongly influenced by the separate spheres ideology, this period marks the beginning of a significant shift in the public behavior of conservative women, as well as in the way they perceived their relationship to the nation-state. Some of the shift was a response to changes in suffrage rhetoric around the turn of the century. A new layer of arguments, focused on expediency, supplemented the arguments based on equal-rights principles. Nineteenth-century woman suffrage arguments had been seen as radical, limiting their appeal.[3] Now native-born, white, middle-class suffragists argued that their votes "could counteract the votes of the undesirable part of the electorate," reflecting racism as well as anxiety about the influx of immigrants. Not only did women need the vote for "self-protection," suffragists claimed they should expect "self-reliance, personal responsibility, and individual citizenship" from enfranchisement. By enlarging women's interests with some of the responsibility for government, women would be better mothers, better wives, and better citizens. Increasingly, suffragists stressed women's differences from men, claiming they had the "duty to contribute their special skills and experience to government."[4] Rev. Anna Garlin Spencer, for example, asserted that when "the State took upon itself any form of educative, charitable, or personally helpful work, it entered the area of distinctive feminine training and power, and therefore became in need of the service of woman."[5] It was women's duty to participate; women needed the vote for the good of society, as well as for their personal development.[6] Suffragist arguments became more acceptable as they deliberately sought to appeal to a broader spectrum of the public.[7]

Over time, anti-suffragists reluctantly gave up their long-established reform techniques, based on volunteer activities and personal influence, to actively and publicly resist the woman suffrage movement. In spite of their initial reluctance, New York anti-suffrage women eventually made use of many of the same political techniques used by suffragists. They formed dedicated organizations, testified in legislative hearings, gave speeches to mixed audiences, debated their suffrage opponents, wrote articles and books, and appropriated some of the exciting new mass-marketing techniques to disseminate propaganda in their effort to protect what they saw as their unique place in the polity.

Yet theirs constituted a "negative organization," as Josephine Dodge aptly termed it. To her, this meant that anti-suffragists would not crusade in any new areas of controversy, for it was their responsibility simply to resist suffrage in every way they could. They would bombard the public with press releases, speakers, and literature to make it clear that woman suffrage was not the panacea the suffragists made it out to be, but they would not attempt to influence new directions for women. Specifically, Dodge promised, the organization will "endeavor to stamp out the pestilence . . . where the contagion is rampant the association will endeavor to check it. Where the malady is only threatened, we will inoculate against it."[8] Anti-suffragists were forced to resist a movement

composed of exciting and transformative ideas and managed by far more politically astute and experienced women, a movement increasingly appealing
to women benefiting from enlarged educational and career opportunities.

Those confrontations forced anti-suffragists to realize how ineffectual their
public speaking abilities were compared with those of suffragists. By 1908, anti-
suffragists founded the National League for the Civic Education of Women
to study questions of women's civic rights and responsibilities "from an anti-
suffrage point of view," and the Guidon Club to train women to articulate
their views on the "woman suffrage problem." These additional anti-suffrage
organizations marked a noteworthy shift in their thinking about political
involvement.[9] While conservative anti-suffrage women certainly wished to
preserve the existing order, they nonetheless accepted, celebrated, and even
advocated the entry of some women into the public sphere. By 1910 antis
solicited New York's governor for political positions for women. As antis
politicized and strengthened their opposition, suffragists responded in ever
more sophisticated ways. The actions of anti-suffragists and their influence
on suffragists during this period constitute important steps in the direction
of women's equality with men as well as their own political development.
Suffragists no longer faced only men in their quest for the right to vote; now
their primary foes were members of their own sex. As anti-suffragists politicized their movement, countering their growing influence became a significant
challenge for suffragists.

Once New York anti-suffragists realized that the 1894 constitutional convention had not settled the question of woman suffrage, representatives from
the original committees of Brooklyn, New York City, and Albany convened
at the home of Sarah Amelia Cooper Hewitt on April 8, 1895, and established
the New York State Association Opposed to Woman Suffrage.[10] Hewitt (1830–
1912) was the only surviving daughter of Peter Cooper, industrialist, philanthropist, and founder of Cooper Union. Raised strictly and modestly, she was
imbued with full knowledge of housekeeping, cooking, washing, and sewing.
Brought up in the Unitarian Church, she was educated at public schools, Mrs.
Meer's Select Classes, and Miss Kirkland's School in New York City, and she
learned dance from the Italian dance instructor and choreographer, Edward
Ferrero. In 1855 the "tall, statuesque young woman" married Abram S. Hewitt,
once her brother's tutor. With her family's support, Abram Hewitt made his
fortune in the iron and steel industry, served as Democratic representative
for New York in Congress for twelve years, then as mayor of New York City

(during which time he planned the financing and construction of the subway system), and he managed the Cooper Union. The couple had three daughters and three sons.[11]

The Hewitt family spent winters at Peter Cooper's house at 9 Lexington Avenue and summers at their beautiful estate at Ringwood, New Jersey, just outside of New York City. Amelia concentrated much of her creative energy on her homes and gardens, creating beautiful surroundings to please her family and many guests. Their New York City home operated as one of the most fashionable of social centers, the site of many teas, dinners, musicales, and large dances, especially in the 1890s. The same was true of Ringwood in the summers, when there might be as many as thirty guests at the Hewitt dining table. Amelia's "placidity, kindliness, and practical common sense" contrasted with her husband's "fire and energy." She loved art, music, and her gardens, while he loved talk and activity. Nevertheless, he preferred entertaining guests in his home, while she loved going out into society.[12]

Two of the Hewitt daughters, neither of whom married, were also involved with anti-suffrage: Sarah (Sally) Cooper Hewitt (1858–1930) and Eleanor Garnier Hewitt (1864–1924). Both daughters were primary forces in establishing the Cooper-Hewitt Museum in New York City. Anti-suffrage ideas had long been aired in the Hewitt homes. Abram wrote two articles on the topic; the New York State Association reprinted and distributed his "Statement in Regard to the Suffrage." He argued that since men were by nature more "combative" than women, government relied on men for the maintenance of civil government. Woman, conversely, had the function of maternity, so "love and not force is the source of her power."[13] Amelia Hewitt was surrounded by anti-suffrage sentiment, although she was primarily a patron of the movement rather than an active promoter of her anti-suffrage views.

Most of the women at this first organizational meeting on April 8 had signed the "Protest" the previous year.[14] They selected Lucy Parkman Scott to serve as chair of the organization, which sought to "increase general interest in the opposition to universal woman suffrage, and to educate the public in the belief that women can be more useful to the community without the ballot than if affiliated with and influenced by party politics." Anti-suffragists claimed that people did not understand the issues connected with women voting and that the public was emotionally caught up in suffrage rhetoric. They argued that if people understood what woman suffrage really meant, they, too, would oppose women's enfranchisement. Antis would speak publicly, disseminate literature, and engage everyone they knew in conversations about suffrage. They claimed they did not intend to convert anyone, nor would they "carry on an aggressive campaign" because they believed public opinion was on their side. The association would consolidate the "focus of a great sentiment which would otherwise be too diffused to exert its full influence" and "be a mouthpiece for the earnest home-loving woman."[15] They argued that education and "all its acquired wisdom" would enable more women to recognize the vital need for "a division of the world's work between men and women."[16] Interested people could obtain copies of anti-suffrage speeches, pamphlets, and books by applying to the secretary at the office of the association. The anti-suffragists established their formal headquarters at 29 East 39th Street, remaining at or near that address for the duration of the movement.[17]

The New York State Association Opposed to Woman Suffrage had five presidents during its tenure. Scott held the office of chair, then president, for the longest period, from 1895 to 1910, except for brief periods during 1902 and 1907, when Abby Hamlin Abbott served in her stead.[18] Josephine Jewell Dodge served as president in 1910, and Carolyn Putnam relieved her when in December 1911 Dodge became the president of the National Association Opposed to Woman Suffrage.[19] The final, most politically active and dynamic president, serving from January 1913 until December 1917, was Alice Hill Chittenden.[20] Once New York State women began organizing an anti-suffrage movement, they were "relatively more adventurous" than antis in other states, according to Susan Marshall, historian of the Massachusetts anti-suffragists.[21] Thomas Jablonsky noted also that organized New York antis "surpass[ed]" Massachusetts antis "in aggressiveness and temerity."[22] Men always dominated the Massachusetts anti-suffrage organization; the New York anti-suffrage association was all the more remarkable for being dominated by women, and for intentionally resisting male dominance.[23]

The president convened the executive committee at least annually, initially in December and later in April. At first they met in the home of one of the members, but increasing membership necessitated their meeting in larger and more public venues. The women elected officers, heard reports on the previous year's activities and work, and listened to speakers on a range of topics of interest to anti-suffragists.[24] They restricted active membership to women elected by the executive committee, and each member paid annual dues of three dollars, an amount eventually increased to five dollars.[25] Sustaining members, who could be women or men, were those who contributed any amount to the annual funds of the organization. Men could donate money, but could not hold official positions; the New York State Association anti-suffragists were determined to be seen as free of the control of men. The executive committee also elected honorary members, women characterized by "distinguished service in opposition to woman suffrage."[26]

In the years that followed the meeting at the Hewitt home, women founded other anti-suffrage organizations in New York, most as auxiliaries of the state organization, including those in Albany, Buffalo, Brooklyn, Hudson, Mt. Vernon, Rochester, Syracuse, Schenectady, Westchester, Utica, and later, in Oneida and Cazenovia. Some anti-suffrage organizations focused on political education or reform work, yet ideologically opposed suffrage. Women dominated the organizational opposition to the granting of the women's vote in New York State during the period between 1895 and 1911. Initially, its official policy was to avoid public debate with suffragists, but soon they sought confrontations and debates.[27]

The New York organization quickly became the vanguard of anti-suffragists throughout the United States. From its earliest years, the New York State Association Opposed to Woman Suffrage received messages of "sympathy and encouragement," as well as requests for information, advice, or assistance from women in at least twenty different states.[28] Articles published in anti-suffrage journals show an awareness of the suffrage situation outside the United States; in 1910, the executive committee appointed Lilian Bayard Taylor Kiliani, wife of the prominent surgeon Otto Kiliani, to the position of international secretary.[29] The state organization created auxiliaries by following the boundaries of the state's judicial districts, a convenient method of organization also used by suffragists.[30] Members of the auxiliaries set up headquarters in the largest city in the district, with one or more branches if the cities were large enough. Each auxiliary elected its own leaders, organized its own activities, and periodically held informational meetings.[31]

For example, the Anti-Suffragists of Albany and Vicinity, an organization formed on May 14, 1895, dominated the movement in upstate New York and was especially active until 1909. With a population of around 94,151, the state capital had already hosted many rousing discussions of woman suffrage.[32] Less bold and assertive than the antis in New York City, the Albany antis elected a board of officers, including a secretary, treasurer, a seven-member executive committee; they also named one hundred honorary vice-presidents so as not to offend anyone of their wealthy and affluent social circle. For president, they chose Anna Parker Pruyn, and her home served for a number of years as the headquarters of the Albany organization. Pruyn continued as president until 1900, and she offered moral, strategic, and financial support until her death in 1909.[33] Pruyn's daughter, Huybertie Pruyn Hamlin, claimed that her mother wanted the committee in Albany to head the state organization, since "New York is only the Port of Albany after all."[34] However important the Albany Association was to the New York State anti-suffrage movement, members of the Albany group were not as extensively involved in other regions of the state as the women of New York City were. Yet, as a tribute to the influence of the antis in Albany, suffragists considered the city an anti-suffrage "stronghold."[35]

Most of the work done by the "large and enthusiastic" Albany group was in the state legislature.[36] A close Pruyn family friend, Bishop William Croswell Doane, supported and encouraged the anti-suffrage movement in Albany.[37] The president of the Albany anti-suffrage organization after 1909 was Mrs. George Douglas Miller, and Sarah Rodgers Sloan Henry, wife of Nelson H. Henry, Republican adjutant general for New York State, led the group through the 1910s.[38] At its annual convention in Washington in 1896, the National American Woman Suffrage Association reported that there were sixteen hundred suffragists in New York. However, according to the anti-suffragists, there was "more than five times that number" enrolled on the lists of anti-suffragists in Albany alone.[39] Either many of the names were kept confidential or the group inflated its numbers, for in 1905 the Albany Association published the names of only 241 members, featuring several members of the Fenimore Cooper family, as well as many other prominent residents, including Gertrude Thomson Dix, whose husband, John Alden Dix, would be New York State governor in 1911.[40] Speakers from New York City and elsewhere presented at the Albany anti-suffrage annual meetings of well over 250 people.[41]

Members of the Albany anti-suffrage association published and distributed pamphlets and broadsides, and, from July 1908 until April 1912, produced the monthly periodical, the *Anti-Suffragist*. Elizabeth [Mrs. W. Winslow] Crannell served as editor, in spite of frequent speaking engagements in the western states. Harriet Pruyn [Mrs. William Gorham] Rice, another daughter of Anna Pruyn, and Margaret Doane Gardiner, the granddaughter of Bishop Doane, were associate editors.[42] The goal of the periodical was to be the "mouthpiece of a no longer silent majority."[43] In response to the many requests they received from people, the press, and libraries, in 1905 the Albany antis published a selection of their pamphlets encapsulating and disseminating their beliefs about the proper role of women. They distributed this bound collection to college libraries and public libraries around the state.[44]

The Albany antis also extended the proper role of women beyond that of "true" womanhood, sending members to speak to interested groups within the state as well as in other states. In 1896, Crannell represented the antis at both the Republican National Convention in St. Louis and at the Democratic National Convention in Chicago. Anti-suffragist groups of New York City, Brooklyn, and Boston often financed her trips.[45] When the suffrage vote was pending in South Dakota in 1898, Crannell traveled to the state to help Marietta Bones, that state's leading anti-suffragist, defeat woman suffrage.[46] Crannell debated Carrie Chapman Catt in what must have been a rousing— the newspaper termed it "almost exciting"—discussion of woman suffrage at a meeting of the Nineteenth Century Club of New York City in 1900. Catt spoke on the need for women's rights, including suffrage, to which Crannell responded that it was "libel to say that woman must have the ballot to secure her rights." Woman suffrage, she said, meant connections with socialists, a desire for elective office, and led to "an aversion to motherhood."[47] Crannell also gave the principle address at the annual meeting of the Buffalo Association Opposed to Woman Suffrage in 1910. Few Albany members traveled in the service of anti-suffragism as much as Crannell, although Gardiner seems to have come a close second.[48]

As the influence of the New York State anti-suffragists spread, the number of people attending the anti-suffrage meetings increased. In 1896, the state organization claimed 12,324 members; by 1914, it claimed thirty thousand members.[49] In 1898, fifty people attended the annual meeting held at the Putnam home; by 1911, the size of the audiences outgrew the parlor meetings, and it became necessary to rent public buildings.[50] Beginning in 1898, members of the association established a subcommittee to conduct "a series of entertaining and useful meetings for wage earners" in an initial effort to influence working class women.[51] In due course, antis established Junior Leagues to encourage the next generation of elite women to oppose enfranchisement.[52] The names of the most prominent members peppered newspaper reports of anti-suffrage activities.[53]

The full range of their activities might suggest sound financing, but it is difficult to determine the funds available to the antis. In 1896, they reported a balance of $218.72, and a partial accounting in 1913 claimed a $20,000 budget, most of which had been paid out for the salary of the secretary, rent, telephone, and publishing expenses. Some of the money came from annual membership fees, the rest from supporter donations.[54] Members of the executive committee wrote letters requesting financial support for their cause. Those written to men included requests for legislative support; letters to women promised that their names and membership in the anti-suffrage organization would remain confidential.[55] Anti-suffrage leadership learned to petition outside their membership for money, but they had to be careful in their choice of donors.[56] With few published financial reports, it was easier for suffragists to accuse antis of accepting money from brewers, liquor dealers, and manufacturing interests. These accusations discredited the anti-suffrage women, but there is no evidence that anti-suffrage women's groups ever knowingly accepted money from liquor dealers or brewers.[57] Business and liquor interests believed that their profits would suffer if women, with their stated intentions of reforming all aspects of society, had the power of the vote. While there were divisions in both suffrage and anti-suffrage organizations regarding temperance and the benefits of prohibition, prominent antis had long opposed liquor. As Jablonsky asserts, "the depiction of anti-suffragism as a fanciful dressing for the real opponents of woman suffrage was timely rhetoric and nothing more."[58] If these powerful interests—brewers, liquor dealers, and manufacturing firms—actually financed anti-suffrage organizations, they were decidedly stingy with their support. In most years the New York State Association lacked operating funds, and the headquarters was reportedly small and austere.[59]

Initially, the antis promoted a narrow range of methods for resisting woman suffrage.[60] In a speech made before the Albany Anti-Woman Suffrage Society, Abby Abbott articulated the grounds for opposition to suffrage, and set out some methods for success. She suggested using the voice and pen, and most particularly the press, to present "carefully prepared literature" to the public. She cautioned anti-suffrage advocates to not fall into "hysterical quarreling," or react adversely to the accusations of "unrighteous alliances." Anti-suffrage women must remain dignified and proper and, yet, aware of the need for their activities to adapt to changing conditions.[61] Abbott, like most other New York anti-suffrage leaders, recognized that the public position of defense was not an easy one. Anti-suffrage methods changed and expanded as time went on, adapting to shifting circumstances and suffrage responses.

Within days of the founding meeting of the New York State Association, Lucy Scott, Helena de Kay Gilder, and other antis appeared before the senate judiciary committee in Albany to assure legislators that true women did not want to vote.[62] Antis also paid close attention when in June the state legislature introduced the "Nixon Resolution," named for Samuel Frederick Nixon, Republican speaker of the state assembly from Westfield, that would allow voters to decide the suffrage question. Widely expected to pass both houses in 1896, the resolution prompted even more action from anti-suffrage women.[63] The battle for women's suffrage had changed; women who opposed suffrage had officially entered the contest, and the pro-suffrage camp now faced "an unexpected attack from the rear."[64]

By 1907, the *New York Times* observed that "the old days when a gaunt, masculine, and forbidding appearance seemed to fit the woman with thoughts have long since passed; the old-time 'war horse' of woman suffrage has passed." The broader acceptance of woman suffrage by more-well-known (and attractive) women alarmed the anti-suffragists as it helped make suffrage more broadly appealing.[65] Actually, most New York State anti-suffrage leaders bore a marked resemblance to suffrage leaders. They had wealth, education, membership in social clubs, and supported any number of charities.[66] In New York, anti-suffrage leaders seem to have had more college education than antis elsewhere in the country, yet virtually no anti completed her college program if she did attend. Like suffragists, most anti-suffragists were philanthropists. In spite of some contrasting characteristics, anti-suffragists attempted to create a "viable political strategy" out of their "public female sphere," just as Estelle Freedman describes suffragists did.[67] Both antis and suffragists attempted to recruit other prominent women to their organizations, and both groups held parlor meetings, typical meeting places for elite and middle-class women, to encourage women to join their organizations.

Even suffragists argued that elite women "most fully embodied" the virtues—"benevolence, morality, selflessness, and industry"—necessary for politics. Their inherent abilities, therefore, made their enfranchisement critical. Antis agreed with suffragists' basic premise regarding the special qualities of elite women, but argued that "woman suffrage would decrease elite influence, rather than enhance it."[68] Anti-suffragists contended that successful legal reforms, such as those related to factory laws, property laws, custody laws, and age of consent laws, in which many elite women were involved, proved that women were highly effective without the vote.[69] Anti-suffragists argued that the vote had done nothing to improve the wages of workingmen, so the argument that suffrage would improve the wages of working women was false.[70] Although anti-suffragists attempted to appeal to working women, they were naïve in their approach to them. Antis argued that women either forced their way into the male-dominated professions, or they frivolously worked for extra money to buy clothing.[71] Worse, as the antis also pointed out, working women competed with men, driving down their wages and making it more difficult for men to support their families.[72]

Both anti-suffrage and suffrage women used similar techniques of political activism as they signed petitions, appeared before legislative bodies, published literature, and held meetings. As Michael McGerr points out, between 1900 and 1920, when women began to rely on education and advertising to promote popular politics, their political behavior changed considerably.[73] Although he focused on suffrage women, anti-suffrage women, particularly in New York State, learned to use those same techniques by mimicking many of the innovative ideas of the suffragists. New York anti-suffragists adjusted those techniques as they deemed appropriate to maintain propriety, resisting suffrage with suffragists' mass marketing and political activist tools.

Anti-suffragists would not have considered themselves political activists, for the concept of political involvement has changed in the last century. Any work related to their "social housekeeping" activities, as heavily involved as women were in them, would not have been considered political activism. Membership in political parties was one of the exclusive domains of men, as Paula Baker has said, and most anti-suffragists strove to keep the female sphere separate from the masculine realm.[74] However, anti-suffragists, by virtue of their family connections to the politicians in power, were probably highly influenced by party politics in spite of themselves. Maintaining their independence from the self-aggrandizing nature of political parties was a notion closely connected to their philanthropic activities and views on public motherhood. The articles anti-suffrage women published encouraged and celebrated the nonpartisan position of unenfranchised women.

Anti-suffragists differed from suffragists most particularly in their fundamental belief regarding the use of the vote as a tool for change, but they also argued that most women were not interested in voting. Whether or not women actually wanted to vote was an argument raised periodically during the nineteenth century, as well as during the 1894 New York State constitutional convention, and in November 1895 Massachusetts conducted a nonbinding referendum on the question.[75] The proposed referendum pleased neither the suffragists nor the anti-suffragists. Suffragists were angry that the poll would not count, and anti-suffragists were angry that they were required to use the ballot to make their views known. Massachusetts antis encouraged as many women as they could not to vote; as a result female voter turnout was very low. Of about 612,000 women who were eligible, 42,676 (just under 7 percent) registered to vote, but only 23,065 (about 4 percent) of the eligible women actually voted. Of those women who did vote, only 4 percent, or 861, voted against woman suffrage; the rest of the voting women supported the measure. In some fifty-seven towns, not a single woman voted for suffrage. The male vote in opposition was 186,976 out of the 273,946 votes cast; almost 70 percent of the male voters opposed woman suffrage.[76] As Sara Hunter Graham has noted, the 1895 referendum "cast a long shadow." Suffrage won, but women's turnout was low, indicating female apathy or resistance to voting. Suffragists would never again call for a vote from the disenfranchised class, and anti-suffragists would never again believe suffragists' arguments that most women wanted to vote.[77]

Most anti-suffragists and suffragists, while they heartily disagreed on the fundamental value of the vote and frequently criticized each other in print, usually tried to be respectful of each other. Moving in the same social circles, they often met at social and club functions. Both groups frequently found ways to confront each other directly but courteously, debating the topic in parlor meetings, on college campuses, and in other public forums. Suffragists invited antis to their meetings, as when they invited Annie Nathan Meyer, well known for her anti-suffrage stance, to a luncheon at the Hotel Astor to honor Susan B. Anthony in 1907. After all, her sister, Maud Nathan, a prominent reformer and suffragist, was one of the speakers. The suffrage disagreement between the sisters became increasingly public over time.[78]

Annie Nathan Meyer (1867–1951) was one of several Jewish women in the New York anti-suffrage movement. Educated in public schools until she was about fourteen, she married Dr. Alfred Meyer in 1887 and had one child, Margaret. She was the impetus for the founding of and fundraising for Barnard College for women in 1889, having been frustrated by the inadequacy of the Collegiate Course for Women at Columbia College. A prolific writer, Meyer published several books, including *Woman's Work in America* (1891), *Helen Brent, M.D.* (1893), and an autobiography, *It's Been Fun* (1951), as well as numerous short stories, essays, plays, and articles. Meyer also wrote quite a number of articles in opposition to woman suffrage, including the often-reprinted "Woman's Assumption of Sex Superiority."[79] The more prominent in society the women confronting each other during the suffrage battle were, the more they enthralled the popular media.[80]

The outspoken Annie Nathan Meyer, founder of Barnard
College, opposed woman suffrage all her life. Courtesy of
the Jacob Rader Marcus Center of the American Jewish
Archives, Cincinnati, Ohio (http://americanjewish
archives.org).

Anti-suffragists were aware of the incongruity of the "true woman" asserting
herself in public, and they knew they were often targets of criticism on this
score. Margaret Doane Gardiner of Albany, for one, acknowledged that suffragists criticized antis "for going into public life to say they can't go into it."[81]
She and other anti-suffragists rejected this criticism, asserting that a public
life for women was an entirely different matter from having the burden of
the ballot. Some antis encouraged women to participate in government, yet
not by using an instrument as masculine as the vote, and laid groundwork
for women to enter public roles wherever possible. For example, New York

anti-suffrage leaders wrote a letter to Governor Charles Evans Hughes in 1909 requesting that "all offices on charity, reformatory, and educational boards" appropriate for women be filled by them. They asserted that too few women sat on the advisory boards, and they thought that appointing women to those boards was the best way to utilize the "capacities of women."[82] Albany antis reiterated this goal the following year, both to the governor and to the mayor of New York City.[83] Meyer addressed this issue in an editorial to the *New York Times* by pointing out that anti-suffragists stood "not against woman's influence in politics, not against her concerning herself in all matters vital to the best interests of her country." Still, she professed herself and all antis as "firmly against all women being forced to take this interest in politics against their will."[84] Once enfranchised, she argued, all conscientious women would feel obligated to vote; their right to stay out of politics would be forfeited.

Once the New York State anti-suffragists had an organization, they took action whenever the members of the state legislature considered the suffrage question. When the senate and judiciary committees debated suffrage in 1897, Elizabeth Crannell, Lucy Scott, and Louise Caldwell Jones attended in order to counter the claims of Susan B. Anthony, Harriet May Mills of Syracuse, and other suffragists. They were very pleased when the legislature again took no action on the measure.[85] A dozen antis attended the joint legislative hearing on suffrage in February 1899, when the committee still took no action on the woman suffrage issue.[86] During March 1906, Jones and Helen Kendrick Johnson, joined by Mrs. Julian Heath, Mrs. George Phillips, Meyer, and Crannell, attended the joint meeting of the judiciary committee in Albany. The following year there was "standing room only" at the joint judiciary hearings.[87] Helen Kendrick Johnson (1844–1917) often attended the hearings, which constituted major events for both anti-suffragists and suffragists.

Born in Hamilton, in upstate New York, Helen Kendrick was educated in both Rochester and Clinton. She married Rossiter Johnson, an author and editor of encyclopedias and literary collections. They had four children, but only one daughter survived. Helen authored several children's books series, a novel, and edited a number of books on a range of topics. She maintained membership in more than one anti-suffrage organization, supported in her views by her ardently anti-suffragist husband.[88] Between 1894 and 1896, Johnson edited the *American Woman's Journal*. Soon after she assumed the position of editor, her office was inundated with letters from women who wanted the vote. She felt honor-bound to publish the pro-suffrage articles submitted to the

Helen Kendrick Johnson, photographed in 1891, carefully
studied the suffrage movement and published *Woman and
the Republic* in 1897. She also founded the Guidon Club to
help train anti-suffrage women for public speaking. Photo
originally appeared in *Helen Kendrick Johnson: The Story of
Her Varied Activities* (New York: Publishers Printing, 1917).

journal, but she also felt obliged to respond to the articles, telling her readers
that pro-suffrage arguments were "completely wrong." In 1897 she published
*Woman and the Republic: A Survey of the Woman-Suffrage Movement in the
United States and a Discussion of the Claims and Arguments of Its Foremost
Advocates.* She concluded that woman suffrage was not related to progress for
women or the government. One of Johnson's primary arguments, frequently
used by anti-suffragists, insisted that the ballot must be backed by the ability
to serve one's country in times of war, echoing her husband's article, "The

Blank Cartridge Ballot," on the same topic.[89] Johnson, with her conservative and antisocialist perspective, influenced many anti-suffragists.

In their struggle to define the proper roles for women in the polity, anti-suffragists would sometimes disagree even with each other. In March 1904, for example, at a hearing before the state judiciary committee, anti-suffragists, including Crannell and Meyer, opposed giving urban women the right to vote for school officers or to "make them eligible for School Trustees or Commissioner." Women in New York, outside of New York City, had been granted school suffrage on February 12, 1880. Although the wording was somewhat unclear, and changes were made to the statute in subsequent years, women who met the legislative requirements were allowed to vote in school board elections and on bond issues. Many women were unaware of this right, many of those who knew of the right faced transportation difficulties; others were not interested in voting for any reason. Additionally, since voting was held in "male enclaves," women were often intimidated enough to stay away from school voting.[90] By opposing even limited suffrage to influence educational decisions, Crannell and Meyer contradicted the anti-suffrage argument that arenas such as education required the attention of women.[91]

In addition to their concerns at the state level, the New York State Association took on what work was necessary at the federal level, sometimes alone, and sometimes with assistance from antis of other states. Anti-suffrage delegates from New York, Massachusetts, and Delaware appeared before the congressional committees in Washington for the first time in 1900 and thereafter whenever woman suffrage was to be discussed in Congress. A highlight of their first trip to Washington was a visit to President William McKinley at the White House. Mrs. Elihu Root presented Johnson, Dodge, Jones, and six other antis to the president, who entertained them, reportedly expressing interest in their anti-suffrage arguments. The women pronounced themselves well pleased by the meeting.[92]

Meeting with members of Congress was less comfortable for this contingency of anti-suffragists, however. The antis were unaware that they needed tickets for admission to the Senate hearings. Susan B. Anthony, on learning who the women were, "persuaded the doorkeeper to admit them."[93] Anthony then saw to it that the suffragists gave some of their allotted speaking time to the anti-suffragists. Her courtesy did not continue, however, and later that same afternoon in the House she would not give up suffrage time. There, the Representatives postponed their adjournment until the anti-suffragists had time to speak. According to the *New York Times*, the antis were "elated" that Congress failed to pass the proposed amendment enfranchising women, convinced of the persuasiveness of their arguments.[94] Circumstances at the federal level were similar for the campaign in the next few years. Each year anti-suffragists and suffragists would present arguments. Each year antis expressed triumph when the measure did not pass, and suffragists found encouragement in the increasing attention paid to woman suffrage. Meanwhile, the New York State suffrage campaign gathered momentum and support, requiring increased attention from anti-suffragists.

Part of the momentum was related to the death of Susan B. Anthony on March 13, 1906. By February 15, 1907, in honor of the day of Anthony's birth and her memory, suffragists received a large sum of money to support their cause.[95] Because New York was so important to the suffrage movement, suffragists earmarked most of the funds for the state campaign. But that year, anti-suffragists outnumbered the suffragists at the New York State judiciary committee hearing to discuss the Raines Bill, which would allow women taxpayers to vote at special tax elections in cities of the third class.[96] Class-conscious antis argued that any extension of suffrage would increase the opportunities for "disreputable women" to vote. Elizabeth Crannell, for example, complained that extending the suffrage to the "unwieldy," "uniformed," and "ignorant" people would be disastrous to the nation-state.[97] It is not clear how influential the anti-suffragist arguments actually were, but the bill did not pass.[98] In 1908, anti-suffragists and suffragists used four hours to present their arguments before the senate judiciary committee, as part of the consideration of another woman suffrage amendment to the state constitution.[99] Anti-suffragists presented papers at a joint hearing in Albany that next year, but they admitted that the "palm for oratory goes unquestionably to the suffragists," acknowledging, with some pride perhaps, their own lack of professional speaking experience.[100] Year after year, anti-suffragists presented their arguments against a woman suffrage amendment, now an annual event in the state legislature.[101] Eventually, antis would gain, and be proud of, greater speaking abilities.

By this point, anti-suffragists could present evidence that in states where women agitated for the vote, such as Oregon, polls showed that suffrage support had decreased over time rather than increased. Additionally, no state had enfranchised women since Colorado had done so in 1896, a point that Alice Hill Chittenden argued had proved a diminishing interest in woman suffrage. Well aware that the opposition of women to woman suffrage "at once differentiates it and sets it apart from all the other so-called woman's movements," Chittenden asserted that "there is no economy in having two people do the same work."[102] This argument was in keeping with those related to improving efficiency in government, as Chittenden's colleague Bertha Lane Scott (1860–1938) also publicized. In her February 1909 address before the joint senate and assembly judiciary committee in Albany, Scott argued that women had evolved to be better suited for nonpolitical rather than for political "occupations and modes of thought." She believed that the "non-political and politically non-partisan woman" must remain "instrumental in maintaining high national ideas." Bertha Scott also defended the anti-suffrage women's entry into the public realm; she argued that by directly confronting legislators in their sessions, the antis were able to realize their reform-oriented aims.[103]

Bertha Lane, born in Cincinnati, Ohio, married William Forse Scott, a Civil War veteran and a lawyer, in 1891; the couple moved to Yonkers and had one son. Involved in several educational clubs and organizations, she frequently spoke publicly on topics such as "Practical Limitations of Democracy," English literature, and women's social status, as well as on woman suffrage. Serving on the executive committee of the New York State Association Opposed to Woman Suffrage, she would also participate in public debates held between antis and suffragists.[104] Scott wrote several articles and editorials on woman suffrage; her "Woman's Relation to Government" was first published in 1904 in the *North American Review* and reprinted in pamphlet form by the New York State Association. In it, she argued that the demands on women as mothers required all of their strength and abilities; the strife of political involvement would tax them beyond their limits. Instead, she advocated higher education for women to bring about social and political reforms.[105]

By the second decade of the new century, the subject of woman suffrage seemed virtually inescapable. Suffragists said that the antis wanted the same things they did, but were only being stubborn about the necessity of the vote.[106] As an indication of the seriousness of the New York State campaign, the National American Woman Suffrage Association temporarily relocated its headquarters to New York City. Carrie Chapman Catt contended that 1909 marked the year New York State became the "storm centre of the movement."[107] The increase in suffrage-related activity that year prompted Anna Howard Shaw to remark in a letter to her Dutch friend, Aletta Jacobs, "We never had such a suffrage boom in our lives. It is either suffrage or anti-suffrage meetings continually, until I should think the people would get sick and tired of them."[108] It was also in 1909 that anti-suffragists reorganized the New York State Association Opposed to Woman Suffrage, incorporating it under state laws and adding more political behaviors to their repertoire.[109]

In addition to facing legislators and suffragists directly, anti-suffragists slowly appropriated some of the other political techniques of suffragists. Suffragists had been using automobiles, trolleys, and trains to spread their message for some years, well aware that a group of women traveling for a public purpose was newsworthy.[110] Anti-suffragists eventually followed suit. About one hundred anti-suffragists rode a special train from New York City to Albany for the 1911 joint assembly and senate judiciary committee hearing on suffrage. Josephine Dodge, Alice Hill Chittenden, Charlotte E. Rowe, and Louise Caldwell Jones were aboard.[111] They joined anti-suffragists from Buffalo, Rochester, Schenectady, and other nearby cities; women of the Albany anti-suffrage association hosted them throughout their stay.[112]

Meantime, some anti-suffragists established additional but independent organizations to oppose enfranchisement for women. In 1907 Helen Kendrick Johnson founded and presided over the Guidon Club in New York City. Guidon, the name Johnson chose for her club, suggests a military influence. It was taken from the "small ensign which, while it does not flaunt itself, is never absent from the fore-front of a marching column." The vice-president, Bertha Lane Scott, outlined the campaign plan, pointing out that the members must "meet yelling with music and parading with high class entertainments."[113] The group included socially prominent women, many of whom, like Scott and Johnson, held memberships in other anti-suffrage organizations as well. The club would educate members on "women's right relationship to the Republic, to social life, and to the home," through "study, discussion and speaking." To further the connection of women to the Republic, the members of the club were intent on exposing what they believed were links between the pro-suffrage faction and socialism. One of various responses to the many social, economic, and political changes taking place during the Progressive Era, socialism seemed threatening to many people. Arguing that "woman suffrage must lead inevitably into communism," Johnson was particularly opposed to socialism because she believed it would destroy the patriarchal family.[114]

According to Johnson, the Guidon Club was the only New York anti-suffrage organization of the time that had both women and men as members, which may hint at a serious point of contention in the female anti-suffrage ranks. Rather than encouraging cooperation between anti-suffrage organiza-

tions, Johnson considered her club the "most important organization in opposition to woman suffrage." Members gathered on a weekly basis to study
the "raison d'être" of the suffrage crisis though a series of lectures. Guided by
strict rules of conduct at meetings, women gathered into several study groups.[115]
Each member of a study group would draw a number, and after listening to the
presentation of the main topic, would rise to present her own view, thereby
gaining confidence in public speaking. According to their organ, *The Reply*,
their literature and speakers were in demand in many states. In 1908, the New
York City Federation of Women's Clubs welcomed the Guidon Club as a member.[116] The Guidon Club apparently kept an exclusive membership, although
its members oversaw a branch of young people, and held weekly meetings at
the home of Louise Caldwell Jones, one of the vice-presidents.[117]

Louise Caldwell Jones (1858–1929) also founded the National League for
the Civic Education of Women in 1908, even as she served as a vice-president
of the Guidon Club and as press chairman of the New York State Association
Opposed to Woman Suffrage. Born in Buffalo, she married Gilbert E. Jones, a
banker and one of the sons of the founder of the *New York Times*, a newspaper
clearly opposed to woman suffrage. Living on fashionable Madison Avenue,
she raised two sons. Heavily involved with anti-suffrage since the 1890s, the
outspoken Jones often spoke and wrote in defense of woman's anti-suffrage.[118]
At the public meeting to announce the formation of the league, Richard Watson Gilder argued that women's unique ability to effect change was "in their
peculiar relation to public opinion." The women of the league would study
local and state needs and ascertain how best they could improve social conditions.[119] Members included many prominent New York women, including
Carolyn Putnam, most of whom retained their membership in the New York
State Association.[120] Jones' husband would often arrange for publicity for the
reform work in which his wife was involved.[121] An all-male advisory board
consisting of Lyman Abbott, Rossiter Johnson, Richard Watson Gilder, Francis
S. Bangs, and Francis Lynde Stetson assisted members of the league.[122] This
board made the league, like the Guidon Club, significantly different from the
New York State Association Opposed to Woman Suffrage, which especially
in its early years avoided male influence.

Its prospectus stated that the National League for the Civic Education of
Women made its priority educating its members "on all questions affecting the
political, economic, and social position of women." Sustaining members paid a
fee of five dollars a year, associate members three dollars, and general members

Louise Caldwell Jones, head of the National League for the
Civic Education of Women. This photograph was originally
published in "Why Women Oppose Woman's Suffrage,"
Pearson's Magazine 23, no. 3 (March 1910), along with the
photographs of other prominent anti-suffrage women.
Courtesy of the Sophia Smith Collection, Smith College,
Northampton, Mass.

one dollar. The league encouraged the membership of women teachers and
philanthropists by offering them a special membership fee of fifty cents, but
they did not offer a membership rate specifically for working-class members.
It maintained an office and meeting room in the basement of the Jones's home
and kept an extensive library of suffrage-related books, newspaper clippings,
and statistical information. Louise Jones opened the library to people interested in learning more about the arguments of suffrage and informational
pamphlets could be had free of charge.[123]

Members listened to lectures on various topics related to women's rights and politics, and they invited such notables as members of Theodore Roosevelt's cabinet, United States senators, members of the federal and state judiciary, and university professors to speak.[124] Prominent speakers such as Rabbi Joseph Silverman, Dr. Lyman Abbott, Rossiter Johnson, Margaret Deland (a popular novelist and short story writer), and Leslie L. Thompkins (a professor of law at New York University) spoke at their meetings.[125] These speakers encouraged women to think more deeply about their important roles as reformers and members of the state while continuing to remain outside of politics. Assuredly, the debate regarding voting rights for women frequently arose. Members were entitled to a range of educational courses, held at the Jones residence, to learn the "fundamental principles against woman suffrage."[126] In addition to training and hosting speakers, the league, like the Guidon Club, provided speakers to interested groups around the country.[127]

To reach a broader public, Jones scheduled several series of public lectures.[128] For example, early in 1910 Jones hosted a series of seven lectures on various topics related to women's civic interests at the Berkeley Lyceum. She cancelled the five remaining lectures of another series at the Cooper Union because of reports that suffragists would heckle and throw eggs if the lectures continued. Perhaps there was something about Jones in addition to her connection to the *New York Times* that antagonized suffragists, for she seems to have drawn more public censure than most other New York anti-suffragists. Suffragists criticized her for being deceptive in advertising her talks and series of lectures, which were initially listed under the general topic of women's suffrage. Jones defended herself by arguing that suffragists did not "have a mortgage on the title 'woman suffrage.'" "To say that one cannot speak against woman suffrage," she argued, "without giving warning that the negative of the proposition will be upheld, under penalty of being deceitful, is ridiculous."[129] Even so, in advertising her next series of lectures, Jones made it clear that the topics were in opposition to suffrage.[130]

Aware of the need for anti-suffragists to expand their influence to other groups of women, Louise Jones and other members of the National League deliberately targeted college students. In the spring of 1910, the league scheduled a "College Day," when Professor Mary A. Jordan of Smith College spoke on "Some Overlooked Issues of the Ballot." Annie Nathan Meyer, who headed a college branch formed later that year, also delivered a speech.[131] College women were as divided on suffrage as they were on any number of issues, but most campuses "were not potent breeding grounds for the cause." Vassar College, for example, banned public meetings on the topic.[132] Interest in suffrage and anti-suffrage in college reflected the interest in the greater society, and the league sought to promote its views to the next generation of leaders.

The National League for Civic Education of Women remained at the forefront of an array of other activities during the next few years, clearly desiring both national and international influence.[133] For instance, it financed an investigation of the four western suffrage states to prove the ineffectiveness of women's enfranchisement.[134] Richard Barry, a journalist who had traveled around the world to report on wars and other topics for a number of magazines and newspapers, apparently found nothing in the suffrage states that showed improvement in the condition of women. He reported little support for woman suffrage even in those states.[135] In addition to disseminating information about the state of woman suffrage around the nation, members used their influence to draw support from overseas.

When Mary Augusta [Mrs. Humphry] Ward (1851–1920), the foremost anti-suffragist in Britain, accepted the vice-presidency of the National League in 1909, it generated some excitement for broadening the influence of anti-suffragism beyond the borders of the United States.[136] Ward, a noted anti-suffragist since 1889, authored more than thirty popular novels, including *Delia Blanchflower* (1914), specifically about the woman suffrage movement in England. Moderate in its perspective, the book was not directly anti-suffrage. The main character, Delia, had been deeply influenced by Gertrude Marvell, a driven leader of the Daughters of Revolt, the most violent and militant branch of suffragism. Other characters reflected more complicated views of woman suffrage, both for and against, but the book's main message encouraged patience on the issue of the vote. In the meantime, women should make use of their abilities to help those in need.[137] The novel clearly reflects Ward's stance on the suffrage question, as she focused primarily on "encouraging women to use what liberties they already possessed to work for public causes in their own localities." However, she served as president of the British Women's National Anti-Suffrage League in 1909, speaking widely for her cause.[138] Her connection with the cause in the United States was negligible but nevertheless important for the reputation of the new organization. Both the National League and the Guidon Club focused on self-improvement and education, yet they duplicated many of the efforts of the New York State Association and its affiliates.[139]

Some of the antis holding membership in the National League or the Guidon Club also belonged to organizations other than the New York State Association Opposed to Woman Suffrage. One such organization was the short-lived National Society for Maintaining American Institutions, which also opposed woman suffrage. The goal of the society was patriotic, to "promote the aims cherished by the founders of this republic."[140] Antis stayed away from clubs with obvious alignments with suffrage but were members of women's clubs such as Sorosis, the influential women's literary club founded in 1868 by Jane Cunningham Croly, not a supporter of woman suffrage. Additionally, anti-suffrage organizations belonged to national, state, and city levels of the General Federation of Women's Clubs. The General Federation of Women's Clubs, founded by Croly to mark the twenty-first anniversary of the founding of Sorosis in 1890, initially connected twenty thousand women through their membership in two hundred clubs.[141] Within ten years of its establishment, the federation claimed a membership of 150,000 women.[142] Like Sorosis, the federation subscribed to "domestic feminism" and influenced its members through the invocation of women's traditional domestic qualities.[143] Eventually, anti-suffragists became confident about their ability to join in debating woman suffrage before groups such as the General Federation and the Empire State Federation of Women's Clubs. Mrs. Julian Heath, president of the National Housewife's League, chaired an anti-suffrage committee of the City Federation of Women's clubs, which held regular meetings during the summer of 1909.[144]

Members of the General Federation were still reluctant to fully endorse woman suffrage, for it was not compatible with the primary goal of the federation to encourage "women's traditional qualities," which were those often used to justify women's reform work away from home.[145] When the federation held its fall convention, the committee responsible encouraged membership from every club "except those of avowedly suffrage convictions."[146] The situation at the convention became "lively" when suffragists began handing out literature and, not to be outdone, antis responded in kind.[147] The "very able anti-suffragist" Alice Hill Chittenden delivered her address on "educated or enlightened public opinion" at the Tenth Biennial Session of the General Federation of Women's Clubs in Cincinnati in 1910, the first time the topic had been presented at the convention. She was paired with the vice president of the National American Woman Suffrage Association, Kate M. Gordon.[148] Suffrage, discussed in virtually every club to which women belonged, seemed pervasive.

One reason for the existence of so many separate organizations in opposition to suffrage was that the New York State Association Opposed to Woman

Suffrage persisted (at least until 1914) in its rejection of the formal influence of men. Both the National League for the Civic Education of Women and the Guidon Club prominently included men on the board or as active members. An additional reason was that until 1907 the New York State Association usually declined to participate in public debates with suffragists. It confined itself to personal appearances in legislative halls and distributing literature to libraries, newspaper and magazine editors, and interested individuals.[149] Members of the National League and the Guidon Club must have disagreed with those policies, for both groups scheduled more public lectures than the New York State Association did during these years. Another reason perhaps influencing the development of other anti-suffrage organizations was that the New York State Association sought to include working-class women in its membership. Even in their statement to the constitutional convention in 1894, anti-suffragists had made a point of claiming that the signatures they obtained on their petition "are confined to no class, but represent those who are obliged to work for their self-support, as well as those more fortunately situated."[150] As early as the winter of 1897, members of a subcommittee carried out a "series of entertaining and useful meetings for wage earners."[151] The membership of the league and the Guidon Club seem to have included the wealthiest and most elite of the anti-suffragists. Constitutional historian David Kyvig suggests that anti-suffragists may have promoted the formation of many organizations to help give the impression of widespread opposition to woman suffrage.[152] Still, it was probably a disadvantage to the anti-suffrage movement that antis were not more publicly cooperative and spread themselves among so many different associations.

Anti-suffragists must have been aware of this problem, for late in 1911 they attempted to develop a greater organizing force to combat the increasingly influential suffrage contingent. By that time the New York antis had the wherewithal and enough political expertise via their confrontations with suffragists in state and national legislative bodies to create the National Association Opposed to Woman Suffrage. Founded in the Park Avenue home of Josephine Jewell Dodge on November 28, just one month after the pro-suffrage California referendum passed, the association shared headquarters with the New York State Association Opposed to Woman Suffrage. Representatives from anti-suffrage groups in eight states (New York, Massachusetts, Pennsylvania, Maryland, Rhode Island, Illinois, Oregon, and California) elected Dodge as president. Carolyn Putnam took over her position as president of the New York State Association.[153] The National Association shared the resources of

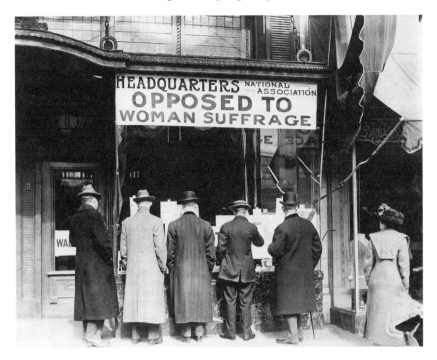

Headquarters of the National Association Opposed to Woman Suffrage, very likely at the 29 East Thirty-Ninth Street, New York City, address. Courtesy of the Library of Congress, Washington, D.C., Prints and Photographs Division, 01453.

the state organization throughout its tenure, including its leadership, although ostensibly they remained separate organizations. It attempted to offer some co-hesiveness among the many anti-suffrage groups that had formed throughout more than twenty-five states. However, from the beginning, the members of the National Association determined that they would not interfere with the activities of state or local organizations; they would wait to be asked for infor-mation and advice, which they would readily make available.[154] This stance, of course, limited their leadership potential and influence. Anti-suffragists, even at the national level, persisted in choosing activities in line with the proper role of womanhood, although that role had been significantly updated for the new century.

Both anti-suffragists and suffragists claimed to represent the dominant view of women in the United States.[155] On garnering public attention, suffragists drew from long experience and their deeply committed membership. The priority of most New York anti-suffragist organizations was to "educate the public in the belief that women can be more useful to the community without the ballot than if affiliated with and influenced by party politics."[156] But they were limited by their lack of funds and incapable of matching suffrage talents in fundraising. Compared with suffragists, antis were politically awkward and inexperienced, although their techniques did improve with practice and as they emulated the mass-communication methods used by suffragists. Antis did not have speakers with the eloquence of Anna Howard Shaw, nor did they benefit from leaders with the organizational brilliance of Carrie Chapman Catt, and they certainly did not have a "potent symbol" like Susan B. Anthony to revere.[157] While anti-suffrage women did not have the panache of the suffragists, they certainly challenged the suffragists to do their utmost to win the right to vote. By 1911, anti-suffrage leaders in New York State developed a higher level of political acumen, were more willing to "assert themselves publicly," and they had become a force to challenge the suffragists.[158] "The fight was hot and heavy," according to Huybertie Pruyn Hamlin, and woman suffrage amassed a lot of attention and publicity.[159] Anti-suffragists were as ready as they would ever be for the intensity of the fight for woman suffrage in New York State.

3. Antis Win the New York State Campaign, 1912–1915

When the *Titanic* plunged 1,513 passengers and crew members to their deaths on April 12, 1912, people ascribed various meanings to the event in an attempt to make sense of the tragedy. Even before the survivors made it to New York City, belief in the exemplary behavior of the "first-cabin" men aboard the ship provided evidence for anti-suffragists that men would follow the law of the sea—"Women and Children First"—in politics as they had in the icy North Atlantic.[1] The myth of male heroism reinforced traditional gender roles and served as ideal support for anti-suffrage arguments. The debut issue of the *Woman's Protest*, the anti-suffragists' national organ, claimed that not only did men obey the law of the sea, "the women admitted that they were not fitted for men's tasks."[2] If a man in terrible danger accepted his own death as "a holy sacrament, sanctified by bravery, self-denial and unequalled consideration" for those weaker than himself, men could certainly be trusted to take care of women's political needs. It proved that the existing gender roles were "natural and eternal," that paternalism was "commonsensical and universal."[3]

Contradictorily, suffragists argued that the evidence of the tragedy clearly indicated that women needed the vote because "male chivalry was exceptional and inadequate." An article published in the *Progressive Woman* asserted that suffragists struggled against the very class of men celebrated as heroes after the disaster. These men undoubtedly "opposed the idea of the rights of women in participation in government affairs" and exploited women in a range of other ways.[4] For suffragists, the tragedy "raised practical issues about power and social responsibility."[5] The women who were victims of the tragedy had "no voice in making and enforcing the laws on land or sea." As far as suffragists were concerned, "only empowered women could initiate the real work of lifesaving."[6] Although unrelated to politics or woman suffrage, the *Titanic* disaster provided grist for the propaganda mills of women on both sides of the issue.[7]

The response to the *Titanic* disaster highlights the pervasiveness of the woman suffrage controversy as it drew increasing attention and debate. The legislative conditions required to submit a referendum regarding the removal of the word "male" from Section 1 of Article 2 of the New York State Constitution had passed two consecutive legislatures.[8] Although the woman suffrage referendum was due in 1916, Democrats, taking advantage of their increased power in the state, pushed for an earlier date for the convention to prevent an alignment of the Republican and Progressive parties against them.[9] Awareness of the 1915 referendum on woman suffrage inspired mounting propagandizing and politicization on the part of suffragists as well as anti-suffragists.

Anti-suffragists recognized the national importance of New York to the woman suffrage issue, and they were long past assuming that their silence would protect them from enfranchisement. Suffragists knew that victory in the state would encourage victory in other eastern states and prepared eagerly for the campaign.[10] They became ever more creative in the use of mass media techniques and promoting their cause. As public support for woman suffrage increased, anti-suffragists also appropriated the newest forms of technology and fashionable amusements to vie with suffragists for the attention of the electorate. Emulating the suffragists in sometimes unexpected ways, anti-suffragists challenged suffragists with their efforts. It was a lively campaign as anti-suffragists and suffragists sponsored dances, teas, parties, debates, speeches, and countless fundraising events throughout the state. New York harbored some of the most politically developed organizations of anti-suffragists in the nation, although antis certainly lacked the experience, resources, sophistication, and creativity of suffragists. Still, anti-suffrage organizational strategies and political rhetoric helped to convince strong majorities to vote against woman suffrage in 1915, especially in upstate New York.[11]

The extraordinarily energetic, innovative, and experienced suffragists facing the antis highlighted the political ineptitude of anti-suffragists. Yet New York anti-suffragists were far from being the quiet, retiring women one might expect of a group who professed to believe in—and promote—the directives of "true womanhood." While anti-suffragists sought to preserve the traditional role

of women as caregivers of homes and families, by 1912 they readily accepted
the need for the public presence of women who would represent that view.
Members of the New York State Association Opposed to Woman Suffrage
behaved in bold, confrontational, and sometimes even outrageous ways, especially as suffragists came closer to success. Harriot Stanton Blatch, the youngest daughter of Elizabeth Cady Stanton and leader of the New York–based
Women's Political Union, was unquestionably a dynamic force in New York
City, and there were many enthusiastic, competent, and deeply committed
suffrage workers across the state of New York.[12] In addition, the New York State
Woman Suffrage Association recruited the formidable Carrie Chapman Catt
as chair of the state campaign committee.[13] Catt's most outstanding character-
istic was her ability to encourage separate suffrage groups to collaborate under
her leadership; she oversaw a movement that reached a level of cooperation
and organization never attained by anti-suffragists.

No longer naïve enough to take legislators' support for granted, anti-suffragists deemed it necessary to be a presence in Albany whenever a legislative
committee of either branch of state government met. The month before the
Titanic disaster, at least twenty-five antis attended the discussion of woman
suffrage before the assembly's judiciary committee. Suffragists posted "silent
sentinels" outside the judiciary committee meeting room during the sessions
of the state legislature all that year. The Women's Political Union described
"silent sentinels" as "typifying the patient waiting that the women of the Empire
State have done since Elizabeth Cady Stanton made the first demand for our
enfranchisement in 1848."[14] Their presence reminded legislators of suffragists'
unity and determination. Suffragists also upped the ante, arranging private
meetings with legislators to lobby for woman suffrage. Anti-suffragists, often
boasting familial and social connections to politicians, found it necessary to
respond in new ways to counter suffrage influence. Sometimes antis lost their
decorum. Estelle R. [Mrs. Robert] McVickar of Mount Vernon, for example,
leapt to her feet and, ignoring interruptions, challenged a sponsor of the bill
under discussion who had reversed his position on woman suffrage. The days of
quietly deferring to men as anti-suffragists had in 1894 had passed. The judiciary
committee handed in a report opposed to granting suffrage to women, in spite
of Blatch's promise that they would have "no peace until women had the vote."[15]

When the issue resurfaced in May 1912, antis and suffragists met before the
state senate. Anti-suffragists had the support of Robert F. Wagner, "one of the
most determined, serious, and critical opponents" of woman suffrage in the

New York legislature.[16] A key reform Democrat and one of the "rising stars" in New York politics, he would serve as a delegate to the 1915 constitutional convention.[17] Many other New York politicians shared Wagner's opposition to women's enfranchisement. Suffragists criticized Assemblyman William S. Coffey, who represented McVickar's district of Mount Vernon, arguing that he did not accurately represent his constituency. Confident that the majority of women opposed the vote, he organized a mock referendum for the women of his district. Of the 360 votes cast, 230 votes were against woman suffrage.[18] He concluded that he had proved his point.

Suffragists and anti-suffragists all sought to influence the development of state party platforms. Neither the Democratic Party nor the Republican Party officially endorsed woman suffrage, although the newly formed Progressive Party did. When the Republican Committee on Resolutions met in Saratoga in the fall of 1912 to consider its platform, antis and suffragists attended the meeting. Although committee members listened for an hour to the women of both sides, the men were clearly eager to focus on the "real work of platform building." They harbored no more interest in woman suffrage than they had in 1894.[19] The main goal of the Republican contingency was to preserve the apportionment they had established at the earlier convention, assuring the continuing domination of their party in the state legislature.[20] Elihu Root would again serve as chair of the constitutional convention; the same "intense conservatism of the Republican members" would dominate in 1915.[21] Although Root remained "steadfastly opposed to woman suffrage," he agreed that the question should be submitted separately to the voters.[22] He eventually appointed a pro-suffrage chair to the committee on suffrage and remained consistently polite, even accommodating, to women suffragists who requested hearings. He had no fear that the measure would pass. Soon after, antis announced they would not oppose a referendum on the constitutional amendment removing the word "male" from the description of a voter, as they, too, expressed confidence that voters would soundly defeat it.[23]

As antis and suffragists sought the support of lawmakers and the electorate, they used increasingly provocative methods to reach the public. Truly masters of drawing attention, suffragists held a suffrage parade on May 4, 1912, just three weeks after the *Titanic* sank. Ten thousand marchers drew a huge crowd, and the newspapers and periodicals kept up a constant barrage of commentary. Anti-suffragists expressed outrage that suffragists ignored the tragedy to promote woman suffrage.[24] But parades were not the only venue suffragists used to draw attention. They sponsored balls, organized a maypole dance for young people, and did their laundry at a "washing bee" to poke fun at the often-heard criticism that women's place was "at the washtub."[25] Suffragists caused quite a stir another time when they sold "bombs" made of old-fashioned doughnuts and talcum powder. Marked "Vote for the Cook," their suffrage cookies sold very well during yet another fund raising event.[26] Suffragists also drove automobiles, still a remarkable sight in rural areas, to relay their message into areas of the state seldom confronted with political campaigners. Anti-suffragists eventually used automobiles for media attention, although more seldom and with less finesse than did the suffragists. The more exciting the suffragists' behavior became, the more difficult it was for the antis to amass attention and enthusiasm. Many suffragists clearly enjoyed themselves as they crossed the borders of decorous behavior that most antis only rarely, if ever, thought of breaching.

Still, anti-suffrage behavior did adapt as the behavior of suffragists influenced them. Radical changes in the attitude toward women's appropriate behavior appeared during the 1910s, affecting views on women in politics. Increasingly, women's access to higher education, exciting new amusements, and a developing consumerism challenged conservative nineteenth-century ideas about women's special but separate sphere. Physically, women gained freedom of movement as they shed corsets and petticoat layers and wore the slimmer silhouette of new fashionable garments.[27] Benefiting from new social freedoms, they could be seen in a wider array of public places, often without male escort. Indicating a bolder and more expanded phase of thinking about women's place in society, the concept of feminism also emerged in the early 1910s.[28] Anti-suffragists perceived suffragist agitation for the vote and the spreading of feminist ideas as obscuring the real threat to the patriarchal family.[29] However, the changes facilitated new ways of reaching people, and the innovative tactics encouraged men to listen more carefully to suffragist claims rather than to those of anti-suffragists.[30] As press coverage of woman suffrage activities increased, anti-suffragists pushed against old-fashioned restrictions to respond as best they could.

The key to influencing the electorate in time for the referendum necessitated increased political organization. Signifying the critical importance of the state to the woman suffrage movement, in 1913 Carrie Chapman Catt established the Empire State Campaign Committee. The committee coordinated the efforts of the New York State Woman Suffrage Association (with Gertrude Foster Brown as president), New York City's Woman Suffrage Party (with Catt's longtime colleague Mary Garrett Hay skillfully managing the presidency), the Men's League for Woman Suffrage (under the presidency of James Lees Laidlaw), the Equal Franchise Society (with president Mrs. Howard Mansfield), the Collegiate League (under Mrs. Charles L. Tiffany as president), and other groups. Organized into twelve campaign districts, each leader reported to Catt. The campaign districts were divided into nearly 150 assembly districts, and further divided into 2,127 election districts, each with an assigned leader.[31] Vira Boarman [Mrs. Norman de R.] Whitehouse, with the help of a press and publicity council, submitted articles to the newspapers and skillfully countered all anti-suffrage charges in articles and editorials.[32] Suffragists also had an uncanny ability to raise large sums of money fairly quickly, an indication of their increasing influence and stature, as well as a clue to their own class status.

Anti-suffragists responded to the more politicized suffragists by improving their own organizational structure and broadening their membership.[33] Antis also divided the state and New York City into districts to be overseen by annexes and local anti-suffrage clubs, although membership numbers always lagged compared with those of suffrage groups. The New York State Association Opposed to Woman Suffrage also broadened the publicity of their meetings to reach more people. No longer satisfied with the limits of the parlor meetings of the previous decade, they held their first open meeting on April 15, 1912, drawing about eight hundred people, perhaps a third of them men.[34] Antis continued these public meetings throughout the campaign. Like suffragists, anti-suffragists actively sought and published opinions of well-known men, although they still refused them active roles in their organizations.

In an attempt to highlight their unity, in 1912 anti-suffragists adopted black, white, and rose as their colors and a blooming rose to stand for anti-suffragism. Proud anti-suffragists wore small anti-suffrage lapel pins and coordinated the colors of their apparel when they gathered in public.[35] By 1913 they would prominently display a flag with the word "Anti-Suffrage" in white on a black and rose background to symbolize their unity.[36] As the campaign progressed, they used the color pink for roses, paper, hundreds of letters and enrollment cards, and leaflets.[37] They distributed fliers, buttons, and reams of anti-suffrage literature at every public gathering. Billboards and kiosks, highlighted with the anti-suffrage colors, announced their opposition to suffrage. Issues of increasing importance to anti-suffrage women included retaining the special privileges the "benevolence of male suffrage" granted women, the view that most women did not want to vote, that little had changed in states that had woman suffrage, and, increasingly, that suffragists had close connections with socialists.[38]

New York anti-suffragists also became politically more adept at challenging suffragists when they scheduled their meetings. On November 19, 1912, marking their seventeenth annual meeting, they held a luncheon to discuss strategy for the November 1915 referendum campaign at Sherry's; suffragists would hold a "jubilee meeting of welcome" for Carrie Chapman Catt at Carnegie Hall that evening.[39] Carolyn Putnam, president of the New York State Association Opposed to Woman Suffrage that year, publicly acknowledged that it was "high time there should be no silent women." Anti-suffrage women would not "go out in carts or speak on street corners," as suffragists did, but Putnam promoted greater anti-suffrage activity. She encouraged antis to tell every man with whom they came in contact, including men who worked for them, of their stance. They must never say, or allow it to be said, that suffrage was "sure to come." Putnam also encouraged donations for the cause from the audience.[40]

The election of Alice Hill Chittenden (1869–1945), who served as president from January 1913 to December 1917, initiated a period of even greater politicization for New York anti-suffragists. Chittenden represents the conservative anti-suffragists who began the movement in the nineteenth century, but also epitomizes the bolder, more assertive anti-suffragists of the early twentieth century. She personally shouldered much of the burden to prevent the 1915 referendum from enfranchising New York women.[41] The granddaughter of Simeon Baldwin Chittenden, an importer and a prominent Republican who served in the House of Representatives from 1874 to 1881, Alice Hill Chittenden was born in Brooklyn, where she lived most of her life. Her father, named for his father, graduated from Yale Law School; her mother was Mary Warner Hill, a prominent anti-suffragist. The family was financially and socially secure.[42] Alice attended Anna Brackett's School in Brooklyn, a popular school for elite daughters of the men of the city. Interestingly, Anna Brackett had announced her support of woman suffrage during the preparations for the 1894 New York State constitutional convention. Brackett told a reporter for the *New York Times* that she signed the appeal because she thought that the time had come for women to have the ballot. While she was not active in the movement, she did remember yearning for the ballot the second time that Lincoln ran for president.[43] Perhaps she did not relay that sentiment to the youthful Alice Chittenden.

Chittenden attended Miss Porter's college preparatory school in Farmington, Connecticut, from 1886 to 1888.[44] The Farmington Female Academy for girls ages fourteen to eighteen was less "rigorous, intellectual, [and] religiously-oriented" than Emma Willard's Troy Seminary or Mary Lyon's Mount Holyoke Seminary, but Sarah Porter taught the accomplishments considered suitable for young ladies along with English, mathematics, languages, and science.[45] Alice's father was billed for books in music, drawing, grammar, physics, geometry, Latin, composition, moral philosophy, and history during those years.[46] Porter's lessons and spiritual talks were infused with a strong sense of the "19th century evangelical world ... some would call it noblesse oblige," as a later graduate recalled, which also seems to have influenced Chittenden. Like the vast majority of Sarah Porter's students, Chittenden did not pursue formal education beyond that she obtained at Farmington.[47] It is not clear if she longed for more education. She did love to read books, and often said, "How I do wish it were possible to read two books at once."[48] An afternoon reception at her family home in Columbia Heights in 1888 drew four hundred guests and launched Alice Chittenden into society, but she never married.[49]

Like most of the women who were concerned in one way or another about woman suffrage, Chittenden was interested in a number of reforms, including the Friendly House Settlement of Brooklyn and the Brooklyn parks and playground committee.[50] She served on the executive board of the National League of Women Workers, frequently contributing reports of the club's events on Long Island to its journal, the *Club Worker*.[51] She also served as secretary for the Brooks Vacation School Association, a six-week summer school that taught manual arts to children who could not leave the city and "to whom life in the streets offers many temptations beside that of idleness." Its goal was to decrease juvenile crime.[52] In 1911, Connecticut Governor Simeon E. Baldwin appointed her to a special committee to investigate the hours and working conditions of women and children in that state.[53] An observer remarked that Chittenden "was never content with the status quo if there could be improvement."[54]

It is not clear if Chittenden attended the first meeting of anti-suffragists with her mother, but she did sign the 1894 "Preamble and Protest" and attend other early meetings.[55] Chittenden devoted much of her time and energy to overseeing anti-suffrage activity in New York. Usually featured as one of the speakers, she attended anti-suffrage activities around the state and assisted as auxiliaries formed in upstate cities, towns, and villages. She traveled extensively for the association, as when she spent three months in the spring of 1913

Alice Hill Chittenden, with her lifelong passion for
politics, was the most dynamic of the anti-suffrage leaders.
Photo originally published in the *Woman Republican* 4,
no. 2 (February 1926), 9. Image courtesy of the Women's
National Republican Club, New York, N.Y., and the New
York Public Library, New York, N.Y.

preparing a report on woman suffrage in California.[56] Described as "tall and
extremely good looking," Chittenden had a "rich contralto voice," which she
used "to good advantage" in expressing her resistance to woman suffrage.[57]

Chittenden's influence, as well as increased experience on the part of other
antis in public speaking and debates with suffragists, helped to further the anti-
suffrage politicization process. New York antis and suffragists began publicly
debating when they met under the auspices of the Women's University Club in

1909, and within a few years, antis regularly organized and accepted invitations to debate with suffragists. In April 1912, Louise Jones of the National League for the Civic Education of Women arranged for the use of the grand ball-room at the Waldorf-Astoria for a debate on woman suffrage, charging both antis and suffragists a one-dollar admission fee.[58] In January 1913, the Woman Suffrage Party of the Twenty-Fifth Assembly District invited anti-suffragists Charlotte E. Rowe, Minnie Bronson, Estelle McVickar, and Chittenden to exchange views with suffragists Harriet Laidlaw, Elizabeth Freeman, Fola La Follette, and Beatrice Forbes-Robertson before a great crowd at the Metropoli-tan Temple. There was "some heckling, but no friction," and questions from the audience indicated interest in the topic.[59] A few days later, the Republican Club arranged a woman suffrage debate at its luncheon.[60] In March 1913, the Colony Club hosted Mrs. Francis S. Bangs, Bertha [Mrs. Fritz] Achelis, Lucy Scott, Alice [Mrs. A. J.] George, Chittenden, and Prestonia Mann Martin, who had recently returned from a yearlong tour debating woman suffrage with Forbes-Robertson.[61]

The women wore anti-suffrage colors, had American Beauty roses pinned to their frocks, and seated themselves among more roses on the platform. They handed out cards and little rose-colored pencils in an appeal for subscrip-tions.[62] For its 1913–14 season, the Rochester City Club sponsored a suffrage debate between Grace Duffield Goodwin and Carrie Chapman Catt. It was an extremely popular event: 452 people attended the luncheon, and so many people crowded into the gallery to observe the debate that its structure suf-fered some damage.[63] During the summer of 1914 Lucy Price and Belle La Follette held a series of sixty-five debates on woman suffrage at the Coll-Alber Chautauquas in Ohio, Pennsylvania, Indiana, and Michigan.[64] Originally from Ohio, Price graduated from Vassar College in 1905 and worked as a journalist. She spent a good deal of her time in New York, although she kept her position as secretary for the Ohio anti-suffrage league. Described in newspaper reports as "charming," "captivating," and as having "a remarkable command of a seem-ingly endless array of data on the subject," she is one of the few anti-suffrage speakers for whom there is evidence of being paid to speak.[65]

It is difficult to determine how much training anti-suffrage speakers had in the art of public speaking and debate. Debaters' manuals were eventually available; for example, in 1915 Ethel Brigham [Mrs. Albert T.] Leatherbee published an *Anti-Suffrage Campaign Manual*. The same year Edith M. Phelps published a *Debaters' Manual*, which is a source for debating methodology and lists references for affirmative and negative suffrage arguments. A year later, the Man-Suffrage Association Opposed to Woman Suffrage published *The Case against Woman Suffrage*, also a manual for speakers. Dr. Ernest Bernbaum, an English professor at Harvard affiliated with the Massachusetts Association Opposed to the Extension of Suffrage to Women, organized anti-suffrage schools.[66] Suffrage speakers, conversely, were well trained in political organization, campaign methods, debating, and raising funds in schools developed to instruct those who had no experience working for the suffrage cause. Suffragists in more remote areas could take correspondence courses, apparently not available to anti-suffragists.[67] A confrontation between highly trained and experienced suffragists and less well-trained and experienced anti-suffragists had vicious potential.

As an example of that viciousness, in September 1913 Catt invited Chittenden to speak before her suffrage school at the Hotel McAlpin and to allow herself to be "heckled" by the suffrage students. Chittenden, "cool and dignified," wearing her colors, an American Beauty rose in her hat, and a black, white, and rose "anti ribbon" pinned to her dress, presented her anti-suffrage arguments during one session. The audience, "tame lions" (a reference to the anti-suffragist being a "modern Daniel in a lion's den"), erupted into laughter or hearty applause during various parts of her speech. Chittenden remained composed, even during the heckling period, as she attempted to answer the questions of the audience. She read letters from brewers' associations denying any monetary support to anti-suffrage organizations, while suffragists told of liquor interests that they knew had contributed to the antis. Some of the applause at the conclusion of the session had to have been out of admiration for Chittenden's composure during an obviously stressful situation.[68]

Confrontations between anti-suffragists and suffragists were usually far less harrowing and, for a time, seemed rather commonplace. In January 1914, antis and suffragists debated their topic under the auspices of the Economic Club before eleven hundred people at the Hotel Aster.[69] Just a few days later, the Civic Forum sponsored a debate on "What Men Think about Woman's Suffrage." According to the newspaper report, both anti-suffragists and suffragists "cheered loudly at every telling point made against their opponents."[70] Anti-suffrage gatherings in New York City were very popular with or without debates, drawing as many as five hundred, eight hundred, or even a thousand or more eager listeners for both female and male speakers.[71] At another event in January 1914, some interested parties were turned away from a luncheon and anti-suffrage mass meeting at the Hotel Biltmore, a venue large enough for only a thousand people. In a room resplendent with the anti-suffrage colors, hosted by 150 luncheon committee members wearing ribbons in those same colors, the guests sat at tables decorated with American Beauty roses and lilies as they listened to anti-suffrage speakers.[72]

Under the rose and black banner of anti-suffrage, crowds of people read the anti-suffrage broadsides covering the windows of an annex on Fifth Avenue, opened in May 1913, four weeks before the annual suffrage parade. Some automobiles displayed anti-suffrage pennants, and antis obtained a permit to sell their literature, buttons, and flags during the parade and another permit for men to carry sandwich signs as suffragists marched by. Anti-suffragists, convinced that suffragists exaggerated the extent of their support, decided to gather their own statistics. They stationed men with counting machines along the Fifth Avenue parade route to record the number of marchers. The men swore to the "truthfulness of their count" before a notary; the *Woman's Protest* compiled and published the "true" figures of suffrage marchers. The *New York Times* reported that a statement released by the National Association Opposed to Woman Suffrage called the "sex appeal" of the marchers "flagrant," making up the "dominant note" in the parade.[73] Anti-suffragists frequently criticized suffragists for flaunting themselves in public.

For anti-suffragists turned away from the elaborate luncheons, unable to attend anti-suffrage events, or who hesitated to participate publicly, Chittenden suggested alternative ways to promote anti-suffrage views. Readers of the *Woman Patriot* must enclose a piece of anti-suffrage literature in every letter they wrote and with every bill they paid. They should supply every local politician with anti-suffrage literature as well. They must make sure every library owned anti-suffrage books, see that every newspaper used anti-suffrage material, tell every man they met of their opposition to woman suffrage, and discuss anti-suffrage every time the topic of suffrage was raised. These ideas and many others make up a list on a broadside printed by the New York State Association: "Some Things Every Woman Who is OPPOSED to Woman Suffrage Can Do to Help Defeat It in New York State in November, 1915."[74] The primary task of anti-suffragists was to communicate to male voters their opposition to woman suffrage.

Anti-suffragists and suffragists sought to best each other in the public impact of their accusations. Suffragists continued to accuse anti-suffragists of being supported by liquor interests, publishing any whiff of a connection between liquor and anti-suffrage.[75] Although Catt explicitly warned suffrage speakers not to state that the "liquor interests are fighting us," for they had "seen no sign of it," it served as a favorite theme for many suffragist speakers.[76] Anti-suffragists denied the charges in every way they could, although liquor interests did oppose woman suffrage for fear that women voters would support prohibition. For their part, anti-suffrage speakers accused suffragists of fighting a "sex war," by which they meant that suffragists sought the destruction of the patriarchal family.[77] They also accused suffragists of immoral behavior and free love, which suffragists continually refuted. One anti-suffrage accusation that suffragists did not deny was the charge of feminism, although suffragists attempted to clarify the meaning of the term.[78] As feminists such as Edna Kenton and Winifred Harper Cooley explained, not all suffragists were feminists and the "vote was only a tool." The goals of feminism were to eliminate "all structural and psychological handicaps to women's economic independence, [put] an end to the double standard of sexual morality, release [them] from constraining sexual stereotypes, and [offer an] opportunity to shine in every civic and professional capacity."[79] Simply put, feminists called for a "complete social revolution."[80]

Anti-suffragists railed against the feminism of suffragists in speeches, print, and public venues. In March 1914, for instance, Prestonia Mann Martin presented "Feminism and Her Master," a short play she had written about the power of commercialism for the League for Political Education in New York.[81] Later in the month she delivered her "famous" lecture, "Why Women Should Not Want the Vote" at the Curtis Lyceum.[82] Martin was increasingly active in anti-suffrage during this period, tearing "to tatters the great new Cause" of feminism at a large gathering on April 2, 1914, at the home of Mrs. Henry Seligman. Pointing out that "politics is intensely uninteresting to women," she aligned feminism in opposition to the family and claimed that it put the "father out of business," rendering him virtually unnecessary. Her comments elicited numerous editorial responses, and the *New York Times* reprinted the entire text of her speech in the Sunday issue.[83] In spite of the efforts of mainstream suffragists to qualify the meaning of feminism, anti-suffragists insisted on conflating feminism and suffrage as a way to intensify fears of the radical changes in family and society that would come with the vote.

As suffragists strengthened their appeal to male voters, anti-suffragists could not help noticing the enthusiastic response of parade observers and the increasing appeal of woman suffrage. One anti-suffrage reaction included opening another annex at 39 Broadway. Calculated to draw the attention of business-men during lunchtime, speeches by able anti-suffragists could be heard daily between twelve and one o'clock. Their appeal to men was apparently successful, for 575 men entered their names as members of a newly formed men's anti-suffrage organization.[84] Chair Everett P. Wheeler (1840–1925) claimed that he organized the Man-Suffrage Association Opposed to Woman Suffrage at the request of the New York State Association leadership.[85] A Harvard Law School lawyer who helped found the New York Bar Association, Wheeler, a Democrat, served on the boards of a wide array of civil service and reform organizations. He played a major role in founding the East Side Settlement House in 1891.[86] His first wife, Lydia Lorraine Hodges, involved with the anti-suffrage movement beginning in 1895, died in January 1902. His second wife, Alice Gilman, the daughter of the first president of Johns Hopkins University, served on the executive committee of the New York State Association and regularly supported anti-suffrage activities.[87]

Wheeler, well known as an "ardent anti-suffragist," persuaded some of the most powerful men of New York to help him organize a Society for the Prevention of Cruelty to Women in May 1913. They actually named it the New York State Association Opposed to the Political Suffrage for Women, but it was often called the Man-Suffrage Association Opposed to Woman Suffrage.[88] The men's association held its opening meeting at Acme Hall in September.[89] Ostensibly, its goal was to keep the "mothers of the state" from having to bear the burden of the ballot.[90] While Wheeler called for "coordination and cooperation among the anti-suffrage organizations," he claimed the "entirely independent" men's organization served as the "primary weapon of anti-suffragism."[91]

Members of the women's anti-suffrage organization probably did ask for male assistance, but it is very probable they did not expect the men's anti-suffrage organization to dominate the movement as it soon would. While there had always been men who opposed women's enfranchisement, and men had long been organized in Massachusetts, these men represented the first organization of its kind in New York.[92] Membership in the men's anti-suffrage association, which crossed party lines, included United States Senator James W. Wadsworth Jr., a Republican who, with his wife, Alice Hay Wadsworth, dominated anti-suffragism in the Genesee Valley of western New York. In the U.S. Senate Wadsworth consistently and vehemently opposed woman suffrage.[93] Other powerful members of the Man-Suffrage Association included Elihu Root, Lyman Abbott, Charles S. Fairchild, and George W. Wickersham (former attorney general of the United States, leading Taft advisor, leading figure in New York legal circles, and a delegate to the 1915 New York State Constitutional Convention).[94] The association claimed 309 members by 1914, a highly concentrated cadre of powerful and conservative elite men who, arguing that suffrage should remain in the power of individual states to decide, would virtually take the anti-suffrage fight away from the women.[95] It is difficult to comprehend the extreme animosity to woman suffrage that these men harbored.

The men's association immediately flooded the reading public with their literature opposed to woman suffrage. They issued questionnaires, pamphlets, briefs, legal arguments, articles, and speeches, as well as the manual for writers and speakers.[96] Wheeler's articles frequently appeared in the editorial pages of the *New York Times*, the *New York Sun*, the *Suffolk Bulletin*, and other newspapers. He was often patronizing in his critiques, such as the time he wrote to the *New York Times* about suffragists: "When she gets this bee in her bonnet she loses all sense of proportion and see[s] everything through colored glasses." He referred to suffragists as "fanatics," and wrote that "the pessimists who think everything existing is evil are generally suffragists.[97] Regularly called upon to speak at events in New York City, Brooklyn, and elsewhere, Wheeler eventually traveled to speak outside New York, and the men of a few other states organized loosely affiliated groups, but the organization never became national in scope. In addition to its fierce opposition to woman suffrage, the association consistently endorsed states' rights.[98]

Along with an increasing connection with male anti-suffragists, members of the New York State Association targeted wage earners as when they gathered on the *Starina* during a one-day river excursion on Decoration Day, May 30, 1913, for an "Anti-Suffrage Picnic." Aimed at working girls, allowed to invite their young men friends to join them, the excursion generated a lot of excitement. More than twelve hundred people paid thirty-five cents each to participate in an adventure that featured an orchestra, a luncheon, and dancing. Although they said they welcomed suffragists, antis strictly forbade suffrage speeches on the barge decorated with the anti-suffrage colors.[99] Mrs. George Phillips, Mrs. K. B. Lapham, Mrs. Burnham, Mrs. Everett P. Wheeler, and Mrs. Church, all members of the New York State Association, posed for a photograph on the deck of the huge barge.

Within weeks, members of the New York State Association Opposed to Woman Suffrage founded a separate Wage Earners' Anti-Suffrage League,

The deck of the *Starina*, a barge used by anti-suffrage leaders who took twelve
hundred people up the Hudson River on May 30, 1913, for a Decoration Day
excursion. L to R.: Mrs. George Phillips, Mrs. K. B. Lapham, Miss Burnham, Mrs.
Everett P. Wheeler, Mrs. John A. Church. Bain Collection. Courtesy of the Library
of Congress, Washington, D.C., Prints and Photographs Division, 51500.

another organization created to broaden the support for anti-suffrage.[100] As
early as 1898, anti-suffragists had established a subcommittee to act as a liaison
with wage earners; the committee seems not to have been very active.[101] Still,
they paid some attention to the working-class. Antis had, however, long argued
that the ballot would not increase women's wages, just as it had not been able
to raise men's wages.[102] In an effort to expand their appeal to working-class
women, they sought to make a connection, although they had virtually nothing
in common with the "foreign born or wage-earning woman." Many of these
women were Catholics who believed they had nothing to gain by suffrage.
Even so, antis did little to attract the support of Catholics, whether of Irish
or Italian extraction, or any other working-class group. As far as antis were
concerned, these women served as "a potential reservoir of housemaids and
cooks."[103] Nevertheless, they claimed that the Wage Earners' Anti-Suffrage

League included a composition of "women engaged in all sorts of occupations and industries," as proof that not all self-supporting women wanted the vote.[104]

The elite anti-suffragists were really not interested in a close connection with wage-earning women, of course. Their link to self-supporting women was primarily to professional, college-educated women or those who managed their own businesses, not to those of the working class. Alice Edith Abell, the president, Edith Drescher, the vice president, and Marjorie Dorman, the first secretary, certainly did not belong to the working class.[105] Prominent anti-suffragists, including Dodge, Chittenden, Lucy Scott, Wheeler, and Church served as patronesses for a Business Woman's Hotel at the corner of Lexington and Thirtieth Street in New York City, which opened in April 1914. Catering to the "upper grade of business women," the hotel and its restaurant were not open to the public.[106] It was to this class of women antis referred when they used the term "self-supporting," clearly indicating the limits of their appeal. Their elitism damaged their cause, for antis missed important opportunities to broaden their support.

New York women antis sporadically organized "special sessions" for working women, and they printed a few publications.[107] However, the primary function of the organization probably had far more to do with preserving women's legislative protection in property, conjugal, and parental rights than with crossing class lines.[108] One spokesperson for the league, Miss I. Pearse, contended that because women "suffer" physical disabilities related to childbearing, they must have protections and privileges, which she feared would be taken away if they gained the right to vote.[109] This theme appeared frequently in anti-suffrage literature. The Wage-Earners' Anti-Suffrage League functioned as an auxiliary of the New York State Association, sharing headquarters with the state and national associations. Members of all three associations represented anti-suffrage at the same events.

Marjorie Dorman represented the Wage Earners' League through both her writing and her travel. It is not clear if the New York State Association or the league financed Dorman's speaking tours. She authored several editorials for the *New York Times*, bemoaning anything she saw as "leveling the sexes to a mediocrity of similarity," as when the teachers college affiliated with Columbia University became coeducational.[110] In another editorial she pointed out that increasing the electorate would significantly increase the cost of elections, arguing that it would also result in increases in taxes, food prices, and rent. She insisted on the incompatibility of public service and motherhood, contending that public service did not further the best interests of the race or the state. In spite of ostensibly representing self-supporting women, she argued that most women were wage earners only until they married; she naïvely considered the married wage earner an "anomaly."[111] Blinded by their elitism and lacking an understanding of working class women's lives, it is no wonder anti-suffragists struggled to reach these potential adherents. To reach working class men, antis sent speakers to taxpayers' associations, to the Fifth Avenue Bus Drivers, to the Knights Templar and the Knights of Columbus, to the Pierce-Arrow Automobile Works and the Snow Steam Pump Works in Buffalo, and to the Central Electric Company in Schenectady.[112] Dorman and other league members planned a number of events and "entertainments" for the working classes during the campaign.[113]

Anti-suffragists met with constitutional convention committee members during the summer of 1914; women of both anti-suffrage and suffrage contingencies each had fifteen minutes to reaffirm their views on suffrage.[114] Although Republicans were even less committed to a consideration of woman suffrage than they had been two years earlier, Alice Hill Chittenden considered the meeting highly successful. As she announced in the September issue of the *Woman's Protest*: "We might paraphrase Caesar's famous utterance and exclaim: "We went; we were heard; we won." Republicans promised to submit the woman suffrage question to the voters, although they were more fearful of losing support to the Progressive Party than they were interested in supporting woman suffrage.[115] Anti-suffragists, like suffragists, occasionally expressed eagerness for a vote on woman suffrage to be submitted to the electorate, certain the issue would be decided once and for all with the coming referendum. New York antis also continued to call for a referendum for women only, as Chittenden did again that year, feeling confident that the majority of women in the state still did not want the burdensome responsibility of voting forced on them.[116]

Anti-suffrage women did, however, encourage advancements for women, including the appointment of women to governmental positions. Chittenden and Dodge offered their official approval when Katherine B. Davis accepted her appointment as Commissioner of Charities and Correction of New York. They considered Davis's appointment a "distinct recognition of the anti-suffrage contention that in such appointive positions the State will have the benefit of valuable women citizens."[117] When Mrs. Henry P. Griffin was appointed head of the school board in White Plains, the antis contended that her nonpartisanship was the key to her "success in her fight for reforms and community betterment." If enfranchised, anti-suffragists pointed out, she must become a member of a political party and her reform issues would necessarily become political.[118] Many antis supported Chittenden's view that women should be involved in "civic and municipal affairs" just as they had long been in "charitable, philanthropic, and educational activities." They argued that women provided better service to the state as a "non-partisan body of disinterested workers" than they would if they had the ballot.[119] At every opportunity, the New York leadership encouraged attitudes that promoted cohesiveness between women and their public-interest groups as well as separation from men and their politics.

This coordination facilitated the domination of the New York State Association anti-suffragists nationwide by the end of 1914. They held their nineteenth annual meeting in December at the home of Bertha Achelis. Combining the state and national annual meetings, she hosted guests from Massachusetts, Connecticut, New Jersey, Pennsylvania, Ohio, and Michigan. Anti-suffragists unanimously re-elected the previous year's officers. They boasted that one thousand new members joined the state organization every month, that they had widely distributed forty thousand pieces of literature and thousands of "dodgers" (handbills), and that they had sold countless ribbons, buttons, and pennants to help raise operating funds. The women reaffirmed their policy of "active educational work" and discussed strategies to win the 1915 referendum.[120] They also voted to withdraw their membership from the New York State Federation of Women's Clubs to protest its recent endorsement of woman suffrage.[121]

The state federation endorsement must have been painful to anti-suffragists, for the Federation of Women's Clubs officially validated "domestic feminism," a modern term for the social sphere anti-suffragists proudly inhabited.[122] Woman suffrage had long been a complicated issue for the state federation, and anti-suffragists had been instrumental in preventing it from supporting the measure.[123] For a few years, the woman suffrage controversy prompted investigative committee assignments at each level of the federation. For example, the City Federation of Women's Clubs appointed Mrs. S. Baruch to the standing committee on anti-suffrage and Maud Nathan to the committee on suffrage.[124] Josephine Dodge served as chair of the state federation's anti-suffrage committee, even asking it to postpone all public discussion of woman suffrage until anti-suffragists were prepared to furnish speakers.[125] When rumors spread that the General Federation endorsed woman suffrage, Dodge wrote an editorial to the *New York Tribune*, reprinted in the *Woman's Protest*, denying the claim.[126] Then, in June 1914, after twenty years of opposition, the General Federation formally announced that it would give the "cause of political equality for men and women its moral support," and within a few months the New York State Federation of Women's Clubs had done so as well.[127] Dodge and other anti-suffragists issued an objection, pointing out that the "magnificent work done by the women's clubs all over the country is of far more importance than the entrance of women into politics." She argued that endorsing woman suffrage "jeopardized" the "solidarity" of women.[128]

A strong indication of the lack of solidarity between women anti-suffragists appeared in a notice printed in the February 1915 issue of the *Woman's Protest*, stating that the directors of the National Association Opposed to Woman Suffrage did not "endorse nor approve of " the *Reply*, the organ of the Guidon Club.[129] Helen Kendrick Johnson's anti-suffrage organization had become ever more focused on the perceived socialist connection to suffrage. Independent of the New York State Association or the National Association, members of the Guidon Club also submitted a bill to Albany, stipulating that if woman suffrage was granted, "as a matter of simple justice" women should rightfully lose the "special privileges they enjoyed under the law."[130] A defiant gesture, it reminded suffragists of the value of protective legislation. But the New York State Association leadership assuredly disagreed with Guidon members' perspectives and methods.

Anti-suffragists and suffragists had long closely followed actions at the legislative level. News in January 1915 about the extensive woman suffrage debate and vote that followed in the House of Representatives pleased suffragists, while antis saw an "end of hysteria" when their side won.[131] Rumors flew furiously during May 1915 that the members of the New York constitutional convention might decide not to submit the referendum on woman suffrage to voters that fall after all. The Democratic Party in New York, through Tammany head Charles Murphy, had agreed to support woman suffrage after a meeting with Harriot Stanton Blatch.[132] By this time, the Progressive Party, which supported woman suffrage, was clearly fading out of power. New York Republicans, the party with the greatest power in the state, had moved away from progressive reform. Republicans blamed Democrats for the recession at the same time the onset of the war in Europe "intensified GOP traditionalism."[133] Anti-suffragists and suffragists traveled to Albany yet again; by this time antis were as eager as suffragists for the issue to be decided one way or the other. An observer pointed out that it would have been "inconceivable" and a "gross abuse of delegated authority" not to submit the question to the voters in the fall.[134]

In the final year of the first referendum campaign, anti-suffragists sponsored luncheons, lecture series, and presentations such as Martin's on "The Menace of Feminism" during a period averaging fifty to sixty meetings per month.[135] To raise money to support their opposition, members of the anti-suffrage association often wrote letters asking for contributions. They also held fundraising events including the *café dansant* at the Hotel Astor, and they introduced a new hybridized pink rose, named after Josephine Dodge, the National Association president. Antis from three neighboring states attended and the event raised at least $2,500 for the anti-suffrage cause.[136] Chittenden and Price spoke at a *thé dansant* at the Gramatin Inn; dancing and socializing accompanied the anti-suffrage promotion.[137] Anti-suffragists reportedly raised $2,000 at another meeting, and gathered pledges for several thousand dollars more. Antis held card parties, some by invitation only, others requiring an admission fee, to raise funds for the anti-suffrage cause.[138] They placed posters reading "Vote NO on Woman Suffrage November 2d" at every station of the Long Island Railroad and elsewhere. The money they raised did not always go to the anti-suffrage cause. When the New York State Association organized a "Historic Women" tableaux and tea dance at the Hotel Astor, they sold Belgian lace to raise funds for war relief efforts.[139] Still, observers could see the "strong opposing force to woman suffrage" in New York.[140]

The 1915 summer campaign commenced with a large, open-air meeting held Saturday, May 29, at the John and Prestonia Martin home on Grymes Hill, Staten Island. Both Prestonia Martin and Alice Hill Chittenden spoke.[141] While antis organized other garden parties and events in and near New York City, a great deal of anti-suffrage energy was spent elsewhere in the state. With a three-week notice, the New York State Association would send speakers anywhere in the state, although antis boasted that the demand was greater than they could supply.[142] Anti-suffrage speakers Chittenden, Price, Dorman, Rowe, and Margaret C. Uhl all spent considerable time on the traveling circuit.[143] They spoke at labor organizations, Rotary Clubs, Elks Clubs, Masonic organizations, and at the Young Men's Hebrew Association. They presented at a Normal College, at a philosophical society, and at girls' clubs, mothers' clubs, women's clubs, and cultural clubs. Antis accepted invitations to speak at political clubs, especially Republican Clubs, at granges, and in churches in

Anti-suffragists displayed posters like this one in Buffalo all over New York State in preparation for the 1915 woman suffrage referendum. Image courtesy of the New York State Library, Manuscripts and Special Collections, Albany, N.Y.

upstate New York. These activities were a response to the increased activity of suffragists, but they also represent the distinct change from the circumspect opposition of just a few short years before.

As she had the previous summer, Lucy Price covered eight weeks on the Chautauqua tour, the tremendously popular speakers' circuit through New York, speaking in places such as Perry, Moravia, Ovid, Cazenovia, Hamilton, and Plattsburg, for a total of thirty-four speeches, often debating suffragists such as Helen Todd of California.[144] Unfamiliar with the topic, many audiences indicated their open-mindedness and eagerness to learn more about woman suffrage.[145] Price's speaking schedule included Glens Falls, a legislative meeting in Albany, and the Dutchess County Association Opposed to Woman Suffrage at the Masonic Temple in Poughkeepsie.[146]

Local and regional fairs and Old Home Days allowed for a multipronged attack on suffrage and connections with a broader, primarily rural audience. Under the direction of Clara Markeson and Margaret Uhl, anti-suffragists distributed literature and buttons, secured signatures, and presented anti-suffrage speeches at more than forty-five fairs around the state. Usually welcome at every fair, they initially had difficulty convincing the secretary of the Tompkins County Fair, held at Ithaca, to give them space for a tent or booth.

Apparently, a strongly-worded letter and an announcement in the *New York Times* naming the important men who supported their organization finally convinced the secretary that fairgoers should be able to hear both sides of the suffrage issue.[147] They distributed copies of their *Weekly News Bulletin* and plate matter to simplify the printing of anti-suffrage articles and advertisements in more than five hundred New York newspapers.[148] In July, Marian Williams Perrin [Mrs. Henry F.] Burton, wife of a University of Rochester professor, and president of the Rochester auxiliary in Monroe County, spoke on anti-suffrage at the Livingston-Ontario carnival at Livonia.[149] Anti-suffragists secured a booth for their literature at the Corning Fireman's Convention held in late July 1915.[150] Suffrage leaders monitored a booth during the 1915 Farmers' Week at Ithaca, while Lucy Price spoke to students at Cornell University. Chittenden, Dorman, and Price presented speeches on the last day of the week, designated as Anti-Suffrage Rally Day. They set up another booth at the "Made in the U.S.A." exposition where they collected more than one thousand signatures, distributed literature, and sold roses, pennants, and buttons. Most communities appeared happy to have anti-suffrage booths and literature at their fairs.

The New York State Fair, held annually in Syracuse since 1890, served as a favorite venue for antis and suffragists.[151] As early as 1908 anti-suffragists distributed literature and explained their views to anyone "who detached themselves from the living stream that passed" their booth.[152] Another year, Chittenden personally supervised the anti-suffrage booth set up in a large tent decorated with anti-suffrage colors. According to the antis, visitors from all over the state heard anti-suffrage arguments, many for the first time, and bought buttons and pennants "in great numbers." The anti-suffragists had the foresight to acquire a license to sell their items, raising money for their cause, while the suffragists, who apparently had not thought to get one, had to give their items away.[153] Many people registered in support of anti-suffrage at the booth, and some prominent Syracuse citizens attached anti-suffrage pennants to their cars. Anti-suffrage and suffrage speeches were heard almost continually, with antis "leading [a] lively attack" on suffragists, according to the local newspaper. They received many letters requesting that booths be set up at fairs throughout the state, as well as at the Rochester Exposition.[154]

Anti-suffragists at the New York City headquarters prepared a set of "Silent Speeches" printed on strips of cloth and mounted on rollers so that interested passersby could read them when a speaker was unavailable. The rollers proved quite popular, probably most especially with rural women unused to speaking in public.[155] Elizabeth Huyck [Mrs. Jerome B.] Moore, chair of the Syracuse branch of the New York State Association, supervised the anti-suffrage booth at the 1915 state fair. Women distributed buttons and literature, and played a recording of "The Anti-Suffrage Rose," made by Alice George and Minnie Bronson. The lyrics of the song, written by Phil Hanna, claimed that the red rose worn by an anti was a far better flower than the yellow jonquil worn by a suffragist:

> Lovely Anti-Suffrage Rose,
> You're the flow'r that's best of all!
> You're better far than jonquils are,
> We are going to prove in the fall.
> Sweetest flow'r in all the world,
> Everybody knows;
> You're the chosen emblem of a noble cause!
> You Anti-Suffrage Rose![156]

Produced as a phonograph recording, antis played it at fairs throughout the state that fall.[157]

Anti-suffrage speakers at the state fair, including Burton, Chittenden, Price, and Margaret Stebbins, countered the arguments of suffragists from both the Empire State Campaign Committee and the Woman's Political Union. Anti-suffragists congratulated themselves on their success, especially on Governor's Day when both Republican and Democratic politicians predicted the failure of the woman suffrage amendment.[158] Antis claimed great success at the Cortland fair in 1915, and committees in Albany, Utica, Rochester, Buffalo, Geneva, Hudson, Poughkeepsie, Troy, Glens Falls, Plattsburg, Cazenovia, Boonville, Palmyra, Canton, Gouverneur, and a host of other places represented anti-suffrage at the fairs. In the last week of September the Westchester county fair opened with a parade of automobiles, many decorated with anti-suffrage pennants. Anti-suffragists set up their white tent to look like a little cottage, offered chairs for weary visitors, played "old-fashioned home melodies," and had pretty young girls sing the "The Anti-Suffrage Rose."[159] Anti-suffragists at the Olean county fair hired "Flying Johnson," an aviator, to distribute pink flyers as he circled above the fair grounds, attracting a great deal of attention for the movement.[160]

Clearly, woman suffrage was a popular topic even in remote areas. Because suffragists used the same opportunities as anti-suffragists did to influence voters, sometimes innocent actions resulted in misunderstandings reported in the local papers, such as the one during Old Home Days in Skaneateles. Old Home Days, like fairs, are, even today, an annual event in many rural towns and villages. The weather was pleasantly fine late that August, so the entire program could be carried out for the thirty-five thousand people drawn to the little town twenty miles southwest of Syracuse. There were pie-eating and ladies' nail-driving contests, swimming and sack races, a tug-of-war, fireworks, a baseball game, and a parade. Suffragists and anti-suffragists set up booths on opposite sides of Genesee Street; the anti-suffrage booth, identified by a large sign, "The Home, Heaven, and Mother Party," and decorated in pink and white, displayed pennants and anti-suffrage literature. According to the *Syracuse Herald*, two women passersby suddenly began to "tear down the hangings and to demolish things generally" at the anti-suffrage booth. Although for a few days the incident caused an uproar in the community, the women had, according to one of the "culprits," only taken down a single paper lightly tacked to a post describing anti-suffrage views, the better to read it. Antis and suffragists soon returned to their usual campaign, according to the newspaper, for they were all "good friends," after all.[161]

Josephine Dodge had long been confident about the victory in the 1915 New York referendum. She won five dollars in a bet with a newspaperwoman (apparently the only one recorded between an anti-suffragist and a suffragist) stating that the amendment would be lost by 150,000 votes.[162] The margin was far greater than she predicted. The New York Department of State final count, listed by county, showed a total of 1,304,340 votes cast in sixty-two counties. Of those, 750,956 votes were cast against woman suffrage. Only six counties approved woman suffrage: Tompkins and Broome (51 percent), Chemung (52 percent), Schenectady (55 percent), Chautauqua (58 percent), and Cortland (61 percent). The block of support was in the southern tier of the state, although Chautauqua, the most western county, came out for woman suffrage. The rest of the counties opposed woman suffrage by a fairly wide margin. Opposition ranged from 52 percent (Oswego) to 73 percent (Columbia), with one-third of all counties, including Albany, Rensselaer, and Oneida, coming out against suffrage at 60 percent or greater. In the New York City area, specifically, the counties of Bronx, Kings, New York, Queens, and Richmond defeated woman suffrage by 57 percent of the total vote.[163]

The activities and outreach during the summer and fall of 1915 constitute the high point of female anti-suffrage activism in New York. Yet, even at the

An anti-suffrage booth at the 1915 Old Home Days in Skaneateles, N.Y. It was directly across the street from the suffrage booth. Image courtesy of the Skaneateles Historical Society, Skaneateles, N.Y.

crest of their success, hints of the demise of female-dominated anti-suffragism appeared. Money anti-suffragists raised was far more likely to go to charity than it was to the anti-suffrage cause, and increasingly, anxiety about the war in Europe crept into their festivities. Just days before the election the Guidon Club, located opposite the headquarters of the Woman Suffrage Party, went out of business, reportedly considering its work complete.[164] Then, unexpectedly, the *Woman's Protest* announced that the women would "put into the hands of the men's organizations opposed to woman suffrage the direction of the campaign." The purpose of the women's anti-suffrage organizations had always been "educational rather than actively political," antis said, and canvassing political leaders was taking its toll.[165] It is not at all clear why the policy of keeping men in supportive, not dominant roles, changed just before Election Day. It may have been the result of intense pressure from Everett P. Wheeler and the men's organization. Just as likely, the war, quintessentially masculine and dominating the media, intimidated the anti-suffrage women into retreating into traditionally supportive roles. In their determination to protect and serve the patriarchal family structure and the nation-state, antis would have assuredly felt more useful in war preparedness than in the suffrage controversy.

4. Suffragists Win the New York State Campaign, 1915–1917

On April 23, 1914, Josephine Jewell Dodge, president of the National Association Opposed to Woman Suffrage, sent telegrams to President Woodrow Wilson and Mabel Boardman of the Red Cross affirming that anti-suffragists believed in leaving the "decision of the policy of peace or war to the men of the nation, but in case of war" the organization stood "ready to render to the nation such service as American women have always rendered in like emergencies."[1] It was one day after three marines were killed in Veracruz during the invasion and occupation of Mexico by the United States.[2] That same day, suffragists held a mass meeting at the Cooper Union; although invited, the antis declined to attend. Suffragists insisted that Wilson "withdraw our troops from Mexico and thus with true courage and a high sense of honor repair the harm he has already done."[3] After the June 28, 1914, assassination of Archduke Franz Ferdinand and his wife, Sophie, and Germany's August 4 invasion of Belgium sparked the Great War in Europe, anti-suffragists reiterated their support for the nation and war preparedness.

When on May 7, 1915, a German submarine sank the *Lusitania*, sending twelve hundred passengers, including 124 Americans, to their deaths, anti-suffragists reaffirmed their patriotic support of the president and his policies.[4] Dodge announced that the anti-suffrage association would spend $5,000 to oppose woman suffrage instead of the $15,000 they had planned to spend that year. She called for a "truce," saying that if suffragists would agree to set aside their campaign until the war in Europe ended, antis would donate the entire sum to the Red Cross.[5] Issues of the *Woman's Protest* focused on patriotism and war preparedness more than on suffrage, regularly publishing appeals for work for the Red Cross.[6] The anti-suffrage parties, fundraisers, and enthusiasm of the 1915 referendum campaign almost disappeared from the campaign for the 1917 referendum. Although it was self-serving for anti-suffragists to argue that they were more patriotic than suffragists, virtually all anti-suffragists fully cooperated with governmental decisions, committed the resources of their organizations to the government and the American Red Cross, and turned their attention to the war effort. Patriotic fervor dominated and significantly altered the anti-suffrage movement in New York.

The almost total immersion in war relief work was detrimental to the anti-suffrage campaign. Anti-suffrage women essentially reframed their organization as the patriotic choice for women. But new alignments with relief and war preparedness organizations, the American Red Cross, and nativist patriotic leagues usually obligated female antis to defer to male leadership. These alignments, as well as American entry into the Great War, constitute the most significant reasons anti-suffragists lost the 1917 referenda campaign. The tone of anti-suffragism changed drastically in this campaign as the men's anti-suffrage organization strong-armed itself in to fill the void, ultimately dominating the campaign to oppose women's suffrage.

Little attention has been paid to the importance of the passage of the 1917 New York State referendum, yet it opened the gate to the passage of the federal amendment, especially in the heavily populated eastern states.[7] Carrie Chapman Catt wrote in her memoirs that the nation's suffrage workers hung on New York State "all their hopes for winding up referenda campaigns and compelling federal action by the Congress."[8] War in Europe distracted suffragists as well, but they harbored a greater range of attitudes to it than did their adversaries. Individually, suffragists' views ranged from full support of war to absolute pacifism, but officially, the National American Woman Suffrage Association did not commit to the war effort until February 1917, when the executive board and council members finally reached a compromise.[9] Throughout the war years, suffrage organizations spent vast sums of money and energy refuting anti-suffrage accusations of disloyalty.[10] Even though many suffragists joined the peace movement, the suffrage movement was fortified by the visible involvement of its members in various war relief efforts.

It was not that anti-suffragists favored war. Rather, they argued that war was the business of men and relief was the business of women. But anti-suffrage women could not effectively campaign against suffrage and do war work simultaneously. Individually and collectively, anti-suffragists put extensive efforts into war relief.[11] From the fall of 1914 the New York State Association Opposed to Woman Suffrage turned its headquarters over to the Red Cross Auxiliary Committee every Monday afternoon. Sewing machines were installed in place of typewriters; headquarters served as often for sewing military and relief items as for disseminating anti-suffrage literature.[12] Antis sold pink roses to raise funds for the Red Cross. The women also donated all proceeds from the Cort Theater presentation of the play "The Spur," by well known and outspoken anti-suffragist Annie Nathan Meyer, to the Belgian Relief Fund.[13] As early as December 1914, Dodge issued a letter to New York newspapers calling for women of "all shades of political faith" to support the work of the Red Cross.[14] Long before the suffragists offered their assistance, the National Association Opposed to Woman Suffrage dedicated the "entire machinery" of organized anti-suffrage to support the work of the American Red Cross in Europe.[15] The *Woman's Protest* published lists of work accomplished, garments made, and dollar amounts donated to war relief by anti-suffrage organizations around the country and encouraged all anti-suffragists to do everything they could for relief efforts.[16] Antis continued to refer to the power of a nonpartisan and "united womanhood" in their literature, but their focus on the war opened them to the suffrage criticism that they were war mongers.[17]

While anti-suffragists put their energies into doing what they saw as their patriotic duty—supporting war preparedness and relief efforts—suffragists wisely kicked their campaign for votes into high gear. Suffragists, like anti-suffragists, knit for the American Red Cross, campaigned for food and fuel conservation and other war measures, raised funds for overseas relief efforts, and participated in Liberty Bond drives. Throughout the campaign for the second referendum, antis persisted in criticizing suffragists for a perceived lack of support for the nation. In her December 1915 article, "Suffragists Traitors to Democracy," Marjorie Dorman argued that "the present year of international strife is not a time for any nation to engage in civil strife."[18] Anti-suffragists also argued that suffragists "put a price on their war-service activities."[19] The accusation bears some consideration because the suffragists clearly generated less enthusiasm about getting involved in the war effort. Anti-suffragists publicly condemned the stance taken by those suffrage women who argued that the United States government had "raised armies and navies without [their] consent" and "declared war without [their] sanction." When some suffragists threatened not to do any type of philanthropic work until women were enfranchised, anti-suffragists condemned their stance. The *Woman's Protest* repeatedly publicized the decision of some New York suffragists to take the "will and won't pledge," whereby the suffragists would support suffrage, but no charities or other interests until they were granted the right to vote. Anti-suffragist M. Eleanor Philips sent a copy of the pledge to the *New York Times* in response to Carrie Chapman Catt's statement that there was no verification of the anti-suffrage statement.[20] It is highly likely that Catt knew nothing about the pledge. Antis, not differentiating between suffrage organizations, accused them all of being "lukewarm" in loyalty and patriotism.[21]

They also argued that those who agitated for "peace at any price" were all "ardent suffragists."[22] Prominent suffragists with known pacifist views such as Carrie Chapman Catt, Jane Addams, and Crystal Eastman drew a great deal of censure from anti-suffragists. Anti-suffragists convinced themselves that "pacifist, socialist, feminist, [and] suffragist" were "all parts of the same movement—a movement which weakens government, corrupts society and threatens the very existence of our great experiment in democracy."[23] Anti-suffragists consistently argued that pacifism was the antithesis of patriotism.[24] The commitment to war caused a dilemma for the Woman's Peace Party, which included woman suffrage in its platform. The link prevented even those few anti-suffragists who supported peace from joining.[25] Annie Nathan Meyer expressed the view that suffragists taking part in peace propaganda "will do their best to try to show the anti-suffragist as a believer in war, or at best one who futilely refuses to lift her hand against it."[26] She argued that anti-suffragists also believed that children "must be trained against warfare" and "taught the ideals of peace and justice while they are young." She claimed that antis placed "the teaching of the ideals of peace above any political propaganda."[27] An article published in the March 1915 issue of the *Woman's Protest* explained that many anti-suffragists already belonged to male-dominated peace societies, for without the "guidance and political experience of men," they could not hope to "establish the right ideas of nations." Nevertheless, their dutiful support of U.S. policy overrode any personal commitment to peace ideals.

The National Woman's Party drew the ire of antis because it ignored the war. Alice Paul, chairperson of the National Woman's Party and a pacifist, refused to allow the war to interfere with her primary goal of women's enfranchisement.[28] At its convention in Washington, D.C., members unanimously agreed that in the event of war, the "National Woman's Party, as an *organization*, should

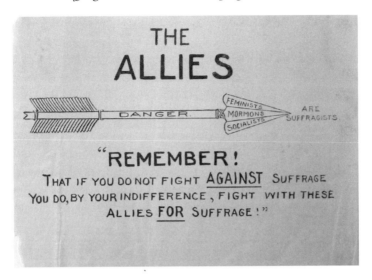

Both suffragists and anti-suffragists frequently published cartoons. This one, using a military motif, makes the anti-suffrage view about suffragists during the Great War very clear. Image courtesy of the New York State Library, Manuscripts and Special Collections, Albany, N.Y.

continue to work for political liberty for woman and for that alone, believing that in so doing the organization served the highest interest of the country."[29] Antis criticized members of the Woman's Political Union of New York City, closely aligned with the National Woman's Party, who refused to give aid to the Belgian noncombatants.[30] They also expressed sharp disapproval of Rep. Jeannette Rankin from Montana, who was one of the fifty-six members of both houses of Congress to vote against the United States' entry in the war.[31]

Anti-suffrage rhetoric of this period was far more often linked to a perceived lack of patriotism on the part of suffragists than it was to the suffrage question itself.[32] They criticized suffragists for trying to "divert Congress from the grave and solemn business before it." Antis claimed suffragists "have proved traitors to the flag which shelters them" because they "would force the majority to do the will of the minority."[33] They also warned that "suffrage agitation may become a menace to the patriotic service of women, even in times of national peril," citing an example of Canadian suffragists who gave up their patriotic war work to return to suffrage agitation. For New York anti-suffragists, these kinds of distractions served further to weaken their organization and increase the public antagonism between them and suffragists.

In sharp contrast to the weakening anti-suffrage organization, Vira Boarman Whitehouse, president of the New York State suffrage organization, and her highly experienced cadre of women supporters oversaw the strengthening state level woman suffrage campaign. The New York City campaign, described as the "finest and most complete in the country," was in the very capable hands of Mary Garrett Hay, known to New York suffragists as "Big Boss."[34] Even after the suffrage organizations committed their resources to President Wilson in February 1917, the dynamic and experienced leadership of the suffragists allowed them to focus on more than one issue. Controversy about woman suffrage continued in the Empire State, however, particularly between the upstate, generally Protestant, rural areas and what was seen as the more "foreign" and radical New York City.

In spite of the antis' belief that far more important issues faced the United States, and that most women did not want to vote, Chittenden and other leaders were compelled to continue resisting enfranchisement.[35] Chittenden, in particular, sought to balance her patriotic duty with the need for her organization to fight the upcoming referendum.[36] She divided her time between three fronts in the two years before the 1917 referendum. On the first front, she oversaw anti-suffrage work in New York. On the second front, she personally represented the state at national anti-suffrage functions. And, on the third, she immersed herself in Red Cross relief work. She contended that although many women approved of anti-suffrage sentiments and activities, most were too busy with their homes and civic activities to be active in the anti-suffrage movement. But anti-suffrage leaders knew that if they allowed suffrage noise to be louder than anti-suffrage noise, men would think women really wanted to vote.[37] Active anti-suffragists adopted the slogan "Where We Work, We Win!" referring to the need to schedule anti-suffrage activities wherever possible and to cheer each other on.[38]

Chittenden began the first year of the second campaign with an "appeal for fair play" in a letter she circulated to the editors of New York newspapers. She argued that since the recent election proved the sentiment of the voters, it was misleading for three-quarters of the state's newspapers to support suffrage. Chittenden requested that each newspaper publish an equal amount of anti-suffrage information to educate the voters. Several editors responded to Chittenden's appeal for fair play by expressing their willingness to publish anti-suffrage material, but they explained that suffragists had conveniently provided a plate box for the printers. The anti-suffragists responded that their organization, too, would provide three galleys of plate every three weeks for the convenience of the newspaper editors.[39] Many newspaper editors would print virtually anything as long as it was readily available, something suffragists knew and antis had to learn. In addition to increasing newspaper coverage, anti-suffragists wrote and solicited letters and editorials in support of their views and distributed literature, arguing that even enfranchised women had contributed nothing to the improvement of politics. They also spoke publicly wherever they could, albeit not on the scale of the 1915 campaign.[40]

Anti-suffragists who had traveled the state during the previous campaign continued to do so throughout 1916. During the summer, the peak of the traveling season, Lucy Price gave speeches in cities and towns around the state, including Pulaski and Watertown. Minnie Bronson continued her speaking tours, as did other anti-suffragists such as Annie Riley Hale, author of several books, including the anti-suffragist *The Eden Sphinx* and a former member of the Guidon Club.[41] Anti-suffragists spoke at various functions, too, claiming in 1916 that they had never before faced such a widespread demand for speakers. Because most of the speakers were needed in the campaign states, anti-suffragists were hard pressed to provide them.[42] Anti-suffragists stepped up their training of public speakers when Minnie Bronson organized weekly classes to dissect each suffrage argument individually.[43] Italian residents of a heavily populated section of Brooklyn reportedly responded enthusiastically to Charlotte Rowe's speeches. She cleverly distributed copies of an anti-suffrage statement prepared by James Cardinal Gibbons.[44] In spite of the antis' enthusiastic comments regarding the progress of their campaign, the number of formal contacts between anti-suffragists and the general public significantly diminished during this campaign when compared to the previous one.

For both suffragists and anti-suffragists, coordinating the work across the state included petitioning and lobbying legislators. The anti-suffrage slogan, "Remember the vote at Albany!" served as the heart of the group's argument to male legislators.[45] Maintaining their official nonpartisan neutrality, New York anti-suffragists sent letters and copies of the *Woman's Protest* to Republican and Democratic state committees, county chairs of both parties, and other prominent politicos.[46] After the 1915 referendum, however, most politicians in the state turned their attention to national and international concerns, even putting aside many of their disagreements on the state constitution.[47] At first, state legislators resisted woman suffrage by keeping the issue in committee, but Carrie Chapman Catt and other suffragists convinced committee members

that they would jeopardize their chances for a federal office if they did not support woman suffrage at the state level.[48] Some legislators reluctantly complied.

Anti-suffragists Chittenden and Price, now frequently accompanied by
Everett P. Wheeler, attended state legislative meetings, such as when the assembly met in February 1916 to discuss yet another version of a woman suffrage
bill. This version, the Whitney-Brereton constitutional amendment providing
for universal suffrage, was designed to be submitted to the general election
in 1917. Henry F. Walters of Onondaga persuaded members to hold off on a
vote until each could determine a change in the sentiments of their constituents, particularly since a similar measure had been defeated just three months
before. Another bill, introduced by George A. Slater of Westchester to the
senate judiciary and the assembly in the same session, would have allowed New
York women to vote for presidential electors in the fall of 1916. If the governor,
known to be pro-suffrage, approved the bill, it would go into effect without the
need to amend the constitution.[49] Chittenden wrote to Controller William
A. Prendergast to protest the actions of the judiciary committee in reopening
the discussion of the woman suffrage issue so soon after the November referendum, contending, "It was an insult to [legislators'] intelligence to raise the
issue again."[50] At a meeting of the state senate on April 5, sixty anti-suffragists
presented a resolution pledging their support through the male members of
their families, as a tribute to the men who had voted against the resubmission
of the suffrage amendment.[51]

Antis publicized any victory, no matter how small. In the fall of 1916, anti-
suffragists waited patiently in the summer heat for a chance to present their
petition to the Democratic platform committee in Saratoga Springs, "outgener-
aling" the suffragists and getting the last word with the New York politicians.[52]
The plank of the Progressive Party included support for woman suffrage at
both the state and federal levels; Republican and Democratic planks endorsed
state jurisdiction only. The planks of both major parties at the state level also
included resubmission of the suffrage amendment to the voters in the fall of
1917.[53] Clearly, the competition between the parties was to the benefit of suffragists, although anti-suffragists would have preferred it was on neither plank.[54]

Early in 1916, anti-suffragists met with the Republican candidate for president, Charles Evans Hughes. Hughes had not yet committed himself on the
suffrage question. Many anti-suffragists thought it probable he would come
out in opposition.[55] In spite of a discussion termed "satisfactory" by the antis
during that morning meeting and another in July to discuss the Republican

platform recognizing the right of states to decide woman suffrage, Hughes declared himself in support of a federal amendment for woman suffrage that summer.[56] Bertha Lane Scott, in an editorial to the *New York Times*, declared that Hughes had taken that extraordinary step in spite of knowing that women would never forgive him, for "he has betrayed them and their future into the hands of a noisy minority."[57]

Suffragists had long emphasized "drama, excitement, 'color and dash'" in their goal to "undercut opposition through emotional stimulation."[58] Increasingly skilled in mass marketing techniques, they seized any opportunity to further their goal of enfranchisement. Hughes' campaign train fit the bill. The first of its kind, the train toured the country from October 2 to November 4, 1916, under the auspices of the Women's Republican National Committee and the Women's Committee of the National Hughes Alliance.[59] Most anti-suffragists emphasized the nonpartisan stance of women, calling for an improved civilization where women remained free from the strife and divisiveness of politics, factions, and parties. However, related to their increased politicization, anti-suffragists made every effort to be wherever suffragists were, and Chittenden was publicly indignant when the train had no anti-suffragists on the roster. It may have been at her suggestion that just before its departure from Grand Central Terminal, Sarah Henry joined it. The women traveled from New York to California and organized 328 meetings along the way.[60] While the campaign train was of little use to Hughes's political aspirations, it drew attention to women as political actors. In spite of the anti-suffrage presence, Republicans as well as Democrats could see the value of women as supporters.

Anti-suffragists commandeered and publicized their own railway excursion a month later. At the December 1916 annual meeting of the New York State Association, anti-suffrage leaders announced that a special train would leave early in the morning to take anti-suffragists to the first national convention of the National Association Opposed to Woman Suffrage, to be held December 7 and 8 at the National Theater in Washington, D.C. Anti-suffragists emphasized the "fundamental principles of patriotism, morality and Americanism," a connection consistently highlighted in anti-suffrage periodicals. Speakers at the convention would address ways that women could serve their country in areas related to "democracy, citizenship, patriotism, and preparedness."[61]

Josephine Jewell Dodge stood under the flag of the United States of America, as anti-suffragists often did at their meetings, and opened the convention by reminding attendees that they represented the majority of women who did not want political responsibilities. She reaffirmed the anti-suffrage belief that women had, as she said, "more power in uplifting civilization through the home than man has through his vote." She reiterated the creed of anti-suffragists, which included "the retention of the best ideals of preceding generations adapted to the advantages and opportunities given to them under modern conditions." Encouraging women to participate in civic and municipal activities, she highlighted the anti-suffrage contention that everything women did could best be done "without the ballot as a non-partisan body of disinterested workers." The audience listened as anti-suffragists articulated the views of Elihu Root, Cardinal Gibbons, and other prominent anti-suffrage leaders in addition to those of Dodge.[62]

Pointedly, speakers at the convention also focused on the questions of relief work and war preparedness in the face of the European war. Dodge introduced two influential guests, Mabel Thorp Boardman, chair of the executive committee of the Red Cross Society, and Louis Frederick Huidekoper, vice president of the National Security League. The overarching theme of the conference was that anti-suffragists had a patriotic duty to further the cause of war preparedness.[63] Boardman, descended from a distinguished family and a member of the Daughters of the American Revolution, had many powerful friends in government, including William Howard Taft.[64] She had been almost solely responsible for restructuring the Red Cross into an organization available for aid during any kind of disaster. Interested in coordinating the efforts of all relief groups with those of the Red Cross, Boardman commended the anti-suffragist organizations for their support.[65] It may have been at Boardman's suggestion that Huidekoper also spoke.[66] Because they were entitled to the protection of their country, he called on patriotic women to encourage universal military training for young men.[67] This anti-suffrage convention showcased the alignments and concerns that distracted anti-suffragists from their work to prevent woman suffrage.

That same month, anti-suffragists took steps to further their resistance to suffrage. To coordinate the efforts of the many auxiliaries throughout New York, and to reduce the burden on Chittenden, state association board members formed a state council. The council represented another distinct change from the state association's laissez-faire policy of a few years before. Council delegates met during 1917 in various cities, discussed strategy, and offered reports, although their activities did not have much of an effect on the campaign.[68] In addition, anti-suffragists moved the headquarters of the state association to a larger and more attractive facility in the Foster Building at 280 Madison Avenue in New York City.[69] With Alice Gilman Wheeler as host, association members invited the public to a housewarming and Christmas sale. A drawing of a young woman holding a ballot as she would an infant, captioned "Hugging a Delusion," graced the front of a calendar offered for sale. Anti-suffragists established a congressional committee, overseen by Mary G. Kilbreth of Southampton, to lobby the members of the state congress. To promote their goal of awakening "non-partisan interest in affairs of immediate concern to patriotic American citizenship," anti-suffragists organized a Public Interest League.[70]

By 1917, the final year of the campaign, anti-suffragists held fewer meetings focused entirely on the suffrage question. As Chittenden wrote, anti-suffragists would have liked to devote themselves full time to service for the state, but they could not as long as suffragists persisted in their campaign.[71] On the anniversary of Lincoln's birthday, Sarah and Eleanor Hewitt held an "Anti-Suffrage Review" at their home in New York City. There Chittenden brought her audience up to date on the suffrage situation throughout the United States.[72] On another occasion Lucy Price accepted an invitation to speak before a Socialist club.[73] By April, the Brooklyn Auxiliary was holding only about ten meetings a month, approximately one-third as many meetings as they held in the previous campaign, while elsewhere around the state, anti-suffragists such as Clara Markeson, Marjorie Dorman, and Charlotte Rowe could be heard at district Republican clubs, at granges, and in a few other venues.[74] Price toured the state under the auspices of the Utica Auxiliary—traveling from Elmira and Little Falls to Middleville, Frankfort, Ilion, Camden, and Richfield Springs— sometimes conducting more than one meeting in each place. Price and Rowe continued their speaking schedules into the fall.[75]

In addition to presenting their arguments in speeches, anti-suffragists once again attempted to engage suffragists in debates. But suffragists usually refused to debate with anti-suffragists, pointing out that the argument was between women and men, not between women. It was so difficult to find local suffragists willing to debate Charlotte Rowe at the Business Men's Club in Nyack that Florence Kelley had to be called in from Chicago to accommodate her. Rowe's arguments apparently convinced some ladies of Nyack to form their own anti-suffrage committee. The antis had more luck scheduling debates in rural areas. Price debated a suffragist in Groton, and when the little town of Weedsport held a festival to celebrate the paving of their main street, anti-suffragist Marjorie Dorman took advantage of the opportunity to debate a suffragist.[76] Sometimes, when suffragists refused to meet with them, antis would simply give speeches or read papers to the audiences.[77]

Debates and speeches were not the only way New York antis drew attention to their cause in this campaign. Alice Foote MacDougall, the millionaire coffee merchant and restaurateur who served as chair of the hospitality committee of the New York State Association, held teas on Thursday afternoons in her shops around New York City. MacDougall scheduled hostesses to address the assemblage on anti-suffrage topics each week. Antis believed the informality of the gatherings encouraged the enrollment of "ardent workers" for the anti-suffrage cause.[78] Patriotic fervor took center stage at most anti-suffrage social occasions. The Junior Anti-Suffrage League sponsored dances, raising money for war-related causes as well as for the anti-suffrage campaign. On March 1, 1916, the league held a fundraising dance at the Plaza Hotel, inviting prominent officials and their wives from the Navy Yard and Governors Island. However, they donated most of the $1,800 they raised to the Aero Club to train two aviators in the interest of national preparedness.[79] In May anti-suffragists held another dance at the Hotel St. George. Brooklyn antis followed suit with a spring dance at the Unity Republican Club.[80] In February 1917, the debutantes of two seasons appeared in fashion-poster costumes, most of them striking a "patriotic note," at the Junior Anti-Suffrage League *Fête de Vanité* at the Plaza Hotel in New York City.[81] An April concert presented in Johnstown, under the auspices of the local anti-suffrage auxiliary, drew an enthusiastic audience. The evening's musical program was followed by dancing and refreshments. The event raised a good sum of money for the surgical supply committee of the Johnstown chapter of the American Red Cross, not for anti-suffrage.[82] When seven hundred people attended a patriotic tea, anti-suffragists sold war cake and war bread with recipes, and members of the Junior Anti-Suffrage League sold red, white, and blue boutonnières instead of their usual red roses.[83]

Because patriotism preempted anti-suffrage activism, patriotic fervor caused many anti-suffragists to change their minds about marching in parades. As the war in Europe escalated, patriotic parades became increasingly common. Some anti-suffragists stayed on the sidelines of any kind of parade. After years of vehemently criticizing suffragists for flaunting themselves in the streets, however, a few antis decided that it was their duty to march in parades held for preparedness or patriotism. Edith Drescher of the Wage Earners' Anti-Suffrage League served as marshal for members of the oil industries division

THE WOMAN'S PROTEST   5

Anti-Suffrage—For Patriotism and Preparedness

THE PARADE PASSING UNDER THE ANTI-SUFFRAGE BANNER   THE FIRST AID STATION AT FOURTEENTH STREET AND FIFTH AVENUE

Images from a parade in New York City. Anti-suffragists raised a banner under which the suffragists had to walk as they paraded along Fifth Avenue. They also set up a first aid station at Fourteenth and Fifth Avenues. Originally printed in the *Woman's Protest against Woman Suffrage* 9, no. 2 (June 1916). Images courtesy of the New York State Library, Albany, N.Y.

in the Citizens' Preparedness Parade held in New York City on May 13, 1916, a parade that drew 135,683 marchers. On May 26, 1917, anti-suffragists, led by Mrs. William McLeod Hanford, marched in a Red Cross parade in Brooklyn. The marchers flaunted red carnations, so their identities as anti-suffragists would not be completely concealed under their Red Cross support.[84] Patriotic organizations like the National Americanization Committee sought and encouraged the participation of women of prominent social status, including antis.

However, antis still condemned suffrage parades. In anticipation of one suffrage parade, for example, they raised a large anti-suffrage banner under which all the marchers had to pass, and they opened an anti-suffrage first-aid station at Fourteenth Street and Fifth Avenue.[85] In 1917, prior to another suffrage parade, antis wrote letters to merchants warning that they would boycott any store displaying windows decorated for the parade. Chittenden issued a protest against the parade, warning members that in spite of divisions for "mothers of soldiers and sailors" and "women rendering patriotic service," it was, after all, still a suffrage parade.[86]

Raising money remained as important a task for anti-suffragists as it was for suffragists. While suffragists spent more than $90,000 for the first referendum campaign, they more than tripled that amount for the second.[87] Chittenden had long condemned what she saw as a gross misuse of money by suffragists. Pointing out that suffragists spent ten times the amount of money to "get women into politics as anti-suffragists have been able to spend to keep woman out of politics," she claimed that the suffrage movement did not move of its own momentum, but only by "extraordinary money stimulation."[88] Suffragists clearly raised vast sums of money for their campaign, especially in its last years. Anti-suffragists found it more difficult to come up with effective fund-raising ideas. For example, in the spring of 1917, Sarah Henry had an idea to raise money for postage. Anti-suffragists displayed adhesive tape, decorated with anti-suffrage colors, in prominent places in offices and libraries to attract the attention of anyone who would attach their coins. The antis considered the technique a huge success, but it could never have raised the kind of money needed for a sustained campaign.[89] Far more often, anti-suffragists needed to rely on the generosity of their wealthier members to support their cause.[90] Also problematic was that even when they were successful in raising funds, they usually split the proceeds with a charitable organization, as they did after the *Fête de Vanité* at the Plaza Hotel.[91]

As they had during the 1915 effort, anti-suffragists sought to reach the rural population at county and state fairs. In September 1916, Elizabeth Moore was able to secure an ideal location for the anti-suffrage tent at the state fair at Syracuse. Anti-suffragists from Syracuse, Rochester, Buffalo, Cazenovia, and other towns handed out pink anti-suffrage fans, a practical and popular souvenir during the three hot days of the fair.[92] That same fall, Charlotte Rowe made a strong impression on the crowd gathered around to hear her speak at the Warrensburg Fair.[93] During the summer of 1917, anti-suffragists attended about forty fairs throughout the state. Following the example of the suffragists, the antis advertised in fair programs, whether or not they had booths there.[94] Rochester anti-suffragists distributed their literature from fair booths at Brockport, Batavia, Avon, Hemlock, Caledonia, Lyon, Newark, Palmyra, and Warsaw. The Albany committee worked fairs at Altamont, Cobleskill, and Nassau. The Troy committee oversaw booths at Hudson Falls, Cambridge, and Ballston Spa. According to an anti-suffrage account, a large crowd enjoyed the anti-suffrage speakers at the booth at the Warrensburg fair.[95] Based on the limited space the *Woman's Protest* devoted to news of the speeches, debates, social occasions, parades, and fairs in New York State, however, it is clear that much of the enthusiasm had gone out of the campaign. The work that remained to prevent enfranchisement seemed less important to most anti-suffragists.

Soon after they attended a meeting of the National Security League Congress in early 1916, members of the board of directors of the National Association Opposed to Woman Suffrage formally dedicated the facilities of all anti-suffrage organizations to the service of "America First" in a June resolution sent to President Wilson.[96] The resolution reaffirmed the antis' commitment to the government, the Red Cross, and patriotic organizations involved in various types of relief and emergency work. The National Association adopted a resolution stating that "every loyal American" should support "adequate measures for national defense." Antis printed and distributed copies of the resolution throughout New York.[97] But the work of the New York anti-suffragists went well beyond resolutions. For example, the group made "pocket packs" of small necessities for soldiers who were called to the Mexican border in 1916. Soon after, the state's anti-suffragists established an Anti-Suffrage Military Relief Committee, housed at the state association's headquarters, with Sarah Henry as chair. It focused on helping women, especially those with children, whose husbands had left to serve in the armed forces. Other anti-suffrage organizations around the state also formed military relief committees.[98] Throughout the Great War, members of the Albany Anti-Suffrage War Relief Committee sent surgical supplies, clothing items, and food supplies to Belgium and France.[99]

Although the antis paid a great deal of attention to the relief efforts overseas, Meyer found a solution to her personal dilemma about whether to join the war preparedness or the peace movement.[100] She became heavily involved on the Emergency Committee of the American Home Economics Association, which emphasized the home as the "first line of defense." Meyer concentrated on educating women in the efficient use of their kitchens to reduce waste. She also disseminated literature, created a film showing ways to eliminate waste, and held meetings to encourage the saving of money that could be used for feeding soldiers. She, like Sarah Henry, Alice Hill Chittenden, and many other anti-suffragists, also joined the National League for Woman's Service.[101]

The league, established on January 26, 1917, attempted to coordinate the work of women and women's organizations along lines of "Constructive Patriotism." It was structured on a military model with "commandants" and "detachments." Members were expected to spend at least one hour per week in physical drill. The drilling was not intended to prepare women for military service but was aimed toward improving physical fitness.[102] By April 1917, the *Woman's Protest* announced that branches of the league had been organized in thirty-five states. The league had already established a Bureau of Registration and Information to compile a list of women trained in industrial, commercial, agricultural, and professional fields, all ready for instant service. The bureau's mission was primarily to assist in the placement and housing of these women and to gather data on the resources of women's organizations for service in connection to industrial preparedness. By September 1917, the league had a motor corps of 150 women in New York alone, ready to transport public officials as necessary.[103] As popular as the league was, and although the women were "trained for real work" and able to replace men who would go to war, the suffrage organization did not announce the league's existence in its publications until the league had been operating for three months.[104] That delay, and the anti-suffrage view that Carrie Chapman Catt "corner[ed]" all organized women's work, added to the list of reasons antis resented the suffragists.[105]

Heavily dominated by anti-suffrage women, the National League for Woman's Service was established four months before the Woman's Committee of the Council for National Defense was created in April 1917. The committee, overseen by suffragist Anna Howard Shaw, was also designed to coordinate women's volunteer organizations during the war. The National League and the Woman's Committee "competed bitterly."[106] The government had no idea about what to do with the outpouring of volunteerism from women. According to Shaw, women were told "to provide the enthusiasm, inspiration, and patriotism to make men want to fight" and to send the men "away with a smile!"[107] The committee registered women for war work, one of several tasks duplicating the work of the National League. Often the tasks assigned to the women through the woman's committee were symbolic rather than practical, such as asking them to knit items that machines could produce far more rapidly, register women for tasks they would never perform, and solicit pledges for food conservation in private homes. The Woman's Committee consisted of the heads of a number of prestigious organizations, two-thirds of whom were active suffragists. Although the committee also included Ida Tarbell and another anti-suffragist, and the National League was publicly critical of the committee, it was another instance where suffragists were highly visible in war-related work, overcoming the antis' efforts to surpass them.[108]

On April 6, 1917, the United States declared war on Germany. A mere six weeks before, when the United States had broken off diplomatic relations with Germany, Catt officially gave the services of her organization, representing about two million members, to Secretary of War Newton D. Baker, who had passed it on to Wilson.[109] The executive board and council members had reached a compromise two months earlier, and Catt, who also actively worked for peace at the international level, finally asked all suffragists to work both for the war effort and for suffrage. She sent a detailed plan of patriotic service to every state organization, calling for everyone to cooperate, confident that her dedicated workers would do as she asked. The National American Woman Suffrage Association, working at multiple levels, included a publishing company, news service, publicity service, an "interlocking chain of suffrage schools" with traveling faculty, bureaus of speakers, an automobile service, and effective organizations at every level in every state. Most importantly, it was able to raise vast sums of money rather quickly. In New York, Vira Whitehouse, president of the New York State Woman Suffrage Party, similarly committed the services of the organization to the governor.[110]

Within a few short months of the United States' entry in the Great War, the New York anti-suffrage movement was altered in ways that drastically affected the entire tone and structure of the organization. Many of the most significant changes came at the national level and included a move to Washington and a change in leadership. Josephine Dodge, president of the national organization since its inception in 1911, stepped aside in June 1917 to allow the well-connected Alice Hay Wadsworth, wife of James W. Wadsworth Jr., the virulently anti-suffrage senator from Geneseo, to take the helm and relocate the entire operation to Washington, D.C.[111] The official resignation was announced in the *New York Times* in July 1917 and to the readership of the *Woman's Protest* in the combined July-August issue.[112] The reasons that Dodge chose this time to retire are not clear, although her six-year tenure as president may have been exhausting. She could have been intimidated by the better-connected Wadsworth, or she may have disliked being away from New York City and having to spend so much time in Washington. Perhaps the combination of overseeing the association and editing the anti-suffrage periodical was simply too much for the sixty-two-year-old Dodge.[113]

Educated in private schools in Washington, D.C., New York, and France, Alice Wadsworth (1880–1960) was thirty-seven years old, younger than most of the anti-suffrage leadership when she took over the position as national president.[114] She was a daughter of John Hay, who had been a personal secretary to Abraham Lincoln, held minor diplomatic posts in Europe, and served as Secretary of State during the Spanish-American War.[115] She moved in powerful political circles and had access to important political connections. Wadsworth, convinced that "Government is a man's job," was far more dominated by men's attitudes than either Chittenden or Dodge had ever been.[116] The change in the location of the national headquarters from New York City to Washington, D.C., suggests that anti-suffrage leadership had already relinquished New York State and would take a more national approach.[117]

Male anti-suffragists became even more dominant in the campaign at this stage. In spite of a number of editorials, a few brief articles and announcements, and several debates with Everett P. Wheeler representing the anti-suffrage view, men made relatively little effort to prevent woman suffrage until just weeks before the 1915 referendum. After that, men displayed virtually no additional activity for the cause until early in 1917, when Charles S. Fairchild of the Men's National Anti-Suffrage Committee publicly announced that the men who had worked against woman suffrage in the previous campaign would again coordinate their efforts for the second referendum.[118] A couple of months later, Ezra Prentice of the Men's Anti-Suffrage Association presided over the Patriotic Anti-Suffrage Mass Meeting at Cooper Union, although it was held under the auspices of the New York State Association. At this meeting, Chittenden reiterated the anti-suffrage support of national preparedness and universal military service, and the willingness of all anti-suffragists to render services to the nation with no expectation of any reward. She was certainly referring to the many announcements that suffragists expected enfranchisement in return for their war work. Marjorie Dorman and George W. Wickersham spoke on behalf of anti-suffragism, Dr. Joseph Silverman focused on patriotic service, and Henry A. Wise Wood of the National Security League argued against woman suffrage and asserted that the "first duty is to remasculinize America" and "stand as a wall against the wave of effeminacy which now threatens the semi-emasculation of our electorate."[119] These male anti-suffrage alignments and their jingoism overshadowed the position of women in the anti-suffrage movement and highlighted their conviction that war, as well as politics, was men's work.[120]

Anti-suffrage women's relations with the Man-Suffrage League, of which James Wadsworth was a prominent member, were complicated. Women anti-suffragists could ill afford to refuse the support of men, but the New York leadership, at least initially, had not wanted men to take charge of the movement.[121] It had once been a point of pride that the anti-suffrage membership was composed only of women. A letter written to Wheeler by J. S. Eichelberger, a former advertising man from Chicago and now the publicity representative and statistician for the National Association, reveals antagonism between women and men antis prior to Dodge's resignation.[122] The letter charged that the "women bosses of the New York anti-suffrage club did knock" Wheeler "unmercifully" because he "did not belong to their outfit, their little clique." According to Eichelberger, the female New York antis did not want the men to hold meetings or make speeches because the women believed that the men did them more harm than good. It is quite plausible that Eichelberger fingered Dodge as the "feminine autocrat who drove thousands of persons away" from the movement.[123] Now, with Josephine Dodge out of the way, male anti-suffragists could dictate the direction of anti-suffragism.

Members of the Men's National Anti-Suffrage Committee had always been critical of suffragists who continued to advocate for enfranchisement during the war. One member, Dr. Charles L. Dana, a neurologist, contended that "it would be the wise, unselfish, and patriotic thing for the women of New York to drop their propaganda just now and try to help their country instead of shouting for their 'rights' and mingling their selfish appeals with the very real demands for sufferers and workers in the great war." By September 1917, Everett P. Wheeler was fully in charge of the men's anti-suffrage organization, and he helped to reorganize and revitalize the group. The group then opened headquarters in the same building with the women's anti-suffrage organizations and began to appropriate the women's limited resources.[124] This further weakened the women's anti-suffrage campaign.

By the fall of 1917, Chittenden had worked with both anti-suffragists and suffragists to raise $46,000 for Red Cross efforts. Although anti-suffragist women had devoted much of their time to Red Cross work, selling Liberty Bonds, and increasing their involvement in every type of relief activity since the declaration of war in April 1917, they were still in a campaign to prevent enfranchisement.[125] Chittenden reminded her audiences and readers, "war or no war," a vote would be held on the woman suffrage question in November. It was the duty of anti-suffrage women to persist in their efforts to convince the men that they did not want the vote. If they remained silent on the topic, men would think the suffragists spoke for all women.[126]

Anti-suffragists made rather desultory efforts to continue their campaigning. In September 1917 Mary Ford, Mrs. John F. Maynard, and other members of the Utica Auxiliary of the New York State Association Opposed to Woman Suffrage hosted a mass meeting at the Colonial Theater in Utica. Elihu Root, as chairman of the event, briefly reemphasized his "unalterable opposition" to woman suffrage. Alice Wadsworth and Grace Duffield Goodwin were also featured speakers. Antis opened an annex in the Bronx to distribute literature to its many residents. On October 1, they held a mass meeting at the courthouse in Newburgh during which Price and Rowe spoke. The Long Island committee, composed of three hundred men and women, conducted meetings in Southampton, Bridgehampton, Sag Harbor, Riverhead, and elsewhere in the few months before Election Day. Wadsworth, Chittenden, and Henry A. Wise Wood spoke at a mass meeting in Gloversville, and Wadsworth was honored at a reception in Brooklyn.[127] But the campaign was already lost.

The final blow to the New York anti-suffrage campaign occurred in September 1917, when suffrage supporters in the upper echelon of the federal government promoted the idea to consider woman suffrage as a "war measure." President Wilson conceded it was a "wise act of public policy" and lent his full support.[128] Perhaps it gave him the opportunity to finally concede to what had been constant pressure from suffragists, for he had long been reluctant to publicly declare his support.[129] The idea of suffrage being called a war measure had been bandied about for some months. Chittenden, Alida B. [Mrs. Barclay] Hazard, and other anti-suffrage commentators argued that giving women suffrage as a war measure, or as a reward for war work, was tantamount to rewarding all women who worked for the war effort by penalizing anti-suffragists. Furthermore, Chittenden pointed out, "a truly patriotic woman wants no reward for her work" because her service is "unselfish, unconditional and unremitting."[130]

At the last stage of the campaign, anti-suffragists simply gave it up in their eagerness to support the war. In the October issue of the *Woman's Protest,* anti-suffragists announced that rather than holding a mass meeting at the end of the campaign at Carnegie Hall, as they had done two years before, they would hold an evening of entertainment to raise money for "Christmas cheer" for soldiers and sailors. Wadsworth was the guest of honor on November 3 at Carnegie Hall. Seated near the Wadsworths were Mr. and Mrs. Robert Lansing, Mr. and Mrs. Elihu Root, and Alice Hill Chittenden. The guest list included quite a number of well known anti-suffragists who enjoyed the evening's musical entertainment and dinner. Yet, Chittenden continued to predict success for the anti-suffragists, saying that she was certain that New York would follow the example of Maine, which had defeated woman suffrage in September.[131]

Suffragists drew energy from the belief that New York State "could not refuse democracy to its own women" as long as the United States was engaged in a war for democracy. According to Gertrude Foster Brown, between the New York State Woman Suffrage Party and the central campaign committee, they raised a total of $525,364.24 to keep the woman suffrage issue in the news.[132] On the last day of the campaign, more than two thousand suffragists listened to Dr. Anna Howard Shaw and other speakers discuss the merits of enfranchising women at Durland's Riding Academy. Five hundred of them had come from marching in a parade, carrying impressive lists of the names of women who wanted to vote.[133] It was the culmination of an extensive campaign to canvas women, circulate special literature, target soldiers in training camps and overseas, and advertise their cause everywhere in the state.[134] Suffragists had worked hard for their enfranchisement, ceaselessly demanding the vote until the very last moments before the state referendum.

On Tuesday, November 6, 1917, New York State male voters gave suffragists what they had worked years to get. The New York woman suffrage amendment passed with nearly 54 percent of the vote. Overall, the vote on the amendment granting the vote to women was 729,793 in favor and 616,636 opposed.[135] The greatest change from the 1915 referendum came in the metropolitan counties of New York, Kings, Bronx, Westchester, Nassau, and Richmond.[136] The combined vote of the five boroughs of New York City and the nearest counties was 293,285 to 419,166 (59 percent) in favor of woman suffrage.[137] The difference in the voting results between upstate—controlled by conservative Republicans—and New York City, was significant. Upstate, the antis actually won by 12,724 votes out of the total 633, 978 cast (51 percent against woman suffrage), in spite of the heavy campaigning on the part of suffragists.[138] When the *Woman's Protest* published the figures, it focused on the increase in the socialist vote, claiming that members of the major parties had voted against woman suffrage.[139] Although the *New York Times* emphasized the supporting votes of socialists and Tammany Hall, it contended that the "suffrage fight was won in the cities."[140]

Woman suffrage was more popular in cities all over the state. The upstate cities of Buffalo, Syracuse, and Schenectady passed the woman suffrage measure. The counties that contain those cities also passed the measure. Voters in Troy supported suffrage, although Rensselaer County came out against woman suffrage. Even in anti-suffrage strongholds, the percentage of oppositional votes declined, reflecting the decline of anti-suffrage organizational effectiveness. The upstate cities that remained the most anti-suffrage were Albany (Albany County), Utica (Oneida County), Rochester (Monroe County), and Newburgh (Orange County). Although Orange County passed the measure, the voters of Albany, Oneida, and Monroe Counties went against suffrage.[141] Counties in the western and southern parts of the states supported woman suffrage, but voters in counties in the southeastern part of the state outside of metropolitan New York defeated woman suffrage from as little as 52 percent to as much as 62 percent. As a general rule, the least populated counties, more rural in population, tended to oppose woman suffrage, although Putnam, Tioga, and Cortland counties were exceptions. Tioga and Cortland Counties are part of a group of counties in the center third of the state—Oswego, Cayuga, Onondaga, Madison, Otsego, Tompkins, Chenango, and Broome— that all supported woman suffrage. Voters in Putnam and Orange Counties were probably influenced by the same factors that influenced the people in the boroughs of New York City.[142]

Suffragists had been excited when "Big Tom" Foley of Tammany Hall confessed at the polls to having just voted in favor of the amendment.[143] Much of the credit for the shift in Tammany support was due to Mary Garrett Hay, suffrage chair of New York City and a "student of local machine politics."[144] Gertrude Brown, writing for the National American Woman Suffrage Association, stated that in the fall, Tammany appointed thirty-four women to political posts. One of those women carried a message to Hay announcing that Tammany Hall was granting "freedom to every voter to express his own convictions on the suffrage amendment at the polls."[145] According to one historian, along with their wage-earning constituencies, urban political machines "were among the staunchest opponents of female voting in the first fifteen years of the twentieth century."[146] A more "docile" and predicable male electorate suited the purposes of machine politics far better than unpredictable and "idealistic" women. By 1917, their fears were assuaged by the lack of influence women voters had in the states where they were enfranchised. Tammany Hall politicos became convinced that woman suffrage would not challenge their power as they had previously feared. Support for woman suffrage was actually part of a "broader process of accommodation" that machine politics underwent in the Progressive Era, coinciding with other ideas about reform encouraged by Tammany leadership.[147] Even so, scholars Eileen McDonagh and H. Douglas Price argue that Tammany dominated only one of the five boroughs (Manhattan) in spite of the "conventional explanation" that Tammany was a key factor. The other four boroughs and nearby Westchester County all showed the same high level of support for woman suffrage. None of them was under Tammany control.[148]

Some suffrage support was certainly the result of the half-million dollars that Carrie Chapman Catt received from the estate of Mrs. Frank Leslie in February 1917. She had immediately handed ten thousand dollars to Vira Boarman Whitehouse for the work of the New York state campaign and fifteen thousand to Mary Garrett Hay for the New York City campaign.[149] The *New York Times* expressed concern that the success of the woman suffrage campaign was due "to the failure of a great many voters to vote," since it was not a major election year.[150] Voter turnout had been steadily declining since the turn of the century. In 1916, for example, a presidential election year, turnout was 62 percent; it dropped even further by 1920, to 49 percent.[151]

Chittenden, refusing to concede defeat until the last ballot was counted, claimed that woman suffrage had won because it had the support of radical, socialist, and pacifist elements. She further declared, "Anti-suffragists always put patriotism and the best interests of their country, State, or city above all other considerations." She then predicted that the men of New York would "rue the day they permitted woman suffrage to carry by default."[152] Alice Hay Wadsworth expressed satisfaction for the way that Chittenden and her co-workers had conducted the campaign, pointing out that "there are many things worse than honorable defeat."[153] Still, the changed anti-suffrage tone was apparent in the November 1917 issue of the *Woman's Protest* when it announced the loss of New York. In addition to blaming radical and pacifist elements for the election results, Wadsworth bitterly blamed Germans, pro-Germans, and socialists. It was indicative of her intention to take the National Association in a far more extremist and conservative direction.[154]

Once suffragists became involved in the war effort their achievements were spectacular. No matter how anti-suffragists criticized them, suffragists clearly had superior capability, thanks in part to the leadership of Carrie Chapman Catt, whose paramount goal was to downplay differences within the ranks and bring credit to suffragists. The suffrage movement attracted many dynamic women leaders and workers who made significant contributions to the cause.[155] They were well organized and highly proficient, which allowed them to make the "most of their 'patriotic' contributions in public meetings, parades, and press releases," garnering the further support of Wilson, who encouraged the men of New York to approve the referendum.[156] In addition, suffragists deliberately targeted the support of soldiers and sailors, a voting group much younger than average civilian voters and one that tended to vote for woman suffrage.[157] By the time of the First World War, woman suffragists were perfectly capable of handling several divergent goals simultaneously without sacrificing their main goal; antis were incapable of doing so. The distraction of the war, coupled with the changes in leadership and headquarters irrevocably damaged the anti-suffrage movement. Although anti-suffragists aligned themselves with patriotic dutifulness while many prominent suffragists challenged U.S. wartime policies, their lack of focus on the anti-suffrage campaign sounded their defeat.

Suffragist Maud Wood Park emphasized the vast importance of the suffrage victory in New York State to the overall campaign, fully aware that winning the woman suffrage referendum was "accepted by the politically wise as the handwriting on the wall."[158] Still, "the victory is not New York's alone," as Gertrude Foster Brown declared. "It is the nation's." New York State representatives in Congress would support the federal measure to appease their constituencies. The number of electoral votes in states where women could vote increased from 172 to 215 after New York women were enfranchised. Once New York "fell into line"—the goal of suffragists for nearly seventy years—success lent encouragement and enthusiasm to suffragists working in other states. As a result, it became easier for voters in other eastern states and politicians at the federal level to justify and support woman suffrage.[159] New York suffragists then committed their state organizations to the passage of a federal amendment, a campaign for which suffrage leaders immediately began to plan.[160] The anti-suffragists must have seen the "tide was turning against them," and although anti-suffrage organizations remained in existence, their campaign to oppose women's rights underwent marked changes.[161]

After 1917, New York men dominated the national anti-suffrage battle, separately or through the new female leadership, and they eagerly used tactics anti-suffrage women seldom, if ever, used. From the beginning, wealthy and politically powerful men had supported anti-suffrage organizations with the loan of their names, the public presentation of their arguments, and their financial contributions. That involvement, however, was primarily supportive of the women antis' activities. Reorganizing the New York State–based Man-Suffrage Association as the American Constitutional League, still under the leadership of Everett P. Wheeler and Charles S. Fairchild, male anti-suffragists became increasingly aggressive as support for a federal amendment increased. Five years earlier the *New York Times* stated that most men really did not care about woman suffrage. The *Times* assured readers that men preferred to "treat the matter as a joke, to let the women agitators go as far as they choose, confident that they will never succeed."[162] But men like Everett Pepperell Wheeler did care whether or not women won the right to vote. The tone of anti-suffrage rhetoric became increasingly bitter when the men took over the fight against a federal amendment after the enfranchisement of New York State women.

5. Using Enfranchisement to Fight Woman Suffrage, 1917–1932

Alice Hill Chittenden vacillated as she contemplated her response to the November 1917 woman suffrage referendum. Her initial public reaction to the lost battle indicated her perspective on the proper role of women during wartime: "Let us all quit being suffragists and anti-suffragists, and just be women backing up the men in every phase of fighting the war."[1] At the November 15 meeting of the New York State Association Opposed to Woman Suffrage, Chittenden encouraged anti-suffragists "to line up with the several political parties." Personally, she would "probably join the Republicans" as her "affiliations have been entirely with the G.O.P."[2] Perhaps suffering criticism for conceding defeat so easily, Chittenden then called a conference for Saturday, December 8, at her Madison Avenue home "to consider how we can reach the New York Congressmen immediately and try to influence them against voting for the [federal] amendment." In letters sent to various anti-suffrage leaders around the state, Chittenden urged anti-suffragists to shift their energies to supporting the National Association Opposed to Woman Suffrage.[3]

Within the next six months, anti-suffragists restructured the New York State Association as the Women Voters' Anti-Suffrage Party. Dodge made its stance quite clear: "While the [Executive] Committee still believes that suffrage is not an inherent right, nevertheless, having once been conferred, it becomes a duty and a responsibility, and as such must be exercised."[4] Chittenden attended organizational meetings of the Women Voters' Party in March and April 1918 and was elected as a vice president.[5] By May, however, she withdrew entirely from all anti-suffrage work. Expanding her volunteer service with the American Red Cross, in August 1918 she traveled to Chicago to recruit canteen workers. Chittenden then headed the first Red Cross unit to work in the huts at the airplane camps in France. She eventually served as a canteen worker for soldiers in Germany as well.[6] Chittenden's departure from the anti-suffrage movement marks the end of an era of anti-suffrage activism. In a period complicated by the pressing needs of wartime, she represents a group of elite, politically active women who, although once opposed to enfranchisement, were now willing to acquiesce to the decision of voters in 1917.

Alice Chittenden and Josephine Dodge were superseded by new anti-suffrage leaders Alice Hay Wadsworth and Mary G. Kilbreth. The change in leadership, along with the relocation of the national headquarters from New York City to Washington, sounded the death knell of the female-dominated anti-suffrage movement in New York State and changed completely the spirit of the national anti-suffrage movement. As the emphasis shifted to fighting a federal amendment, anti-suffragists under Wadsworth and Kilbreth adopted a harsh, almost hysterical tone, linking feminism and socialism to woman suffrage in an evil triumvirate. After the campaign to prevent woman suffrage failed in 1920, Kilbreth and a select cohort of former anti-suffragists focused their energies on other challenges to the Constitution, including the amendment process itself. Those women who continued to publicly oppose suffrage often deferred to male leaders decidedly hostile to women's involvement in the political process.

Kilbreth briefly served as acting president of the New York anti-suffragists during the transitional period. Never married, Mary Guthrie Kilbreth (1869–1957) came into wealthy independence after the death of her father.[7] She had begun her active involvement with anti-suffrage in 1913, and in 1916 she served as chair of the congressional committee of the New York State Association. She had a reputation for being an ardent and energetic anti-suffragist.[8] Kilbreth, outspoken and harsh in her criticism of suffragists, claimed that suffragists were "childless women politicians" fighting a "sex war," and that the "unpatriotic" suffragists were heavily influenced by socialism and other radical ideas destructive to the nation.[9] She dominated a faction of anti-suffragists who publicized their intention to "wage war on pacifism and all forms of disloyalty," alongside their fight against a federal amendment.[10] By February 1918, Kilbreth gave up her temporary position, and Helen Krumbhaar Lincklaen Fairchild (1845–1931) of New York City and Cazenovia became president of the altered organization. Kilbreth would take over the presidency of the Women Voter's Party by the end of the year, however.[11]

Although encouraged to join the major party of their choice, members considered their new organization to be a "political party of women voters organized to fight with our ballots the twin dangers of woman suffrage and radicalism."[12] They used the name "party" to emphasize its potential power as a viable political entity in the manner of any other political party.[13] Encouraging their members to vote as the state's "anti-socialist, anti-radical force," they were aggressive in their denunciation of radical ideologies: pacifism, socialism, communism, and feminism. In addition to working against a federal amendment and preserving states' rights, these newly enfranchised anti-suffragists determined to use their votes to elect men who had not yet lost, in the words of Kilbreth, "all the male instincts of domination and sovereignty."[14] Additionally, they would push for the question of woman suffrage to be resubmitted to the people, arguing that with women voting, it would not pass. Three hundred delegates from nineteen congressional districts adopted resolutions to challenge the state suffrage amendment. A couple of weeks later, five hundred male and female anti-suffragists held another meeting in New York City to "organize the anti-suffrage vote."[15] The Women Voters' Anti-Suffrage Party sent petitions to the United States Senate requesting that body to set aside the woman suffrage issue until the war in Europe ended.

The executive committee broadly publicized the opinion that it was now a duty for a woman to vote, "to qualify herself for political action and efficiency by enrolling in whatever party she likes best—or dislikes least." Conservative women would use the vote itself to prevent further detrimental political changes.[16] Fairchild made it clear that anyone who failed to vote joined the ranks of "moral shirkers." They promoted their so-called "Cazenovia Idea," to register as members of political parties and attempt to vote out of office any politician who had previously supported woman suffrage.[17] No longer advocating nonpartisan status for women, by early 1918 anti-suffragists established both Republican and Democratic sections of the Women Voters' Party. In the meantime, whenever they were criticized for voting, anti-suffragists argued that it was their duty to vote, or else they claimed that they voted in "self defense."[18]

In addition to their willingness to use their votes, they publicized letters they wrote to any man they perceived as having forced enfranchisement on them. For example, they tried to convince President Wilson that it was a mistake to endorse woman suffrage and protested his decision to support a federal suffrage amendment as a war measure. Members of the Women Voters' Party also issued an appeal to the United States Senate arguing that since woman suffrage was "an essential principle" of socialism and pacifism, they would "protest against the Suffrage Federal Amendment being passed as a war measure."[19] Writing open letters was their primary occupation, an indication of fewer powerful political connections and a loss of their former insider status. Although less politically active than its organizational predecessor, according to its first annual report, the Women Voters had sent speakers and literature to other states, its members had gone to the polls to carry out their civic duty, and it was fully involved with the work of the National Association in its fight to prevent a federal amendment.[20]

New York State anti-suffragists had dominated the suffrage battle at the national level even before they organized the National Association Opposed to Woman Suffrage in November 1911. Under the leadership of Josephine Jewell Dodge, the National Association had slowly developed into a viable political organization, eventually claiming seven hundred thousand members.[21] Involved in anti-suffrage from the beginning of the New York State movement, Dodge was a determined advocate for anti-suffrage, long condemning the suffrage movement as a "sex disturbance."[22] She strongly advocated a nonpartisan stance for women as the best way for them to influence change, particularly in what she saw as their particular area of expertise: social reform that related to their role in the domestic sphere. After serving one year as president of the New York State Association, she had stepped down to take the position as the first president of the national organization.[23]

Josephine Dodge or Minnie Bronson, the general secretary, traveled throughout the United States participating in debates, garnering more support from independent organizations, and assisting those state affiliates who invited them to give organizational assistance. The National Association Opposed to Woman Suffrage, which ostensibly served as an international organization, was never financially secure, although appeals for contributions frequently resulted in cash donations.[24] The association sent representatives to Congress and to state legislatures; antis had long made annual visits to congressional hearings or sent anti-suffrage petitions if a group of anti-suffrage women was unable to attend. Members of the National Association held mass meetings, provided speakers during campaigns, and distributed anti-suffrage literature and information in addition to publishing the *Woman's Protest*.[25] In spite of the need to attend legislative hearings more frequently, it took until December

1915 for anti-suffragists to establish headquarters in the capital. Dodge first set up temporary headquarters at the Hotel Shoreham to facilitate the escalation of the fight in Washington; previously she had traveled back and forth from New York City as necessary. Members of the executive committee usually attended an annual meeting in New York City, and they had waited until December 1916 to schedule one in Washington.[26]

Although the National Association leaders were quite active, especially for women who believed in the mandates of "true womanhood," and promoted and supported the anti-suffrage activities of their affiliates, they were nowhere near as effective as the suffrage movement leadership at the national level. However, anti-suffragist women were always welcomed in both houses of Congress. In the first years of Dodge's 1912 to 1917 tenure, she would simply send a letter expressing anti-suffrage views to the hearings before the joint Senate committee on the judiciary and woman suffrage.[27] But it soon became apparent that a physical anti-suffrage presence was necessary. The National Association then made sure that some representatives of the national organization, most often with Dodge in charge, always testified in person before the Senate and House committees.[28] A senator once remarked that the antis "had shown such a high order of intelligence that it proved that they ought to have a ballot."[29] Comments about the anti-suffragists in the *Congressional Record* were usually pleasant—not surprising, considering the number of anti-suffragists who were married to or related to senators, representatives, and other politicos.[30]

During March 1917, in preparation for Alice Paul and the Congressional Union's demonstration the day before the second inauguration of Woodrow Wilson, anti-suffragists opened temporary headquarters at 1219 Pennsylvania Avenue. Alice Hay Wadsworth, head of the District of Columbia branch of the Anti-Suffrage Association, assisted by Eleanor Foster Lansing, wife of the Secretary of State, prepared for the arrival of delegations of anti-suffragists by decorating the building in the anti-suffrage colors and distributing pink roses.[31] Alice Wadsworth had been gradually taking on a more active and dynamic role in the anti-suffrage activities in Washington. A sense of the contrast between Wadsworth and Dodge emerges from an account of an anti-suffrage appearance before Congress a few months later. The diminutive Dodge "briefly expressed regret" for taking the time of the United States Senate Committee on Woman Suffrage and then introduced Mrs. James W. Wadsworth to the assemblage, who "took charge" of the hearing, complaining that because the suffragists would not put aside their activities, anti-suffragists must continue to defend themselves.[32]

After replacing Josephine Jewell Dodge as president in June 1917, Alice Hay Wadsworth could avail herself of far greater political resources than Dodge ever could. Under her leadership, the anti-suffrage movement became much less dignified as she and her supporters shifted their emphasis, like the suffragists, from the state-by-state approach of the earlier campaign to lobbying in Washington against a federal amendment. Her takeover epitomized the often-bitter tone and shift in direction of women's organized anti-suffragism from this time forward.[33] This shift may be noted at the second annual anti-suffrage convention, when Wadsworth declared that "the keynote of our campaign now is the determination to protect America from the enemies within her borders." They would rid the country of the "socialist-pacifist menace behind the woman suffrage movement."[34] At Wadsworth's direction, the National Association formed an "all-male 'advisory council' composed of 'distinguished and experienced' . . . political figures," including James W. Wadsworth Jr., Henry Cabot Lodge, Charles S. Fairchild, George W. Wickersham, and Ezra Prentice, at the same time it adopted a new national platform and resolutions.[35]

Because they considered that an "increased pro-German, pacifist, and socialist vote" had carried the election in New York, Wadsworth and representatives from twenty-five states resolved that their platform would stand for "home and national defense against Woman Suffrage, feminism and socialism," for "MAN-POWER in government," and for the "ENFORCEMENT OF THE CONSTITUTIONAL RIGHT of each state to settle the question of woman suffrage for itself." The revamped organization also stood for the "CONSERVATION of the best womanhood of all conditions and stations of life." Wadsworth wanted to make the anti-suffrage stance very clear to every man concerned, so she sent copies of the platform to President Wilson and to each member of Congress.[36]

To disseminate their views among the membership and to reflect the changes in the National Association platform, anti-suffragists announced that the *Woman's Protest* would merge with both the Cambridge-based *Anti-Suffrage Notes* and the Boston-based *Remonstrance* to become the *Woman Patriot*. Wadsworth's photograph graced the front cover of the issue announcing both her presidency and a change in format for the journal. The articles in the *Woman Patriot* became accusatory and harsh, sometimes bordering on slanderous. Maintaining that the *Protest* "has always been too crowded with special articles, 'views,' and too far behind on 'news,'" the editors proposed a weekly publication in a newspaper format to "present facts in *proportion* to their value to the *country* and to the *average* woman."[37] Articles written by male anti-suffragists became more common as fewer women contributed articles. The shift from a political lobbying organization to one of "internal discursive exchange" and increasingly hostile and personal attacks made even women who did not want to be enfranchised uncomfortable.[38] Edited for a few years by Minnie Bronson, general secretary of the National Association, and its field secretary Charlotte Rowe, the contributing editors were Colonel Henry Watterson, Anna Katharine Green, Octave Thanet, Annie Nathan Meyer, Elizabeth Ogden Wood, and Margaret C. Robinson.[39] The first issue was published on April 27, 1918, under the auspices of the newly formed Woman Patriot Publishing Company. Stockholders included Mrs. James W. Wadsworth, Carter Glass, and the presidents of state associations opposed to woman suffrage.[40] The company immediately sought more stockholders as well as correspondents and national representatives.[41]

Members of the newly restructured organization touted their conservative stance prominently. Under Wadsworth the anti-suffragists would "enter every State, whether women vote or not, and support the men who, noting the symptoms of decline and degeneration, have the courage and ability to apply a remedy." They were "Dedicated to the Defense of Womanhood, Motherhood, the Family and the State AGAINST Suffragism, Feminism and Socialism."[42] As articulated in an article by Annie Nathan Meyer, socialism was an evil to be prevented because it meant "class rule from below."[43] In spite of their opposition to women voting, it remained the policy of the organization to encourage women to register to vote in every state where women had the franchise. As far as anti-suffragists were concerned, voting had become a useful way to prevent suffragists from dominating at the polls.[44]

Anti-suffragists continued to be distracted by the Great War, especially after the United States entered it. When Wadsworth took over the anti-suffrage organization in 1917, she, like Dodge, was closely connected with the American Red Cross. The National Association, like New York State Association, allowed the Red Cross to use its headquarters once a week for meetings and making bandages.[45] The *Woman Patriot* often published news about the Red Cross and printed requests for women to knit more socks and assemble more comfort kits.[46] Anti-suffragists also continued to publish news and information about the National League for Woman's Service, as when nine women delivered three-quarter-ton trucks to Atlanta without incident.[47]

When their work related to war, anti-suffragists celebrated activity unusual for women, as had been true of anti-suffragism right along. Otherwise, anti-suffragists no longer celebrated the achievements of women in public office. As for the suffrage movement—"a 'cause' culminating in woman's militancy," as Alice Wadsworth warned—it "will no longer be dignified by high-sounding names. A spade will be called a spade, and the doctrine of 'sex equality' will be recognized for the unnatural abnormal thing it is."[48] Suffragists actually came to call this new defamation trend "Wadsworthy."[49] As a conservative, Alice Wadsworth's personal opposition to woman suffrage stemmed from her ideological support for a separate sphere for women. Her husband opposed the vote for women on the basis of the legality of states' rights, continuing his vehement opposition to woman voting long after the voters of his state enfranchised them.[50] From the time antis accepted an invitation to address the House Committee on Woman Suffrage in 1918, male supporters virtually always accompanied Alice Wadsworth and other anti-suffrage women to present testimony.

Alice Wadsworth harbored a particular dislike for Carrie Chapman Catt. In her first public interview as president of the National Association, Wadsworth denounced the sincerity of Catt and other suffragists.[51] The published attacks increased, as in September 1917 when she named Catt and other suffrage leaders as having "discourage[d] patriotism in certain quarters and . . . lower[ed] the vitality of democracy."[52] In February 1918, the anti-suffrage president issued a challenge to Catt to debate the question of woman suffrage under the auspices of the Press Forum of New York City. Wadsworth stated that if Catt refused to debate her, Catt was to "admit without equivocation that the methods, platform and principles of the woman suffrage movement cannot succeed if submitted in any fair way to the sound judgment of the American people."[53] Catt sent a letter to each of the U.S. senators, including James Wadsworth, pointing out the fallacies in Alice Wadsworth's claims, but the two women apparently never met to debate.[54] Wadsworth also repeatedly charged Carrie Chapman Catt, Jane Addams, and other suffragists with disloyalty to the United States.

In addition to personal attacks, there is less evidence of creative thinking after 1917; the *Woman Patriot* primarily reprinted articles from other publications. The vindictive, personal attacks and lack of original writing on the part of the anti-suffrage leadership were signs of a deteriorating movement that had abandoned its earlier ideas in favor of anti-radicalism. Perhaps the lack of inspiration and Wadsworth's maliciousness stemmed from a reaction to the awareness that the antis were losing, for there was a desperate quality in many of the articles anti-suffragists chose to publish in those years. Under Wadsworth and her successor, Kilbreth, who would replace Wadsworth in July 1919, the tone of the National Association rhetoric become "pathologically xenophobic, hysterically despairing at every setback and rhapsodic over every achievement."[55] The publication repeatedly attacked socialism and feminism, and accused various high-level politicians of subversion or treason. Certainly these fears were apparent in many other venues, for the decade following the Great War saw many "broad attacks on civil liberties."[56] Even so, prior to the Wadsworth takeover, there "had always been more to the ideology of anti-suffragism than merely painting the opposition with shades of red."[57] Once supported by quite a few prominent and respected women and men, anti-suffragism had lost its popular appeal.

The remaining anti-suffragists had the added task of defending their champions from increasingly demanding observers. Responding to the criticism of a prominent New York suffrage leader regarding his continuing opposition to woman suffrage, Senator James Wadsworth argued that he did not have to support woman suffrage even if some of his constituents did. The National Association, as well as the Women Voters' Party, justified Wadsworth's opposition by pointing out that the New York referendum vote was for a state amendment, not a federal amendment, which Senator Wadsworth, who had been "elected by antis," continued to oppose.[58] Wadsworth claimed that above all other considerations, the right of states to determine their electorate was a principle he fully supported. Even Alice Wadsworth occasionally found herself having to defend her husband on this issue, and she proudly publicized her support of him.[59] Confident of her position as wife of the senior senator from New York, lulled into a belief that she had continuing support for her views, she initiated her campaign to influence Congress and the president of the United States.

In an acknowledgement that Congress and the president were still occupied with the war, the National Association held a convention at its headquarters in Washington during December 1917 without the banquets or social functions of the past. Alice Wadsworth claimed that the New York State loss furnished antis with "new ammunition." Specifically, members would target "the socialist-pacifist menace behind the woman suffrage movement." They received over $9,000 in pledges to maintain the office in Washington and then resolved to establish a committee to raise additional funds. The anti-suffragists also proudly emphasized "the active support of some of the country's leading men."[60] Although Wadsworth sent letters to members of Congress warning that a federal amendment would destroy the right of the people to vote on the question of woman suffrage, thereby forcing it on unwilling states, the antis announced no exciting new strategies to prevent a federal amendment on woman suffrage.[61]

In addition to their opposition to woman suffrage, conference attendees agreed to continue supporting the policy toward the war in Europe. They boasted that "all anti-suffragists place 'America First' and anti-suffrage second."[62] The state presidents' reports were "strikingly similar," revealing that anti-suffragists all over the country "had practically deserted their own cause during the war to devote themselves to war service." The *Woman Patriot* reported that "anti-suffragists were the first and foremost women in such service" in most states. They claimed that by supporting opposition to woman suffrage and preventing the doubling of the electorate, antis helped save the government "an amount sufficient to buy five hundred million rounds of ammunition a year."[63] Anti-suffragists had eagerly followed the suggestions for war relief work outlined by Secretary of the Navy Josephus Daniels. Their articles urged readers to "make this your war," with the contribution of even small sums of money, to support the work of the Red Cross, and to continue their work for the National League for Women's Service.[64] The chair of the executive committee of the National Association recognized that although anti-suffragists neglected their campaign to prevent enfranchisement for motives of the "purest patriotism," unfortunately for the anti-suffragists, their utter devotion to the war effort allowed suffragists to make significant gains in their campaign.[65]

Women's involvement in the Great War offered justification for more attempts to pass a federal amendment. The House of Representatives passed the federal suffrage amendment in January 1918, despite the arguments of anti-suffragists.[66] Anti-suffragists publicly congratulated the representatives, including three from New York State, who "stood by the principle of local self-government against the policy of surrender to suffrage threats."[67] The *Woman's Protest* falsely claimed that Wilson announced his support for the amendment only the previous evening.[68] Anti-suffragists tried to convince themselves and their readership that the president supported suffrage as a "political maneuver designed to appease the noisy suffragists rather than as a true reflection of his personal views."[69] Wilson contended that the suffragist war effort compelled him to reward them with the right to vote, but the anti-suffragists had worked at least as diligently in the war effort as the suffragists, and they felt betrayed by the president.[70]

Despite their sense of betrayal, anti-suffragists unceasingly publicized their support of President Wilson during the war and after, although, since suffragists "surrounded" him, they claimed they found it difficult to get near enough to express their views to him.[71] Anti-suffrage leaders from both the National Association and the Women Voters' Party continued to send the president letters expressing their opposition to woman suffrage. They were also quite direct in their opposition to suffragists being at the peace table in Versailles during negotiations at the end of the war, as demanded by the International Woman Suffrage Alliance.[72] Wilson, for his part, had difficulty convincing senators to vote for woman suffrage. He argued, "We have made partners of women in this war," and he reiterated his full support for their enfranchisement; but when the Senate voted on the woman suffrage amendment in the fall of 1918, a strong southern Democratic bloc prevented the passage of the measure.[73]

The decline of the anti-suffrage movement and its smaller base of support were reflected in the conference facilities chosen after 1918. The Wadsworth home in Washington, the famous Hay House, hosted the annual meeting on January 9, 1919. Hay House was considered "inviting" by those who had seen it, but Alice Wadsworth was known for her "reticence" as a hostess, which may have influenced the choice of venue even when participation in a war no longer justified a scaling back of organizational events.[74] Wadsworth and her board invited the state presidents or their proxies, supposedly representing five hundred thousand enrolled members, to present their reports and help in planning strategy for the year. Together the seventy-five delegates planned to "conduct a dual fight the following year against the federal woman suffrage amendment and the 'red peril' of Bolshevism." Additionally, they would work for the repeal of the right to vote in states where women already voted.[75]

Members of both the National Association and the Women Voters' Party were outspoken in their opposition to the January 1919 decisions of the National Republican Committee to establish a Women's National Republican Committee and to endorse woman suffrage. Mary Kilbreth, writing for the Women Voters' Anti-Suffrage Party, added her opposition in an open letter to

Will H. Hays, the chair of the National Republican Committee, and in another open letter to the New York State Republican Committee.[76] In spite of the anger directed at the Republican committees, neither the National Association Opposed to Woman Suffrage or the Women Voters' Anti-Suffrage Party advocated for nonpartisanship. Like the Women Voters' Party, the National Association also established a "Republican Section" to represent its Republican members and a "Democratic Section" to represent its Democratic members. The National Association, however, strongly emphasized that its organization "as a whole is strictly non-partisan."[77]

The Women Voters' Party encouraged all antis, men and women, and their friends to write notes thanking those senators of either party who voted no following the February 10, 1919, congressional debate on a federal amendment for woman suffrage.[78] The National Association sent a resolution to the Senate asking that body to investigate the National American Woman Suffrage Association, offering all the evidence in its possession.[79] But these letters and resolutions were rather pathetic, desperate attempts to prevent the now inevitable passage of woman suffrage.

On May 20, 1919, Woodrow Wilson, again recommending passing the woman suffrage amendment, called a special session of the Sixty-Sixth Congress. The House of Representatives re-passed the amendment that day, and the Senate again debated it. Supporters refrained from speaking in an effort to hurry the vote, so the majority of those who did speak used the states' rights issue to oppose the measure. This time the vote was sixty-six to thirty; a large Republican and smaller Democratic majority finally passed the woman suffrage amendment.[80] It had taken more than half a century, the dedication of thousands of women, reams of paper, and hours of discussion and argument for Congress to pass a woman suffrage amendment. Even so, the battle was not over, for the next step was ratification by the states. Thirty-six states needed to ratify it, but only thirteen states were required to prevent the adoption of the amendment.[81] Suffragists, highly experienced in lobbying state legislatures, drew energy from their success in the Senate; they enthusiastically and immediately got to work in the states.

Anti-suffrage forces also "geared up for battle," ceaselessly arguing that the amendment represented a "violation of states' rights."[82] But discouragement in the anti-suffrage ranks was apparent at the highest level. Within days of the Senate vote, the *New York World* quoted Alice Wadsworth as saying that because no time limit was set on the ratification of the amendment, "it would be entirely useless to make any further fight against woman suffrage." Although she stated she was not speaking for the National Association, she was widely reprinted without this disclaimer. For Wadsworth, the strain of carrying on the anti-suffrage fight must have been tremendous; simultaneously, she dealt with the criticism her husband garnered for his persistent anti-suffrage stance.[83] The board of directors immediately called a meeting at New York City's Vanderbilt Hotel to discuss plans to prevent the ratification of the amendment without the aid of Alice Wadsworth. They said they had it on the authority of a number of constitutional lawyers that the amendment could be rejected.[84]

Although concerned anti-suffragists had once urged the National Association to "try to keep New York antis in line," it was the leader of the Women Voters' Party, Mary G. Kilbreth, who was unanimously elected president of the National Association.[85] During several days of meetings, under the leadership of Kilbreth, antis made plans to defeat the suffrage amendment. Wadsworth, who attended, claimed to have had to resign her position for health reasons, and she was elected honorary president for life. Wadsworth also kept her position as president of the Woman Patriot Publishing Company, and the *Woman Patriot* continued to be published in Washington.[86] Anti-suffrage headquarters returned to New York City, where the antis claimed that "opposition has not only the weight of public protest, but the support of men and women voters dissatisfied with the political manipulation of woman suffrage."[87] Antis chose Constitution Day in September 1919 to celebrate combining the National Association and the Women Voters' Party headquarters at 268 Madison Avenue.[88] Mottos on facing walls seemed contradictory—on one wall, "Politics are bad for women and women are bad for politics"; on the other, "You must register and enroll Oct. 6 to 11 to vote in the Spring primaries for President and United States Senators"—but nevertheless serve to illustrate the peculiar position anti-suffragists found themselves in after the congressional vote.[89] Anti-suffragists, as they had pointed out for years, were deeply committed to doing their duty in spite of their original opposition to enfranchisement.

Soon after the move, in a letter to Elihu Root in his capacity as a member of the National Security League, Kilbreth argued that "special interests" were "tampering" with the Constitution, indicating the focus of her overarching argument.[90] She traveled extensively to amass support for her cause, and she continually instigated personal campaigns against suffragists, politicians, and anyone she viewed as attacking the Constitution.[91] Her methods did not have

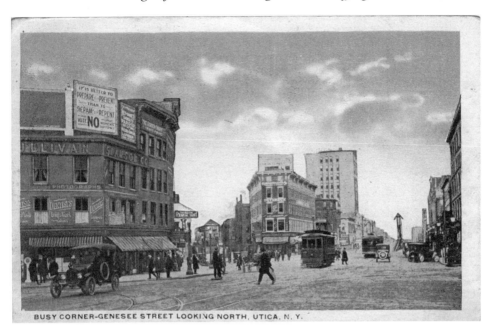

BUSY CORNER-GENESEE STREET LOOKING NORTH, UTICA, N. Y.

Utica Postcard, "It is Better to PREPARE and PREVENT than to REPAIR and REPENT; Vote NO on Woman's Suffrage" on a billboard over the Sullivan Slauson Company, probably erected in 1919. The same location was the site of another billboard stating: "Vote No for Woman Suffrage on Nov 2" on display during the parade prior to the opening performances of the Ringling Brothers Circus when it came to town on June 19, 1915. Courtesy of Evelyn and Melville Edwards, Clinton, N.Y.

enough appeal to attract widespread support, and a great lapse in membership commitments added to the problems of the beleaguered organization.[92]

The dwindling anti-suffrage contingent focused on the ratification process already underway. By the end of June, nine states had ratified the amendment. The New York State legislature had called an extraordinary session and quickly adopted a resolution to ratify the amendment, making it the fifth state to do so.[93] As the ratification process continued around the country, antis vigilantly searched for any action that did not follow state ratification rules. From June 1919 until August 1920, issues of the *Woman Patriot* kept count of the states that rejected or ratified the Susan B. Anthony Amendment. The journal recorded a few anti-suffrage activities, but its greatest concentration was on reprinting anti-suffrage articles and letters of commendation that supporters sent to anti-suffrage politicians.[94] Temporary headquarters opened in cities wherever the amendment was discussed.[95] The May 1, 1920, issue of the *Woman Patriot* reported that the National Association held its "greatest meeting" on the previous Thursday at the Hotel McAlpin in New York City. More than five hundred delegates representing twenty-six state associations "cheered again and again as speeches, plans, legal arguments and political measures against Federalism and Suffragism were advanced." Anti-suffragists also reported a "$55,000 budget for the coming campaign, and a 'surprise fund' of $6,600 for immediate use." Kilbreth was "unanimously re-elected as president" of the National Association.[96] On April 29, 1920, the National Association Opposed to Woman Suffrage announced the "opening of a new national anti-suffrage campaign, stronger and better than any possible in the past, to defend the rights of the States and the people against Federalism, feminism and demoralization."[97] But it was the dying gasp of an organization that had deteriorated under leaders who were distracted by fighting the specter of radicalism.[98]

Around the United States, the pressure for a constitutional amendment to allow women the franchise was simply too powerful to resist, and state after state ratified the amendment. By the middle of August 1920 only eight states had rejected ratification; thirty-five states had approved. The legislatures of both North Carolina and Tennessee were in session, and only one of those was needed for ratification.[99] The atmosphere in Nashville was frenzied as both suffragists and anti-suffragists descended on the city. Charlotte E. Rowe, the chief campaign speaker for the National Association, traveled to Nashville at the invitation of the Tennessee Division of the Southern Women's Rejection League.[100] Each side pinned roses on the lapels of legislators—red roses for anti-suffrage and yellow roses for suffrage. Even at the last, charges of fraud abounded. For example, anti-suffragists claimed that suffragists had offered $10,000 to a Tennessee legislator to change his vote.[101] The amendment passed with exciting drama as young Harry Burn, ignoring the telegrams Kilbreth and others sent demanding that he vote against ratification, changed his vote to support woman suffrage as he promised his suffragist mother he would if ratification came down to one vote.[102] Days later, on August 26, 1920, Secretary of State Bainbridge Colby signed the certificate of ratification, and women throughout the country could vote.[103]

Anti-suffragists continued to resist the ratification. J. S. Eichelberger testified for two hours before a Tennessee Grand Jury investigation into charges that "improper influences" had pressured members of the legislature.[104] Some controversy also existed over whether or not the Tennessee legislators were legally able to vote on the amendment, for the state constitution required the legislative body to be elected after the amendment was submitted.[105] It was regarding this right, along with questions about the legality of the ratification decisions of two other states, Missouri and West Virginia, that provided the impetus for members of the American Constitutional League (the former Men's Association Opposed to Woman Suffrage) to challenge the Nineteenth Amendment in the federal courts.[106] The league's primary argument against a federal amendment allowing all women the right to vote remained focused on states' rights. Their opposition eventually rested on resistance to amending the Constitution.

But representatives of all organizations that challenged the Nineteenth Amendment argued that it "was destructive of the governmental structure and political autonomy of the States."[107] In addition, based on various lawyers' readings of individual state constitutions, they contested the ratification process in five states.[108] The common, outspoken personality in New York continued to be Everett P. Wheeler, the most persistent and aggressive of all the men working against women's enfranchisement. Wheeler worked closely with J. S. Eichelberger, field secretary for the American Constitutional League, business manager for the Woman Patriot Publishing Company, and now editor of the *Woman Patriot*. Even as the final votes were being taken for ratification of the Nineteenth Amendment, league leadership had called for the anti-suffrage organizations to "flood the courts with suits" in a last ditch effort to prevent the passage of the woman suffrage amendment.[109]

By October 1920, the board of directors of the National Association returned its headquarters to Washington. It "pledged to support the letter and the spirit of the United States Constitution" yet argued that the constitutionality of the Nineteenth Amendment was in doubt.[110] In a plea for greater organization and support, the board of directors further elaborated on the role of their organization to fight feminism, federalism, and socialism. It also wrote to ask the Attorneys General of thirty-two states to keep the votes of women and men separated, to separate the votes of those it considered legal from those it considered illegal.[111] Still referring to themselves as anti-suffragists, the board's members remained convinced most women did not want to vote.

In the aftermath of the Great War and the Bolshevik Revolution in Russia, fears of Communism plagued people all over the United States. No longer afraid of the German "Hun," the "red radical" became the threat to eliminate.

Many people thought that the apparent disunity and disorder they perceived indicated an impending socialist revolution. The mood of the period also signified a "backlash" against changes to the existing order through feminist and progressive reform during the previous decades.[112] Conservative women especially feared that newly enfranchised women would advocate for expanded governmental interference in the lives of citizens. Alterations to the existing Constitution seemed to presage ever-greater threats to democracy.[113] As far as anti-suffragists were concerned, the more the government interfered in private lives and families, the greater the risk to the patriarchy.[114] With preserving the patriarchy remaining a priority, former antis positioned themselves at the forefront of the social reaction to these fears during this politically unsettled period.

The combined National Association Opposed to Woman Suffrage and the Woman Patriot Publishing Company became the driving force of anti-suffragism in its new incarnation: a force fighting feminism and radicalism.[115] Determined to "spread the gospel of real democracy," by early 1921 anti-suffragists more frequently referred to themselves as Woman Patriots. Relying on the *Woman Patriot* as their official organ, the right-wing conservative Woman Patriots led the fight against radicalism in several different arenas. In connection to their opposition to women's enfranchisement, they were, of course, fighting the "alleged" Nineteenth Amendment. In their view, this amendment had resulted in the "clamor of the Feminists for a Dictatorship of Education," which they would also resist. To prevent another "lobby" like the suffragists from passing a minority measure, they carried on a fight to restore to the majority the right to alter the constitution of government. Finally, they fought to uphold "morale" and unite the many citizens who realized the "many wrongs which must be corrected" for the system to endure.[116] Enemies of the Woman Patriots included the staffs of the Women's Bureau and the Children's Bureau, which the *Woman Patriot* accused of having communist connections, as well as the League of Women Voters, the organizational descendant of the National American Woman Suffrage Association.[117]

The editor of the *Woman Patriot* closely followed the events leading to a Supreme Court decision on the Nineteenth Amendment. Even before the Tennessee ratification, the president of the American Constitutional League, Charles S. Fairchild, had filed a suit against Secretary of State Colby and Attorney General A. Mitchell Palmer, "seeking an injunction against the proclamation of the proposed Federal Suffrage Amendment." Wheeler, who argued on behalf of Fairchild on July 13, 1920, in the District of Columbia Supreme Court, submitted the testimony of several authorities who argued that the amendment was "not within the amending power of Article V" of the Constitution. Rather than an amendment, he contended, it was a "radical change," "destructive" of democratic government, and it "jeopardized" the "entire theory of a republican form of government."[118] The judge dismissed the case as premature; Wheeler and the Washington attorney for the Constitutional League immediately filed an appeal. Wheeler's argument was reprinted in several issues of the *Woman Patriot*, which, naturally, promoted the suit quite heavily.[119]

In October 1920, after Colby proclaimed the Nineteenth Amendment in effect, Everett P. Wheeler, with William L. Marbury of Baltimore and Alfred D. Smith of Washington, D.C., moved to advance the hearing of their appeal. His request denied, Wheeler expressed confidence that the more time the Court had for considering the case, the greater the chance of victory.[120] Filed with the Supreme Court of the United States on December 24, 1921, the case of Charles S. Fairchild against Charles E. Hughes as Secretary of State and Harry M. Daugherty as Attorney General was heard on January 23, 1922, in tandem with the case of *Leser v. Garnett*, brought by the Maryland League for State Defense for a similar purpose.[121] In regards to the Leser case, the Court held that the Nineteenth Amendment was similar to the Fifteenth Amendment, which had been recognized for half a century. The Court dismissed the Fairchild case because Fairchild was not an election official. Justice Louis Brandeis did not consider that either case required extensive comment.[122] The *Woman Patriot* made available the "Oral Argument" on the Nineteenth Amendment at two dollars a copy.[123]

Once the Supreme Court affirmed that the Nineteenth Amendment was indeed constitutional, the board of directors formally announced the dissolution of the National Association Opposed to Woman Suffrage and prepared for new battles. For some time, the National Association held board of directors' meetings, claiming a large attendance, but rarely, if ever, publishing reports of the proceedings.[124] On March 15, 1922, at the directors' meeting, members discussed reorganization plans and requested proposals from interested persons.[125] The association had already become one of letter writers, rather than functioning as an organization overseeing active political participation.[126] Eventually, it settled on a new structure with a board of five directors. In addition to Mary G. Kilbreth, board members included Mrs. Rufus M. Gibbs of Baltimore, Mrs. Randolph Frothingham of Boston, Margaret C. Robinson of Cambridge, and Mrs. John Balch of Milton, Massachusetts. The board was beholden to no membership, which obviously facilitated working closely with other organizations for any cause that related to protecting states' rights and, with James Wadsworth, preventing any challenges to a "strict construction of the Constitution."[127]

The Woman Patriots claimed that the federal government took too much power from the states and violated the mandates of the Constitution. In addition to disseminating the principles of the Constitution, they would "expose radical activities" and undermine feminist activism.[128] They were nonpartisan and proud that they "challenged and censored" presidents, governors, or any politician who supported what they deemed unconstitutional or socialistic measures.[129] No published list of active members existed because it had no members, and no soliciting of news from any state auxiliaries ensued because most of the affiliated groups had apparently disbanded. The Woman Patriot Publishing Company financially supported the work of the Woman Patriots.[130] Citing a need to reduce costs in an increasing struggle for solvency, in April 1921 they began to publish twice a month rather than weekly. The editors promised to publish "specifications rather than generalizations," and "not simply talk about the 'bureaucracy,'" but to "name the bureaucrats."[131] Cost-cutting measures allowed the Woman Patriots to function but frequently forced them to print apologies for late and missing issues.

The perceived crises of the 1920s stimulated the formation of a number of groups that turned to the *Woman Patriot* for information and publicity. Members of the Sentinels of the Republic, for example, announced the founding of their organization in the *Woman Patriot*.[132] The stated purpose of the Sentinels of the Republic was to "maintain the fundamental principles of the Constitution," to oppose further federal encroachment upon the reserved rights of the states, to stop the growth of socialism, to prevent increasing power in Washington through a "perverted interpretation of the General Welfare Clause," and to "preserve a free republican form of government in the United States."[133] By the summer of 1923, the organization claimed that it had "sentinels" in six hundred cities and towns around the country and had drafted a "Plan of Organization." It required that at all meetings, members "lay stress on the necessity of putting strong men into office during this crisis,—men who believe in our Constitution and institutions."[134] Membership in the Sentinels of the Republic included conservative men and women whose names had long been linked with anti-suffrage.

The Woman Patriots joined with the American Constitutional League in proposing a new amendment to the Constitution that would bypass state legislatures in decisions regarding amendments and provide for ratification or rejection only by popular vote, or through special conventions of instructed delegates.[135] They claimed they wanted to restore the rights of the people, and they promoted a so-called "Back-to-the-People" amendment, although it contradicted their former willingness to limit voting rights on the basis of sex. Wadsworth's name is not connected with the earliest announcements of the proposed amendment in the *Woman Patriot*. It is possible that Wadsworth wanted to gauge the public response through the publication before he presented the Wadsworth-Garrett amendment to Congress in April 1921.[136] A delegation of Woman Patriots expressed support for the amendment to President Harding on the first of June.[137] Significantly, Wadsworth sought support for the amendment before the public was aware of the wording of the final version, for instead of involving the people in the amending process, he and his supporters actually intended that the amendment further reduce the involvement of the average citizen in the amending process.[138] Wadsworth himself "continually placed faith in the judgment of leadership elites," rather than in the people, making a mockery of the amendment anyway.

In January 1923, a Senate subcommittee heard the Wadsworth-Garrett amendment, the so-called "people's amendment." Representatives of the *Woman Patriot* dominated those who spoke for its passage. People closely connected with the Woman Patriots who also spoke in favor of the amendment included Everett P. Wheeler of the American Constitutional League, Mrs. John Balch, who, in addition to serving on the board of the Woman Patriots, spoke for the Massachusetts Public Interests League, and Louis A. Coolidge of the Sentinels of the Republic. The editor of the *Woman Patriot* probably read the statement in favor of the amendment written by Rossiter Johnson.[139] The proposed amendment made adoption of any amendment more difficult, as critics readily pointed out. In response to a proposed alternative amendment, that all congressionally approved amendments be submitted to the people of each state for ratification, a measure not in his version in spite of the name the Woman Patriots used, Wadsworth "grumbled" that the new version "once again had the central government telling the states exactly what to do."[140]

While the former anti-suffragists shifted some of their focus to functioning as constitutional watchdogs, they had not abandoned gender issues. Rendering powerless women in governmental offices was another important goal. Although anti-suffrage associations had once supported the appointment of women to public offices, the Woman Patriots adamantly opposed women in office as promoting communistic and feminist agendas. The Woman Patriots served in the vanguard of those fighting the Sheppard-Towner Maternity and Infancy Protection Act, not only because it was overseen by women, but because former suffragists and the League of Women Voters supported it.[141] The Children's Bureau chief Julia Lathrop designed the act so the federal government would help fund education for mothers in every state in an effort to reduce the high rates of maternal and infant death rates. It moved through several incarnations between 1918 and 1920 before Democratic Senator Morris Sheppard of Texas, who supported both prohibition and woman suffrage, and Republican Representative Horace Mann Towner of Iowa sponsored a version.[142] In its final form, the bill provided matching federal grants to the states "for information and instruction on nutrition and hygiene, prenatal and child health clinics, and visiting nurses for pregnant women and new mothers." The act was weaker than its authors intended; the original request of $4,000,000 for the program was reduced to $1,240,000, and limited to just five years (1922–27) when the bill would have to come up for renewal. Intended for all mothers, not just the poor, it was supported by rural, working-class, and middle-class women, many of whom were "clients" by virtue of reading *Infant Care*, a pamphlet published and distributed by the Bureau, or by attending lectures presented by the Children's Bureau. The act did not challenge the patriarchal structure of families, nor did it encourage women to seek positions in public office.[143]

Herbert Hoover, known for his work with the American Relief Administration, supported Sheppard-Towner and pointed out that the concerns put forth by women would need to be addressed if political parties wanted the support of women. As a result, parties such as the Democratic, Socialist, Prohibitionist, and Farm-Labor endorsed the measure in their platforms. Although the Republican Party did not formally endorse Sheppard-Towner, its presidential candidate, Warren G. Harding, endorsed the measure in his Social Justice Day speech a month before his election.[144] While a few organizations initially objected to Sheppard-Towner, including those linked to the National Association Opposed to Woman Suffrage and the American Medical Association, national groups did not organize in time to oppose it.[145] Around the nation, most women's groups endorsed the program in the five years before it came up for renewal.[146]

Many women's groups, including the Woman's Joint Congressional Committee, were supportive during the congressional discussion related to renewal of the program. However, this time a better-prepared American Medical Association joined the Woman Patriots and other right-wing conservative organizations to preserve states' rights and fight what they considered to be socialized medicine.[147] Additionally, by the 1920s "charges of lesbianism had become a common way to discredit women professionals, reformers, and educators—and the feminist political, reform, and education institutions they had founded."[148] Using "spinster" as her code word for lesbian, the unmarried Kilbreth condemned the "spinsters" of the Children's Bureau and derisively claimed that the "main argument for the bill appears to be that if a number of spinsters can get the Government to pay them high salaries and traveling expenses to go all over the country and *talk*, it will reduce infant mortality!"[149] Florence Kelley, head of the National Consumers' League and a frequent target of the *Woman Patriot*, rightly worried about the harm Eichelberger, Kilbreth, and the Woman Patriots would do to the act.[150] Members of organizations affiliated with the Woman Patriots challenged the act in the Supreme Court, but the cases were dismissed for "want of jurisdiction."[151] Grace Abbott, the new director of the Children's Bureau, accepted numerous compromises in order for the bill to be renewed in any form. A weak version of the bill was renewed in 1927, regardless of the tangible and positive results in improving women's knowledge of childbearing and childcare across much of the United States, but Sheppard-Towner was repealed in 1929.[152] The Woman Patriots widely trumpeted their success.

With the support of the Sentinels of the Republic and the American Constitutional League, the Woman Patriots additionally fought the proposed child-labor amendment.[153] Fearing that it radically challenged the existing social order, the editor of the *Woman Patriot* argued that these changes would allow the federal government to have more power over children than parents had. In addition, the board of directors claimed that it was wrong to prohibit youths up to age eighteen to work for their self-support or that of their parents. The proposed amendment would endanger the future of America because the youth would be put under the guardianship of the Children's Bureau; it would violate states' rights, promote pacifism, communism, and socialism; and it would prevent farm children from doing chores.[154] The Woman Patriots and other opponents celebrated the failure of the ratification of the child labor amendment by three-quarters of the state legislatures. They considered that it marked not only a return to sound constitutional principles, but a great victory for the people over a host of enemies, specifically communists, socialists, feminists, bureaucrats, and pacifists.[155] Like members of the National Association of Manufacturers, however, many people at the time resisted the idea of the government intruding in child-labor issues.

The Woman Patriots left the same legacy of anti-feminism in opposing the proposed Equal Rights Amendment, initially presented to Congress in 1923, which they contended was socialist in nature. The former anti-suffragists saw the amendment proposal as the logical result of the Nineteenth Amendment, sneering that the Alice Paul amendment was "simply a further effort on the part of a small lobby of women to repeal nature by Federal amendment."[156] Later, the Woman Patriots charged that the National Woman's Party did not have "even the political morality of the Communist Party" in presenting candidates for public office. Rather, it behaved as a "parasite," because it supported candidates of other parties.[157] They kept up the arguments throughout the 1920s, claiming that the "pandemonium" that would result from enforcing the amendment "would be nothing less than chaos throughout the structure of the government and society."[158] But as that amendment divided and distracted the feminist forces in the nation for decades and did not make it out of committee until 1946, the opposition of the Woman Patriots was inconsequential.

In addition to its protection of the Constitution, the Woman Patriot Publishing Company was at the forefront of "protecting" the democracy from all radical challenges from non-American citizens. Kilbreth, Wheeler, Robinson, and Gibbs were among those who charged twelve people with communist activities in a letter written to the Attorney General and another written to President Coolidge. The letter presenting their "cases" stated that they and other signers had legal counsel, and that they required the district attorneys in the several districts to "institute prosecutions for the offenses alleged."[159] Articles in the *Woman Patriot* often targeted members of the International Council of Women.[160] They also opposed pacifist Rosika Schwimmer's bids for citizenship, with Kilbreth submitting a petition to the president of the United States entreating him to exclude Schwimmer.[161] Their efforts to prevent Albert Einstein and any other people they believed had connections with the Communist Party from immigrating were widely known.[162] By the end of the decade, however, the organization was faltering, and fewer people were willing to read the *Patriot* diatribes. After years of publication delays, problems with mailing issues, and requests for financial support, the *Woman Patriot* ceased publication with the December 1932 issue. Mary G. Kilbreth and J. S. Eichelberger slipped into obscurity.

The anti-suffrage movement changed significantly after the 1917 referendum enfranchised the women of New York State. The period that followed reflected the mood of the greater society as anti-suffragists sought to resist radicalism more than they did woman suffrage. With changes in leadership and a focus on the federal suffrage amendment, the core argument of what anti-suffragists once believed—that women and men were meant to occupy separate spheres and that they were so different from each other that they should have a different relationship with the government—is less apparent in the Woman Patriots' arguments during its later years. Kilbreth lost sight of those essential anti-suffrage beliefs in arguing for states' rights and against socialism, feminism, and radicalism. In addition, the attitude toward women suffragists had hardened. No longer even pretending to tolerate the women who had once advocated for suffrage, these anti-suffragists projected an animosity they had previously not harbored. Anti-suffrage leadership had once represented a significant majority of the people; support for the hate-filled rhetoric of former anti-suffragists disappeared during the 1920s.

6. Antis Adjust to Enfranchisement, 1917–1932

After spending twenty-five years opposing woman suffrage, Annie Nathan Meyer had some difficulty adjusting to her changed political status. Meyer, an intellectual maverick and one who never backed down from criticism or an argument, fired off an editorial to the *New York Times* ordering anti-suffrage women not to vote.[1] Antis, Meyer declared, should let socialist and radical factions win "just once" to show governmental leaders how widespread radicalism had become. Public censure was swift and brutal.[2] An editor for the *Chicago Herald* wrote that because Meyer believed that "the grant of woman's suffrage having put the country in a bad mess, the anti should see that the country suffers as much as possible." Meyer was, in the editor's words, "acting like a child who has been spanked."[3] An editor for the socialist *New York Call* condemned Meyer as well, contending that "she would rather see this ruin effected, so as to be able to say 'I told you so!' than have the noble patriots like herself step into the breach and by working and voting perhaps save the country she sees so desperately threatened."[4]

Obviously stung by the responses to her idea, a contrite Meyer sought understanding through a more carefully crafted article in the *New Republic*. She wrote that after recommending the scheme in the *New York Times*, she had also suggested the idea at an anti-suffrage meeting. The former National Association Opposed to Woman Suffrage president Josephine Dodge "immediately rebuked" her by saying, "You and I place our country above any controversy; at such a time a question of suffrage or non-suffrage must be of relative unimportance." Meyer admitted that she could see the sense in her friend's words. Regretting her rash decision to dash off her thoughts to a newspaper before privately testing the idea on her anti-suffragist friends, Meyer was as close to a public apology as she would ever get. She concluded the article by asserting that the act of voting contributed to the greater good of the country and promised that she, too, had upheld her duty to register and vote.[5] Although Meyer apparently collected every article, critical or laudatory, for her scrapbooks, she does not mention this specific incident in her 1951 autobiography. In fact, there she assessed women's enfranchisement by writing only, "How could we possibly refuse to vote but permit women whose whole outlook on life differed from ours to have their say, unopposed?" Meyer's question could have just as easily referred to suffragists as it could have to uneducated immigrants. Either way, by the time Meyer wrote her autobiography she was ostensibly reconciled to women voting.[6]

While some women persisted in anti-suffrage activities after 1917, as we saw in the previous chapter, the more typical former anti-suffragists in New York State put aside their old animosities and tried to work with former suffragists in an attempt to create the better world Lucy Price had foreseen through women's participation in politics.[7] Political expectations for women were very high, but whether or not women fulfilled these expectations is far less important than trying to understand the process of politicization for newly enfranchised women. Faced with civic adjustments and new responsibilities, many women—even those who had been anti-suffragists—found it a politically exciting decade. Once most people realized that women's enfranchisement would not significantly alter traditional gender roles (a fear anti-suffragists had long expressed) even anti-suffragists became a part of changing the relationship between women and politics.[8] Just as former suffragists devoted energy to "revitalizing American politics," so too did former anti-suffragists assist in that revitalization in the 1920s.[9] To date, all of the full-length studies of the women's anti-suffrage movement end in 1920, leaving virtually untold the impact enfranchisement had on the women who had formerly worked to oppose the vote.[10] Knowing what former anti-suffragists did in the first decade of enfranchisement enhances our understanding of the political gains and experiences of all women as they moved from disenfranchisement to a fuller participation in politics.

Newly enfranchised women entered the decade with very high expectations for themselves. Their adjustment difficulties were compounded by the expectations politicians and critics had for them. For decades, suffrage activists had encouraged these high expectations while anti-suffragists had denigrated them. Although women faced heavy "burdens of culture, the family, and history" when they entered politics, commentators and political pundits somehow expected women to radically change the political system, rising above those burdens, all in a few short years.[11] Many women were unsure of how to handle their new state of enfranchisement. It was too uncomfortable for some women and would take time to get used to. Others did not take advantage of their enfranchisement, remaining opposed or apathetic to voting rights for the rest of their lives. Still other women claimed to have no faith in any political party. Some women were simply following early instructions like those given to members of the New York City Woman Suffrage Party, who were told not to join political parties until they learned how to behave as voters. By April 1918, the organization lifted the restriction; Mary Garrett Hay pointed out that while individuals could be members of whichever party they chose, the suffrage party hoped to retain members of all political parties.[12]

While all women had to adjust to their new status as voters, for some anti-suffragists, the adjustment was complicated by antis' previous apprehension about the time commitment proper voting required. Lyman Abbott was conciliatory in his September 8, 1920, *Outlook* article regarding the Nineteenth Amendment. He pointed out that if ballot-box duties conflicted with a woman's home duties, she could be excused from fulfilling her political obligations.[13] Even after enfranchisement, many women remained outside of the political process. Between 1916 and 1920 voting by the general population declined by about 30 percent. It is a coincidence that there would be a general decline in the same years that women acquired the vote; and, since most states did not keep separate records of women's and men's voting behavior, it is difficult to know conclusively the behavior of the newly enfranchised group.[14] The Republican Women's State Executive Committee sent requests to each of the sixty-two counties in New York State asking the election districts to divide by gender those who voted during the 1924 election. Half of the counties responded and the committee received widely varied responses. The top five counties—all rural, primarily Republican—reported that between eighty-eight and ninety-five women voted for every one hundred men. The most disappointing report claimed that only thirty-nine women voted for every one hundred men. The data also showed variance in the cities. In one upstate city forty-eight women voted for every one hundred men while sixty-nine women voted for every one hundred men in one of the boroughs of New York City. The three most crowded boroughs showed that between fifty-seven to sixty-seven women voted for every one hundred men.[15]

According to the observers, the informal barriers to women's voting took on more consequence than the formal ones. In 1924, Sarah Schuyler Butler, chair of the Republican Women's State Executive Committee in New York State, published an article in *Scribner's Magazine* on the voting behavior of women. To understand women's voting patterns and determine the reasons some women were not voting, she and members of her committee traveled throughout New York State to speak directly to women. She found that whether or not women voted was more dependent on local conditions than on any "general causes, or even upon the political complexion of the counties in which they live."[16] For those who wanted to vote but who lived in remote areas, many claimed the main hindrance was transportation. Women's homes were often isolated and the roads were poor. In urban areas, with a heavy concentration of immigrants, Butler found that many women had a fear and distrust of government or were merely uninterested in voting. For many of these women, the Nineteenth Amendment simply made no difference. Noting that women "could not be effectively organized by men," she concluded that the solution was to have more female leaders "in whom they have faith" reach out to them.[17] Practicing what she preached, Butler devoted considerable energy during the decade to traveling and speaking throughout the state encouraging women's political participation.

A lack of female leadership was not the only problem women voters faced during the 1920s. An April 1924 article in the *Literary Digest* summarized the views of George Martin Madden (pseudonym of Mrs. Attwood R. Martin), who saw, in her fourteen-month tour of the United States, political apathy on the part of women.[18] Journalist Charles Edward Russell contended that women refused to vote for female candidates, and he accused women of not caring enough about voting.[19] Carrie Chapman Catt, however, was adamant that women needed more than four years to remove the "unsatisfying outgrowths of men's political evolution," and Jane Addams argued that women's voting behavior needed to be assessed in the context of an overall decline in voting nationwide.[20] Vira Boarman Whitehouse, once president of the New York State Woman Suffrage Party, expressed concern that not enough women leaders had stepped forward to "discover the real attitude of the women of the organizations." She feared that the former suffragists would "stand pat" and not dare to take other chances to advance.[21] Former opponent of suffrage Ida Tarbell asked tough questions about woman suffrage. She pointed out that calling suffrage a failure was as prohibitive as lethargy to good voting practices. She suggested that the effects of suffrage could not be accurately assessed until decades, at least, had passed.[22] In a three-month trip through twelve or fifteen states, Tarbell found much to commend in women's "lively concern in public questions," and their aversion to the recently proposed equal rights amendment, which would eliminate protective legislation for women. She also praised the professionalism that women displayed in public office. Tarbell was particularly critical of any woman who did not vote as "intelligently and disinterestedly" as she was able and predicted that women were unlikely to act outside of political parties.[23] Clearly, the path to women's political enfranchisement was complicated by continuing and still-strong public censure.

The majority of former anti-suffragists in New York tended to agree with people like Josephine Dodge and James Cardinal Gibbons, who "strongly urge[d] upon all [women] the exercise of suffrage, not only as a right but as a strict duty."[24] This notion was far more in line with typical anti-suffrage rhetoric than Meyer's imprudent reaction, but voting would take some getting used to. Years before antis had announced their willingness to do their political duty should the need arise, for they considered the vote a responsibility, a duty of citizenship, not the right suffragists demanded it was.[25] Yet, facing the male-dominated political world assuredly intimidated many women, whatever side of the suffrage divide they hailed from. In the minds of most people in the early-twentieth-century United States, popular politics and political parties were inseparably linked.[26] Many women, then, whether or not they had advocated nonpartisanship for women prior to the Nineteenth Amendment, naturally gravitated to one or the other of the parties after state, and then federal, enfranchisement. Although some agreed that remaining independent of political parties would be more useful to women, others claimed women needed to cooperate with a political party to accomplish their goals.[27] Several historians argue convincingly that women had been involved in party politics for many years; it is feasible that most women, whether for or against suffrage, had never truly been nonpartisan.[28] Yet for many newly enfranchised women, developing the habit of voting was a two-stage process. The first step was to overcome gender-related reluctance to physically cast a ballot, and the second was to accept the relationship between voting and political party involvement.

Nonpartisanship, according to some historians, remained a "resilient component of women's approach to politics" during the 1920s.[29] Not so for former anti-suffragists. In New York they usually registered with a political party, most often the Republican Party.[30] Antis had become increasingly politicized in the process of opposing enfranchisement. They were already in the habit of joining women's organizations, and women's political organizations welcomed them, apparently with little comment or censure. The organizations former antis chose depended on their comfort level with party politics. Women outside of the cities could be influenced by the publications of political organizations, further spreading the possibilities of women's political involvement.[31] Just as the understanding of the suffrage movement is enhanced by exploring anti-suffrage activities and behavior, the understanding of anti-suffrage acquiescence in the decade following the passage of the Nineteenth Amendment affords a better comprehension of the process of politicization of all newly enfranchised women.

Rather than joining forces with Alice Hay Wadsworth and Mary G. Kilbreth once the New York referendum passed, the majority of the state's conservative women who had actively opposed suffrage adapted to their changed political status and voted. In point of fact, former anti-suffragists were actually proud of fulfilling that commitment to duty once women were enfranchised. Some anti-suffrage women (or their family members) boasted that these women were among the first to register for the vote after the 1917 referendum. They seemed unashamed of their former perspective, or at least it soon become inconsequential. New York State anti-suffragists such as Elizabeth Huyck Moore, once leader of the Syracuse Branch of the New York State Association Opposed to Woman Suffrage, for example, went to the polls to "cast a vote for prohibition of the liquor traffic" as soon as she could.[32]

Contemporary accounts of these newly enfranchised, former anti-suffrage women stress that most of them extended their political involvement beyond simply placing a ballot in the box and strove to educate themselves and other women about their new role in the electorate. Certainly, a prominent task of the anti-suffrage movement all along had been promoting political and civic education. That this mission would continue after the 1917 New York State referendum or the 1920 ratification of the Nineteenth Amendment should come as no surprise. They, like former suffragists, sought to share in women's newly achieved political power, and they became a crucial part of the transitional phase between progressivism and the New Deal era.[33]

Women were, in terms of politics, doing what men did; no longer did the vote divide the sexes. Gone were the days when women separated themselves into suffrage and anti-suffrage camps; former suffragists and anti-suffragists now participated in many of the same organizations as they had before suffrage became such a divisive issue. That women maintained their separate groups can obscure women's political achievements during the period, although women's groups of the 1920s were inclined to be more specialized than before enfranchisement.[34] Women who belonged to groups that did not work on women's issues alone tended to be undermined in male-dominated organizations. Although women did have the right to vote, and many people encouraged women to register with political parties, changes in mass political participation took place simultaneously with women's entrance to politics, complicating the transition to their political enfranchisement.[35]

Concurrent with women entering politics, political parties lost a great deal of their influence during the early twentieth century. Governments more frequently responded to the pressure individual groups put on legislators. This change exacerbated the difficulties for women's entry into politics as many became disillusioned with political parties and returned to their volunteer organizations.[36] For both suffragists and anti-suffragists, the process of political involvement was slow, and as quite a few historians point out, the political parties themselves remained male-dominated.[37] Still, from the time politicians had come to see the strong possibility of an amendment enfranchising women, members of both political parties had vied to attract women and make use of their partisan support. Democrats reminded women that they had received the vote under the administration of Woodrow Wilson, while Republicans reminded the women that they had "overwhelming Republican support in Congress" and that "twenty-nine of the thirty-six ratifying states were Republican-controlled."[38]

The majority of New York's former anti-suffrage women who chose political party affiliation chose the Republican Party because it was the party of affiliation for many of the families of women who served in the movement.[39] The former anti-suffragist leaders' focus on civic education helped to convince their cohort that acquiring the vote was not as alarming as they had previously imagined. By the time of the 1917 referendum, after carefully studying politics and voting habits in their efforts to prevent enfranchisement, a significant number of former anti-suffragists may have already been less opposed to using the vote. In addition, their experience in war preparedness and relief efforts during World War I may have shifted their priorities. Ever dutiful to the nation, anti-suffragists registered and voted, dropping many of the political divisions between them and suffragists, even working together in the same organizations, as Lucy Price had predicted they would. And although not every woman joined a political party, participation in party politics also served to eliminate some of the divisions between former anti-suffragists and suffragists.

At first, anticipating "a new note in politics," male politicians adjusted their views in an effort to acquire women's votes while both parties eagerly courted the newly enfranchised women.[40] This feared "new note" was the expectation that women "embodied nonpartisanship even when they acted in partisan ways."[41] Intensifying the anxiety of politicians, a significant number of women who enrolled in parties declared that they would not necessarily vote a straight party ticket.[42] It made women's voting behavior unpredictable, and it belied male politicians' attempts to control women's votes through their party affiliation. As Elisabeth Israels Perry defines the general attitude toward party politics at the time, there were those who "warned that as long as women held aloof from partisanship, they would remain politically inconsequential."[43] Yet, those women who were integrated into the political system found it difficult to influence social or political change from within.[44]

Quite a few dynamic women were already fully involved in party politics, and they encouraged the new female voters to register with political parties. These high-achieving women understood that those who lacked confidence or political knowledge might be reluctant to enter the political arena. For such new voters, education was the key to voting responsibly and making a commitment to the political process. One who attempted to influence the new voters was Henrietta Wells Livermore, vice chair of the New York State Executive Committee and a member of the National Executive Committee of the Republican Party. Livermore (1864–1933) graduated from Wellesley College in 1887 and married Arthur L. Livermore in 1893. She served as vice president and on the board of directors of the New York Woman Suffrage Association, as chair of literature for the National American Woman Suffrage Association, and, for two years, on the Leslie Woman Suffrage Commission. She was the first woman to serve as vice chair of the New York State Republican Committee and had charge of the organization of Republican women in the eastern states in the campaigns to elect Presidents Harding, Coolidge, and Hoover.[45] Livermore publicized the Republican Party's facilitation and encouragement of women as they registered to vote.[46] Not only did the party help to educate new voters on the logistics of registering and voting, it provided a motor corps to transport women to the polls to register, and a telephone corps to remind women both to register and to vote.[47] These methods were most effective in reaching middle- and upper-class women, who had ready access to telephones as well as to the party's publications. As organizations and political parties addressed the specific educational needs of inexperienced new voters, they helped to overcome some of the problems the women faced in adjusting to their new political duties.

It does not appear that most anti-suffragists had to face the dilemma of whether or not to join a party once ratification was a reality. Anti-suffragists, unlike suffragists, had never conceived of reforming politics and so were content with the existing system. A significant number of former New York State anti-suffrage leaders became active in the Republican Party and in affiliated organizations. In the 1920s, the Republican Party was "the party of business and property," which appealed to the many elite women who had been connected with the anti-suffrage movement.[48] The Republican Party "began as the party of reform; even when it became dominated by a business elite, it still viewed itself as the party of progress," a perspective assuredly appealing to anti-suffragists. It drew women of the Protestant and educated middle class, while the Democratic Party drew greater numbers of working-class men, whose wives and daughters had received less education than the women drawn to the Republican Party.[49] For many women who joined the Republican Party, "Republicanism was already part of their understanding of themselves as Americans and as social and economic elites."[50] Virtually all of the former anti-suffragists fit descriptions of the typical Republican. With its connections to the business elite and affiliations with Presbyterian or Episcopal churches (denominations generally recognized at the time as Republican), the party was a logical choice for anti-suffragists.[51] Apparently, women who had once been opposed to voting and then joined the Republican Party drew little censure from former suffragists, who may have gleefully welcomed their capitulation to politics.

Following her return to New York after serving overseas during the Great War, it became as common to see Alice Hill Chittenden's name in connection with various Republican political activities as it had been prior to 1917 in connection with anti-suffrage activities. She contended that in spite of having fought women's enfranchisement, once men decided women should vote it became the duty of all women to exercise their right. In her typical way, she wholeheartedly embraced her new responsibilities to the Republican Party.

She was ideal to support the Republican Party for several reasons. She grew up in a Republican family and supported its platform. As savvy as she was, she had absolutely no interest in reforming politics, so she fully accepted the directives of the party. While she once fought enfranchisement, she had made no secret of her willingness to do her duty. As a Republican, she represented the ideal elite female voter: deferential and obedient to the patriarchal system and never threatening or reform minded regarding politics. She also embodied the political perspective of many of the conservative anti-suffragists in the period after women won enfranchisement.

New York State women first exercised their right to vote in a statewide election in 1920. Senator James W. Wadsworth Jr. faced reelection to Congress, and loyal Republican women were bound by their affiliation to support him. However, because Wadsworth blatantly opposed women's suffrage, many former suffragists considered him their "inveterate enemy" and opposed his candidacy.[52] Mary Garrett Hay, serving as chair of the Women's Executive Committee of the Republican National Committee, refused to support Wadsworth's reelection bid. Hay was eventually forced out of the committee and actually went on to support the Democratic candidate.[53] At the same time, Carrie Chapman Catt publicly criticized the candidate for his hostility to woman suffrage, his lack of support for Republican candidates to various committees, his opposition to "special interests," and his support of big business. Loyal Republican Party women such as Henrietta Livermore announced that Wadsworth, regardless of his position on woman suffrage, had their votes. Chittenden had worked with Wadsworth during the anti-suffrage movement and assuredly would have voted the Republican ticket, as would most other former antis. Despite a bitter campaign against him by former suffragists, Wadsworth won reelection.[54] But it soon dawned on many women that their divisions and committees within the parties kept them in auxiliary roles and prohibited them from wielding any real power within the political parties.[55]

Frustration with the 1920 presidential campaign led directly to the formation of the Women's National Republican Club, according to Rosalie Loew Whitney's brief history of the club written in 1928. Independent of the Republican Party, yet fully supportive of it, the club was founded in 1920 by Henrietta Wells Livermore, Alice Hill Chittenden, and other members of the New York Republican Women's State Executive Committee, including Pauline Morton Sabin. Sabin (1887–1955) was educated in private schools and had inherited millions from her family's Morton Salt business. In 1916 she married Charles Hamilton Sabin, president of Guaranty Trust Company. Devoted to the Republican Party, she excelled at fundraising and recruiting new members.[56] These loyal Republican women opened temporary offices in a suite of rooms at the Hotel Vanderbilt, meeting at weekly luncheons to plan their work. After the election, they established headquarters on Thirty-Ninth Street.[57] The goals of the club's founding members including helping other women develop an interest in politics and party affiliation through education, and then to "draw them by education into the Republican Party." This education involved an understanding of the Republican Party platform and the importance of party affiliation.

The club, based in New York City, spread its influence broadly. Quite a few of the members who lived outside the city established branches in their towns and cities around the state. The Women's National Republican Club claimed nearly sixteen hundred members, and by February 1924 was sufficiently popular that a national clubhouse for Republican women opened on East Thirty-Seventh Street. Conveniently situated between Grand Central and Pennsylvania stations, the clubhouse was "in the heart of the shopping and theatre district," surely an advantage to members. The building was a five-story structure with a large assembly hall, two dining rooms, a library, a lounge, committee rooms, and fourteen bedrooms available at "moderate rates" for out-of-town members. The clubhouse was carefully decorated in a style that members considered "suggestive of early American history, closely identified with the Federalist party founded by Washington and by Hamilton, progenitor of the Republican party." Even many upstate women considered membership in the organization worthwhile and valuable.[58] Livermore, Sabin, and other members of the Women's National Republican Club worked hard in their efforts for the Republican Party.

Republicans at any level would have been hard-pressed to find a more loyal adherent than Alice Hill Chittenden in her more than twenty-five years of formal involvement with the Republican Party. Drawing on her experience with the anti-suffrage movement, she organized and assisted with innumerable political affairs for campaigning, fundraising, and charity.[59] She immersed herself in campaign committee activities for local, state, and national Republican candidates, supporting or endorsing candidates that included Major General Leonard Wise Wood in his 1920 bid for his party's nomination to the presidency, Wadsworth in his unsuccessful 1926 campaign for U.S. Senator, the dry candidate for state senator in 1930, the Republican candidate for Supreme Court justice in 1933, as well as the presidential campaigns of Coolidge and Hoover.[60] Chittenden, as chair of the Women's Speakers Bureau of the Republican State Committee, stimulated a great deal of activity in support of Herbert Hoover. Partly because of her efforts, for the first time in history more women than men campaigned to elect a Republican candidate for president.[61]

Traveling throughout New York State and beyond, Chittenden presented speeches on topics related to political campaigns, or on topics such as the success or failure of suffrage, the Constitution and the need to limit amendments to it, or the national park system.[62] She worked with other prominent Republicans, both female and male, on various political advisory committees, including one on prohibition.[63] Chittenden served on the Women's National Republican Club's board of governors from 1924 until 1944, as vice chair of the Campaign Committee, and, for several years, as chair of the National Affairs Committee. For the rest of her life she remained active on committees such as public affairs, luncheon, entertainment, activities, and, especially, political education.[64] Her background in the anti-suffrage movement facilitated her political commitments in the post-suffrage years.

Another former anti-suffragist, Lucy J. Price, also transferred her considerable talents and loyalty to the Women's National Republican Club and support for Republican candidates. Having been both a journalist and on the anti-suffrage speaking circuit for many years, she continued making political speeches all over the state and beyond.[65] As early as October 1920, she was on the campaign trail for Warren G. Harding. "Blessed with a good stage appearance, a fluent delivery and a remarkable command of the language," according to a newspaper report, Price spoke on the necessity of a two-party system but declared that the Republican Party was sufficient to the "practical needs" of the country. Because she knew Senator Harding personally, she could endorse his candidacy for president most adamantly.[66] She also spoke for the Women's National Republican Club on several occasions.[67] Price joined former Senator Henry M. Sage, State Chair George K. Morris, and Sarah Schuyler Butler, vice chair of the state committee, as a speaker at a dinner given at Union College in Schenectady.[68] A month later Price was in Potsdam at an annual organizational meeting of the St. Lawrence County committee. There she spoke on the need for "partisanship among women voters if our government is to be truly representative."[69] She shifted her energies from resisting suffrage to supporting party involvement and Republican candidates without much difficulty.

Price spoke for the conservative former anti-suffragist when she loyally commented that she voted for the man "who holds the same theories of government" as she did, "and so can help to work out the governmental policies" she believed in. Even if the candidate was not charming or interesting, his commitment to uphold the principles of the Republican Party made him the best choice for public office.[70] Her speech made it clear that she was a devoted party member, assuming that the Republican candidate, when it came to politics, believed in the principles she held dear. Women's voting rights also raised other issues of civic responsibility. For example, in a debate staged by the Women's National Republican Club, Price argued against jury duty for women on the basis that women would ignore actual facts because they were "so accustomed to depend upon intuition."[71] Even though they exercised their right to vote, the women who joined the Republican Party still hesitated when it came to voting women into elective office.[72] The offices occupied most often by women included those seen as an extension of women's traditional responsibilities such as those relating to education or charity. Regardless of their reluctance to elect women to office, these new party members wanted a political education, and they celebrated the women who held political appointments and committee responsibilities within the party. Lucy Price's comments, then, represent the attitudes of any number of former anti-suffragists, and even suffragists, who were uncomfortable with or ambivalent about full political participation for women.[73]

Former anti-suffragists agreeing with Price and Chittenden included Josephine Dodge. She supported the Junior Republican Committee of 100, a group for young people, although it was apparently not very active.[74] Alice George of Massachusetts continued speaking at political education meetings, drawing the marked respect of her audience.[75] Alice Foote MacDougall, also a "good Republican," was on the board of directors of the Republican Business Women, Inc. During an interview at the Women's National Republican clubhouse, she contended that she still did not believe that women should take time away from their duties to their families and homes to vote. Since women had the franchise, however, MacDougall insisted, they needed to do their duty to the state and educate themselves on political candidates and issues. She preferred that they would "stay away from the polls [rather] than vote sloppily or think hazily on political questions."[76] These former anti-suffrage leaders continued to embody the views of previous anti-suffrage adherents. In cities throughout the state, Republican women's clubs formed, drawing some of their membership from the ranks of former anti-suffragists.[77]

Members of the Women's National Republican Club asserted themselves in a variety of political ways beyond campaigning. For example, in 1926 the club's State Affairs Committee issued a report on the desirability of limiting the workweek for women to forty-eight hours. Based on 483 interviews with women employed in thirteen different communities, the committee found that the majority of female workers wanted such a law, even if it meant a wage decrease.[78] Club members held conferences, such as the one where the Republican Women's State Executive Committee discussed the proposal to raise the legal age of marriage from twelve to sixteen years for girls and from fourteen to eighteen years for boys. Members also discussed the proposed amendments to the workman's compensation law and the expenditures of the State Charities Aid organization.[79] Other topics included "A Balanced System of Taxation," delivered by the Secretary of the Treasury and "The Protective Tariff," presented by a Connecticut senator.[80] While programs covered a wide range of political topics, areas that could be considered women's special domain (such as those related to the care of minors and the poor) received the most attention.

Annual luncheons provided women with opportunities to hear eminent speakers on a diverse range of topics. Many of those speeches were later published and distributed. Pauline Sabin, presiding at the 1923 luncheon said: "The women here today have proved that they are not playing at politics but that they are in politics for the rest of their lives. We have our ambitions and we have our ideals. Some of us are more active politically than others. But there is one rallying point upon which we are always together—that is our desire that the Republican party should put forward men of the highest integrity, courage and brains for all political offices."[81] It was not unusual for members to have a letter or speech written by an important political figure read aloud at meetings, but those personages often visited the club as well. In the beginning of the decade, male political figures were the most usual speaking guests, but the club hosted a few women as well. Consistently, the goals of the Women's National Republican Club speakers at those events included arousing ever-greater interest in women's public service and voting.[82]

The club hosted events to honor high-level Republican Party members' wives at the club. In September 1926 members of the James W. Wadsworth

Jr. campaign committee honored Alice Hay Wadsworth at an afternoon event.[83] Presidents' wives were often invited to attend club events, as when Mrs. Hoover was honored at the eleventh annual luncheon at the Waldorf-Astoria in January 1932.[84] Members would come from all over the country to attend the elaborate annual luncheons in January (later held in April).[85] It was traditional for the women to hear a talk on some aspect of the life of Abraham Lincoln the day before the anniversary of his birth (scheduled so as not to interfere with the Republican men's celebration for Lincoln). President Warren G. Harding wrote a letter about Lincoln, which was read to the audience during one luncheon meeting.[86] By January 1930, Grace Abbott of the United States Children's Bureau shared the podium with the U.S. Secretary of Agriculture and the Assistant Secretary of War. Abbott spoke to the more than one thousand women and men in attendance. Despite the blame heaped on the Republican president, Herbert Hoover, for the economic depression, the speakers encouraged members of the audience to continue to support and vote for candidates of the Republican Party. Abbott invited women to "overcome their timidity and speak out boldly so as to achieve their rightful places in the government."[87]

Chittenden continued to assert herself politically, applying the various lessons learned when she led the New York State campaign to resist women's enfranchisement.[88] Members of the Women's National Republican Club elected her to the office of president in 1926 and again in 1927, following the tenure of Pauline Sabin, the club's second president. During her presidency, Chittenden, writing for the board of governors, announced the *Guidon*, a new publication to supplement the information contained in the *Woman Republican*. Rather than publishing news of the club, it was intended as a way of "giving Republican women of the country authentic political news from the different states." Its goal was "to strengthen the party organization and develop loyalty and cooperation among Republican women," and to be a "clearing house" of information valuable to the membership.[89] In 1926, President Coolidge appointed Chittenden to the National Advisory Committee of the Sesquicentennial Celebration and placed her in charge of the Philadelphia Exhibition to be held from June until December 1926. Coolidge had chosen two people from each state to work on the exhibition, designed to celebrate the progress made in the last fifty years in "education, art, natural science and industry, in trade and commerce and in the development of the air, the soil, the mind, the forests and the seas."[90] Chittenden was sufficiently well known to acquire such appointments.

Chittenden lectured to audiences all over the Northeast, frequently on topics related to the United States Constitution.[91] She, like many of her fellow Republicans, expressed concern about the increased number of amendments being proposed during the period, including the child labor amendment and the equal rights amendment. The controversy over the amendment process was the direct result of the changes in "fundamental rules for social behavior and gender relationships" developing from the amending process during the "tumult and dislocation" of the Great War period.[92] In one article, for example, Chittenden argued that the Eighteenth and Nineteenth Amendments indicated a "noticeable tendency toward permitting the Federal Government to encroach upon the powers originally reserved for the states," a common response to proposed changes to the Constitution. Many observers thought that the process itself should be changed. Chittenden, who supported the reelection bid of James W. Wadsworth Jr., confirmed that a committee of the Women's National Republican Club had recently appeared before the House Judiciary Committee to show the club's support of his Wadsworth-Garrett amendment, designed to "add barriers to constitutional change."[93] She was so well known for her knowledge of the Constitution that she often served as a judge in oral contests on the Constitution.[94]

Chittenden's forte, however, was educating women in the political process and training them to work for Republican candidates. She was noticeably present whenever Republican women gathered to learn about candidates or to study legislation.[95] Her involvement with political education is notable and seemed to increase exponentially as the initial excitement of women's enfranchisement waned. It was while she was president that the club established a School of Politics.[96] In 1927, Henrietta Livermore, at Chittenden's request, conducted a Speakers' School. The program consisted of all-day sessions that ran from Monday through Friday in which participants learned to prepare and deliver speeches for the coming state and national campaigns.[97] News of the success of the School of Politics spread, and the club received many requests to help inaugurate schools in areas outside New York City.[98]

Another School of Politics was held every Monday for the six months from November 1927 until April 1928. Twenty-three speakers addressed a total of twenty sessions in that time. Usually around one hundred women arrived in the morning to attend the forty-minute talks and the subsequent question-and-answer sessions. During six of the sessions, classes were also held in the afternoons to train future speakers. Chittenden, who had gathered resources for the Political Education Committee, offered books and pamphlets so the attendees could prepare their own ten-minute speeches.[99] By early 1928, the women had held three sessions of the school, distributed a number of informational leaflets, and sent speakers all over the country.[100] During the 1929–30 season, members concentrated on topics such as "American Government," "the meaning of America," and "the study of debate."[101] The program was repeated with varying topics several times throughout the decade.[102]

Some of the lessons of the educational programs were reprinted in the *Woman Republican* and included topics such as political parties and the "History and Basis of the Republican Party."[103] The Committee on Public Education, supervising not only the School of Politics, but also the Library Committee and the Speakers' Bureau, suggested books and magazine articles to the membership. The committee filed clippings related to matters of interest in Congress, collected speeches and addresses of the presidents and other public officials, collected all publications issued by the Editorial Research Bureau, and maintained a complete file of the *United States Daily*.[104] It also kept a list of active speakers, both paid and voluntary.[105] The efforts of the committee during the latter half of the decade of the twenties paid off because it inspired the holding of similar classes around the state.

Occasionally an observer would criticize Chittenden for having once opposed women's involvement in politics.[106] However, she clearly earned the respect of the members of the club, as well as the respect of male Republicans.[107] Her former stance did not stop her from continuing to support public affairs and other social reform issues.[108] Furthermore, she often represented the club in the receiving lines at numerous Republican functions, indicative of the respect her colleagues held for her.

While the Republican Party drew a notable percentage of former anti-suffragists, some women who were interested in politics remained committed to activism and joined nonpartisan associations. Those women, undoubtedly eager to fulfill their political responsibilities, were more likely to join the League of Women Voters.[109] Members of the National American Woman Suffrage Association held their Jubilee Convention in St. Louis on March 24, 1919, before the ratification of the Nineteenth Amendment. Attendees voted to "launch an auxiliary organization in the enfranchised states, and to dissolve NAWSA" as soon as all women in the United States were enfranchised.[110] Catt challenged the women to "finish the fight" after they won enfranchisement. Women still needed to remove legal discriminations, she said, and they should reach out to help women in other countries.[111] With these goals in mind, the women returned to encouraging the ratification of the Nineteenth Amendment.

Once satisfied that the franchise was won, members of the league met to determine the organization's further path the following year. Catt wanted the League of Women Voters to remain heavily involved in politics, to encourage women to join political parties and run as candidates for public office, and to assist in policy formation. Jane Addams, fearing the corruption of "women's principles," wanted the league to facilitate social reconstruction in its communities and to have the group maintain an "identity as a separate interest group."[112] The membership of the League of Women Voters ultimately accepted both roles: to educate their members and to promote social reform.[113] In effect, the organization "consciously acted to extend women's traditional, private, and domestic roles into the public realm." Women would not be prevented from joining political parties, and their political activity was in combination with whatever women as individuals chose to do. Nevertheless, as Kristi Andersen points out, the league exuded a "strong critique, if not an outright rejection, of the party system."[114]

Politicians and the press acknowledged this rejection, expressing anxiety in the first few years after women's enfranchisement that the league was positioned to become a powerful "women's bloc."[115] Some recognized the limits for women in the male-dominated parties but denied the need for separate political organizations for women. Chittenden, for one, challenged the oft-repeated contention that the party system was a "menace" to women and their reform efforts. She insisted that the party system was "a healthy sign in the progress of government, for it has developed along with the growth and ideals of representative government." At the same time, the idea of a nonpartisan stance could be considered a "menace." Almost as soon as members of the Women's National Republican Club learned of the League of Women Voters, they forwarded a resolution to major newspapers and former suffrage leaders "denouncing the new organization" as a "menace to our national life," because of its nonpartisan stance.[116]

This fear of nonpartisanship manifested itself at the 1921 convention of the New York League of Women Voters. The guest speaker, Governor Nathan Miller, shocked the audience by accusing the league of being a "menace" to the institutions of representative government and criticizing its reform programs. While he was speaking, one of three male stenographers who accompanied him periodically left the room to send the transcription of the governor's tirade to the press wires so that everyone could learn of the attack as it was happening. The governor left the meeting before the stunned women had a chance to respond. Catt issued a rebuttal, as did a group of Republican women. Following the outcry, Miller tried to recant, saying "he had been misunderstood," but he never reconciled with the league and he lost the election in 1922. The incident convinced members of the league to no longer support specific candidates but to "remain issue-oriented," as Catt put it, and to be "non-partisan and all-partisan."[117] The league then drew the ire of leading Republican women such as Ruth McCormick and the criticism of members of the Women's National Republican Club.[118] These women argued that voters must affiliate with a party to fulfill their responsibilities as voters.

Although the league focused on preparing women for political involvement, it was in competition for membership with women who belonged to political clubs.[119] Early in April 1919, in a resolution to newspapers all over the country, the Women's National Republican Club denounced the new league as "un-American and a menace to our national life." The club's main argument expressed the fear that the league "would use its power regardless of party principles of government and regardless of safe-guarding our Republic."[120] From its founding, league resolutions made it very clear that the powerful leadership of the former suffrage movement would continue to work against the existing political system.[121] Within a few years, however, representatives of the Women's National Republican Club were less outspoken in their criticism of the league, even accepting its existence.

Occasionally the *Woman Republican* would publish news stories on the League of Women Voters, as in 1924, when the league asked for the help of the Women's National Republican Club in registering new voters as part of the league's "Get-Out-the-Vote Movement."[122] Republican women had carried on a drive to enroll women voters as soon as women had the franchise. They believed they were already very effective, making the work of the league redundant. Even so, Sarah Schuyler Butler responded that a "duplication of effort" in the case of unregistered women voters was "valuable."[123] Another possible duplication of effort was reflected in the fact that both the Women's National Republican Club and the League of Women Voters were committed to the political education of women. Rather than educating women in the value of party membership, however, the league encouraged its members to view "all sides of public issues" to "develop habits of fairness and sagacity to do their own thinking and possess their own viewpoints."[124] The Women's National Republican Club membership, conversely, officially supported only Republican candidates and Republican Party platforms. As a result, relations between the two women's organizations were often strained.

The Republican women were more supportive a few years later when the league announced success in registering many new voters from the ranks of women in college, business, industry, and "at home." League members targeted younger voters, who may not have been as important to members of the Republican Club.[125] Annie Nathan Meyer chose membership in the league once she got over her initial objections to women voting. Although, as she points out in her autobiography, she still did not think that women should vote, she admitted in her later years that enfranchisement had not "brought about the dreadful results that the extremists prophesied." She was, she said, proud of having joined the League of Women Voters. Even for that choice, she and her companions—other former anti-suffragists—sometimes faced criticism. At one time, some women expressed surprise that anti-suffragists had joined the league. Meyer, referring to the creation of the New York League of Women Voters, "retorted that it was an Anti who had first encouraged its start and that more Antis than Suffragists had made it possible."[126] Whether they had started out being for or against woman suffrage, registering and educating voters was clearly a priority for all league members. However, the methods of the league did "little to encourage women to draw connections between their political interests and political actions."[127] Education and familiarity with politics took time, and women's organized political power became more dominant in the next decade.

Inevitably, the first decade of women's enfranchisement stimulated reflection and assessment. A 1927 *New York Times* article represents those evaluating New York State's first decade of women's political participation. Ethel Eyre Valentine [Mrs. H. Edward] Dreier, once a suffrage leader, bitterly pointed out that "to many it has been a disillusionment to find the political parties, through whom all real power comes, comparatively cold." Still, she asserted that the effect on the community had resulted in better conduct at political meetings and polling places, and women had "put their own lives and their homes upon a higher plane" since suffrage. Alice Hill Chittenden assessed the decade by contending that "a large number of intelligent women in every community" took a deep interest in "civic questions" and had "conscientiously assumed their full share of political responsibilities without the least thought of furthering any personal or selfish interest or ambition." These women, as far as Chittenden was concerned, "have proved to be a distinct asset as workers in their respective parties." She qualified her remarks by arguing that most women still were not any more interested in politics than she believed they had been before they had the right of suffrage and "voted or not as suits their convenience." She contended that more political education was needed to arouse all voters, male as well as female. She also reiterated the point that women did not vote as a bloc, that there was as much disagreement among women as among men "on all important political, social and economic problems." Women were particularly divided on issues such as prohibition, jury service for women, the child labor amendment, and the maternity act; the success or failure of any political measure could not be solely the result of women's votes. She concluded that cooperation between women and men as citizens should "bring about far-reaching and beneficial results in our whole political life."[128] Chittenden exuded more optimism than most former suffragists in her assessment of the decade, since her expectations had not been high in the first place.

The decade following women's enfranchisement allowed moderate former anti-suffragists to reconcile themselves to lives that included voting. It was a time of new opportunities for women interested in politics or civic responsibilities. Bertha Lane Scott, for example, became the first policewoman in Yonkers, immediately taking up the "police baton of civil authority." Former suffragists praised her for believing that the proper place for a woman was wherever she could best serve society.[129] Another former anti-suffragist, Prestonia Mann Martin, had an even more far-reaching influence. She shifted her focus from politics to economics. She achieved quite a bit of praise for her book *Prohibiting Poverty*, which she privately published in 1932. Eleanor Roosevelt readily acknowledged that some of the administrative projects of the New Deal stemmed from ideas in Martin's book.[130] For these and many other former anti-suffragist women, reconciliation to their enfranchisement meant exciting new opportunities.

The years between 1917, when women in New York acquired the vote, and 1932, when President Franklin Delano Roosevelt faced the staggering challenges of the Great Depression, represent a period of momentous political adjustment for all women. Party politics eliminated some divisions between antis and pro-suffrage women in the same way that civic work had brought women together before the war. Suffrage, as suffragists had constantly argued, was simply one divisive issue for women. Although it required some time to learn the habits of full enfranchisement, women functioned effectively even during a state of experimentation and exploration. Barred from acquiring real political power, those women who joined political parties found themselves on the periphery of party organizations or relegated to so-called auxiliaries to carry out women's traditional tasks. "Significant resistance" met every attempt by women to enter electoral and partisan politics on a par with male party members.[131] Their volunteer organizations and nonpartisan groups, while effecting some changes, still faced competition with political parties and "echoed the convention of a separate sphere for women."[132]

Some historians of this period cite the "persistence of anti-suffrage attitudes" as one reason inhibiting women's voting.[133] Certainly resistance to woman suffrage did not end with the Nineteenth Amendment. After their enfranchisement by referendum in 1917, however, anti-suffrage attitudes were not expressed by the former leaders of the New York State anti-suffrage movement. Women like Alice Hill Chittenden, Josephine Dodge, Lucy C. Price, Alice Foote MacDougall, Annie Nathan Meyer, and others sought diverse ways to educate women in their new political roles, to encourage them to be involved in politics as much as their household responsibilities would allow, and, especially, to vote. The moderate, more typical leaders of the organized anti-suffrage movement facilitated the politicization of women as much as possible and, in the process, sought to eliminate any residual anti-suffrage attitudes. Although they had all spent years resisting women's enfranchisement, these former anti-suffragists, as soon as they had the vote, dutifully met their political responsibilities.

Conclusion

During the presidential campaign of 1928 the women of the Women's National Republican Club held a mock convention to poke fun at the men who refused to let women into the inner sanctums of real power. It was not unusual for male Republican Party members to hold a "Gridiron Day" or "Amen Corner meetings" to poke fun at themselves. The women's mock convention was an elaborate all-day affair held under the auspices of the Women's National Republican Club National Affairs Committee on the roof garden of the Waldorf-Astoria in New York City.[1] Ostensibly called for educational purposes, participants accurately represented each procedure of the convention. Sixty women made up the cast of the show, helping to prove the point that "the true wit and humor shown in the many speeches proves that the capability for keen insight combined with as keen a wit does not rest alone in the hands of men."[2] Their goal was to choose a well known Republican for president and "a total stranger, as usual" for vice president. While the voters would have to be "legal and qualified" to participate, the delegates did not have to be qualified, although they had to be legal. No delegate would be "discriminated against for age, color or even for membership in the League of Women Voters."[3]

The delegates dressed in a wide range of costumes, including that of a cowboy, a bellhop, a dancer in a grass skirt who represented the delegate from Hawaii, a policeman, and several businessmen.[4] Several delegates had theme songs such as "Maryland, My Maryland," "The Good Old Summertime," or

Image from the "Proceedings of the Mock Convention Held at the Waldorf-Astoria Hotel, New York City, April 24, 1928." This photograph shows members of the Women's National Republican Club dressed in the costumes they wore to poke fun at the male-dominated political process. Photo courtesy of the Women's National Republican Club, New York, N.Y., and the New York Public Library, New York, N.Y.

"Oh, You Beautiful Doll." Alice Hill Chittenden, who played the delegate from Michigan, had as her theme song "Over There," a tribute to her work during the Great War. The platform of the Republican Party included advocating for immigration (citing the need for cooks), foreign relations (the same as in 1924), farm relief (advocating that farmers leave the farms), law enforcement (the necessity of adhering to Emily Post's Rules of Etiquette), Commerce and Navigation (increasing appropriations for Bathing Beauty Contests), and Men in Politics (since the men had yet to get government "right," they proposed to complete the task and "finish off the Government they have set up").[5] Once they had the platform in place, the delegates nominated their candidates for president and vice president.

The delegate from Indiana, played by Henrietta Wells Livermore, announced the nomination of Dr. Mary Walker, "the only self-made man in the United States," for president. Nominated because she was "indomitable, patriotic, unsexed, and unbeatable," she campaigned under the slogan, "Panting for Pants." Elizabeth Arden, the "apostle of beauty" who would "smooth every ugly line" and provide "ice packs for the Cabinet members so that they may be able to relax and their brains will not become overheated when they are discussing the queer things they call *issues*," opposed Dr. Walker.[6] A third candidate, Lydia E. Pinkham, the highly successful creator and marketer of a women's tonic to relieve menstrual and menopausal symptoms, campaigned under the slogan, "A Baby in Every Bottle," and was the "sworn enemy of race suicide."[7] When no candidate received a majority in the first vote, the secretary called for a second one. Dr. Mary Walker and Lydia Pinkham lost to Elizabeth Arden, who had bribed the delegates with "pink-ribboned jars of cold cream."[8]

The delegate from Ohio nominated Dorothy Dix for vice president because the "right to pop the question is the only right that men have now that women do not possess"; she promised to eradicate flapperism.[9] The delegate from Illinois, who proudly stood for men no matter how unpopular the stance, nominated Gene Tunney (the 1926–1928 world heavyweight boxing champion) for vice president since the convention had ignored one-half of the population—those "who bear the trunks of this Nation."[10] Again it took two votes, but the second time Lydia Pinkham won the ballot, although she had not been nominated for the office.[11] Delighted by the witticisms of the convention, the audience expressed the hope that it would become an annual event.

The profound symbolism of the mock convention illustrates the political dynamics and attitudes of women in the decade after their enfranchisement. It highlights the point that at its deepest level, the long struggle over woman suffrage had been an attempt to understand, articulate, and revise the relationship of women to the state as well as to men.[12] Enfranchisement always meant more to women than simply acquiring the vote, just as preventing enfranchisement meant more to anti-suffragists than simply preventing women from voting. The conflict challenged the meanings of gender and of womanhood in the United States. Conservative women stayed out of the fray until they perceived the threat to true womanhood was great enough to require their intervention. Initially, they believed their power lay in the preservation of the separate spheres ideology. As anti-suffragists faced their suffrage opponents, they were frequently wrenched from the security of their womanly sphere and necessarily forced to adapt to expanded roles for women. By acquiescing to the responsibilities of the vote, engaging in an act that had formerly been accessible to men only, women could no longer retreat to their separate sphere.

Still, when these conservative women played significant roles in their organizations and party politics, their unflinching deference to patriarchal thinking and male proprietary relationships remained paramount to their perspective and goals. Certainly anti-suffragists benefited by a continuing acceptance of patriarchal domination on a personal level, and they continued to believe that women were best suited to play supportive—not leading—roles in politics and government. Anti-suffragists had long advocated increased opportunities for the education of women, yet as women became more educated, they were less inclined to accept the restrictions inherent to the anti-suffrage vision of a proper life for women. But the antis' vision of a "proper life" became less tenable in the years just prior to the First World War.

A decade after they won enfranchisement in New York, political women realized that they still did not have the power to pose the questions that, ostensibly, politics should answer. Nor did they have access to the real power in the political parties, although most believed that the only way women would gain political power was through party affiliation.[13] Underlying the hilarity of the mock convention lay a serious goal for these women: "We purpose to take an ever-increasing part in the great questions of National politics, as well as to demand our share of the acclaim that comes to the party that made and keeps the Nation united, prosperous and free, and at peace at home and abroad."[14] Their efforts continue to the present day.

It is between the 1890s and the 1920s that conservative women's politics took root. It was a period marked by the angst of uncertainty and instability, with significant reforms promoted or instituted in response to the tremendous changes of the time. Until the 1890s, few questioned the idea that a woman's place was in the home. The reinvigorated suffrage movement challenged that contention, forcing conservative women to develop a political expertise to protect the patriarchal social structure. While the ideas of the suffrage movement remained somewhat radical, blending those arguments with conservative components was the key to state and federal level changes in perspective. When the suffragists used conservative arguments, those drawing on the idea of the special nature of women as wives and mothers, woman suffrage became acceptable to a great many more people.[15]

From the 1890s to the Great War, anti-suffragists matched their wits and creative energy to challenge the suffragists to ever-increasing levels of political ingenuity. The peak of anti-suffrage activist creativity occurred during the campaign for the 1915 referendum. Without men in charge of their organizations, anti-suffrage women were politically creative in presenting their arguments to the public. To protect what they perceived to be their rights, many anti-suffrage women dared to lecture in front of mixed audiences, debated suffragists, attended conferences and meetings, presented papers, spoke at conventions and at fairs and in a multitude of other public places, and even published books and articles. New York State anti-suffragists supported organizing efforts in cities and towns throughout the state and across the country, providing speakers for all kinds of social and political events. The women who organized anti-suffrage associations voted for officers and on decisions about applications for membership, and in order to determine strategic plans, they followed very closely the political models established by the suffrage organizations for decision making. The momentum the anti-suffragists gained from their efforts, together with an electorate still reluctant to enfranchise women, kept women from acquiring the vote in New York State in 1915.

But, even by 1915, circumstances had changed for anti-suffragists in ways that so distracted them that their organizations ceased to be the threat to women's enfranchisement that they had once been. The coming of war to Europe in 1914 diverted the anti-suffragists from their task to prevent woman suffrage, just as suffragists had been sidetracked by their efforts during the Civil War. The advent of the war, inherently masculine, shook the anti-suffrage movement to its core, and they increasingly allowed men to influence their public activities. The period of the war coincided with the acquiescence of female anti-suffragists to male dominance, making it a markedly different kind of movement than it had previously been. Additionally, many anti-suffragists found the growing anti-socialism and patriotic rhetoric compatible with their ideas of preserving democracy. While it is possible to attribute the hyper-patriotism and ever more hostile demeanor of the antis to a foreknowledge of the inevitability of women's enfranchisement, it makes sense that more moderate anti-suffrage leaders felt out of their element when dealing with the social and political upheaval of war. With the antis distracted, although opposition remained strong in most rural areas, women in New York State won the right to vote in the 1917 referendum. Between 1917 and 1920, most anti-suffragists were well on their way to understanding that an expanded role for women could ultimately benefit the state and nation.

Whether politicians acknowledged them or not, the women of New York State influenced the discussions surrounding voting rights that took place between the 1890s and the 1930s. The last state to grant woman the right to vote by referendum, New York was the first eastern state to grant women the right to vote. Carrie Chapman Catt enthusiastically judged "the battle of New York" to be "the Gettysburg of the woman suffrage movement."[16] To suffragists the state represented their greatest challenge during the campaign and their most meaningful achievement until federal enfranchisement.[17] Although it took another three years of hard work at the federal level, once New York granted women the right to vote, acquiescence by a broader public was inevitable. Decisions made in New York, with its large population and powerful politicos, influenced woman suffrage elsewhere. The suffrage movement also culminated in a political awakening for anti-suffragists, part of a process that encouraged women to transcend the residual boundaries of the nineteenth-century ideology of separate spheres.

Suffragists would have achieved the vote sooner without the keen opposition of the New York anti-suffragists. The length of the struggle and the duration of the opposition related to factors such as fear of the unknown, resistance to changing gender roles, and a general apathy to voting, which had been increasing since the turn of the century.[18] Yet, the organized anti-suffrage movement in New York stimulated increasingly creative, thoughtful, and provocative arguments and activities on the part of women involved in the suffrage movement.[19] During those long years of arguing over women's enfranchisement, women on both sides of the movement found the battle over suffrage thrilling.

Great excitement and activity hides among the words and images relating to the quest for the vote in the publications, letters, press releases, cartoons, and newspaper reports yellowing with age in the archives and private collections. These politically active women, whether for or against woman suffrage, rallied to the side of a cause they believed in, expanded their friendships, articulated their arguments, met new intellectual and political challenges, and focused on women's political well-being. They looked at the work the other side was doing and responded in ever more imaginative ways. Neither the anti-suffrage movement nor the suffrage movement was static. Each movement ebbed and flowed with the progress of the opposing movement. Initially reluctant to publicly articulate their views, but deliberately resisting male dominance, anti-suffragists gradually became more politically proficient, appropriating suffragist methods and publicity techniques in their efforts to prevent enfranchisement. Thoughtful, intelligent, educated women lined up on either side of the struggle, and even women once opposed to woman suffrage relished the politicization process. The anti-suffrage movement served as a training ground for many of its adherents. Their experiences provided the impetus for their activism after enfranchisement. Unashamed of their past involvement in anti-suffrage, these women were highly likely to stay involved in politics and to join political parties. Most former anti-suffragists seemed to recognize the value of their enfranchisement and were part of the same processes that marked the experience of most politically savvy women after 1920.

With the vote, a powerful "symbol of women's political struggle" and a rallying point for many women activists ceased to exist.[20] Neither side had been able to predict accurately what would happen when women were enfranchised. Charlotte Perkins Gilman, who supported suffrage, denied the importance of gaining woman suffrage to "winning true equality for women." She recognized the need for "drastic changes in the family, sex mores, and social organization" before women and men would be equal.[21] And, as Eleanor Roosevelt pointed out in 1928, "there is widespread male hostility—age-old, perhaps—against sharing with [women] any actual control."[22] The long, drawn-out battle for the ballot was only one step in the process of equality for women and men, and the process is still incomplete.

In spite of the acquiescence of anti-suffragists to their new political roles, and that their prediction that the family or the state would be destroyed never came true, in some ways the anti-suffragist arguments were right. The vote was not to be as powerful a tool for reform for women as the suffragists argued it would be. Women never again worked as creatively in their reform efforts with the vote as they had without it, and the connection to party politics also seemed to weaken the power of their reform activism. Women's influence through their philanthropic organizations was significant, although social reforms waned during the 1920s.[23] The division along gender lines that many critics expected when women gained the right to vote never materialized.[24] Women never did vote as a bloc, for as Nancy Cott argues, most politically active women at the time were "in favor of women's diverse individuality."[25] Women did not become a voting force that politicians needed to be particularly concerned about appeasing.[26] Politicians stopped making their "concessions" as soon as they realized that suffragists had promised more from women voting than could be realized.[27] Several historians point to factors such as race, class, ethnicity, and religion as influencing voting decisions to a far greater degree than the gender of the voter.[28]

Although virtually all politically active women during the 1920s agreed that women should have equal political, legal, and economic rights, conflicts developed over which path to follow to get those rights.[29] The essential argument was, from the very beginning, between those who believed women and men should be equal in every way and those who believed the biological differences between women and men require a different set of laws for each gender.[30] Among thoughtful women, alignments changed again when many clubwomen and former suffragists opposed the proposed equal rights amendment. Alice Paul designed the amendment in 1922 as another step in the attainment of equality between women and men. Simple in its wording, it clearly states her goal: "Men and women shall have equal rights throughout the United States and every place subject to its jurisdiction."[31] Her organization, the National Woman's Party, focused on that one issue and used a variety of political techniques to urge support for the amendment. Eventually, however, the organization relied on their lobbying efforts more than on mobilizing women.

Many women's organizations, including the League of Women Voters, almost unanimously opposed the National Woman's Party. These groups differed in their view of the necessity of protective legislation for women.[32] After persistent lobbying, the Woman's Party supporters finally won congressional hearings on the proposed amendment in 1923, but the discussions lay dormant until after the Second World War.[33] After decades of stagnation in Congress, on March 22, 1972, both houses of Congress finally passed the Equal Rights Amendment. As the amendment went to the states for ratification, new anti-feminist groups like Phyllis Schlafly's STOP ERA and Eagle Forum formed to oppose it.[34] Those who fought the ERA also believed they protected the traditional roles of women and men.[35] This time the conservative women's forces won their campaign. The lengthy battle over the equal rights amendment pitted women against women in ways similar to those of the suffrage battle.

Virtually everywhere in the world women have had to struggle against deep-rooted adversity to attain citizenship rights on a parity with those of men.[36] Certainly, there have always been men who have opposed granting women political or equal rights, yet some women have opposed their own equality virtually all over the world, even to the present day. The struggle between anti-suffragists and suffragists was never a simple battle between feminists and anti-feminists, or between conservatives and liberal or radical women. Anti-suffrage women in New York State were not mentally deranged or even women who simply followed the lead of their husbands or male relatives. Virtually all of them sincerely believed that suffrage was wrong for women, or that women generally needed more time to develop political capability.

Initially, anti-suffragists worked to maintain their class status and position on the pedestal of "true womanhood." But as time passed and circumstances required it, anti-suffragists changed their tactics, illustrating their political awakening and new levels of commitment to women's role in the polity.

For a long time, anti-suffragists had been adamant that the vote would accomplish nothing that women philanthropists and reformers were not already able to achieve without the vote. But clearly some prominent women anti-suffragists were caught up in a fight that became less important over time. Like Annie Nathan Meyer, thoughtful antis denigrated the "wild" claims of suffragists who speculated that women's enfranchisement would greatly enhance women's reforming power.[37] While their contentions were themselves idealistic, even outdated, anti-suffragists won enough of the battles to help prevent the granting of voting rights to women for seventy-two years. Anti-suffragists were vitally important to the suffrage movement for they provided an opportunity for suffragists to clarify their arguments and hone their political techniques, even influencing shifts in the ways suffragists presented their arguments. It may have been partly in response to anti-suffragist arguments that suffragists abandoned their egalitarian arguments for arguments that promoted the value of gender difference. Their promotion of gender difference also became part of the reason that women did not significantly change politics in the 1920s as had been expected. Even though women did not make major political gains in those years, significant numbers of anti-suffragists were themselves converted to supporting a political role for women. Understanding the co-constitutive nature of the two movements, and the significant role anti-suffragists played in the process of women's enfranchisement and politicization, is critical to understanding the entire suffrage movement as well as the continuing movement for equality.

Notes

Abbreviations

ANM Papers   Annie Nathan Meyer Collection, Jacob Rader Marcus Center
               of the American Jewish Archives, Hebrew Union College,
               Cincinnati, Ohio
CAKL   Jon A. Lindseth Woman Suffrage Collection. Manuscripts
               and Rare Books, Carl A. Kroch Library, Cornell University,
               Ithaca, N.Y.
CCC Papers   Carrie Chapman Catt Papers, Manuscripts and Archives
               Division, New York Public Library, New York, N.Y.
EPW Papers   Everett P. Wheeler Papers, Manuscripts and Archives Division,
               New York Public Library, New York, N.Y.
Gilder Mss.   Gilder Mss., Lilly Library Manuscript Collections, Indiana
               University, Bloomington, Ind.
HCH   Anti-Suffrage Collection, Historic Cherry Hill, Albany, N.Y.
HKRJ Papers   Helen Kendrick and Rossiter Johnson Papers, Manuscripts and
               Archives Division, New York Public Library, New York, N.Y.
LSHS   Lincklaen/Ledyard Collection, Lorenzo State Historic Site,
               Cazenovia, N.Y.
LHH   Lou Henry Hoover Papers, Herbert Hoover Presidential Library
               and Museum, West Branch, IA.
NYSA   New York State Association Opposed to Woman Suffrage
               Collection, New York State Archives, Albany, N.Y.
SSC   Sophia Smith Collection, Smith College, Northampton, Mass.
URSC   Department of Rare Books and Special Collections, Rush Rhees,
               University of Rochester Special Collections, Rochester, N.Y.

VC   Archives and Special Collections Library, Vassar College,
                      Poughkeepsie, N.Y.

Introduction

1. Women could vote from 1790 to 1807 in New Jersey. Anne Firor Scott and Andrew MacKay Scott, *One Half the People: The Fight for Woman Suffrage* (Urbana: University of Illinois Press, 1982), 5–6.

2. Paula Baker, *The Moral Frameworks of Public Life: Gender, Politics, and the State in Rural New York, 1870–1930* (New York: Oxford University Press, 1991), 28–29.

3. Ellen Carol DuBois, *Feminism and Suffrage: The Emergence of an Independent Women's Movement in America, 1848–1869* (Ithaca, N.Y.: Cornell University Press, 1978), 15.

4. Ronald Schaffer, "The New York City Woman Suffrage Party, 1909–1919," *New York History* (July 1962): 272–73.

5. Judith Wellman, "Women's Rights, Republicanism, and Revolutionary Rhetoric in Antebellum New York State," *New York History* 69 (July 1988): 353.

6. Aileen S. Kraditor, ed., *Up from the Pedestal: Selected Writings in the History of American Feminism* (Chicago: Quadrangle, 1968), 14.

7. Stephanie Coontz, *The Social Origins of Private Life: A History of American Families* (London: Verso, 1988), 210.

8. Kraditor, ed., *Up from the Pedestal*, 13.

9. Carl N. Degler, *At Odds: Women and Family in America from the Revolution to the Present* (New York: Oxford University Press, 1980), 27; Barbara Leslie Epstein, *The Politics of Domesticity: Women, Evangelism, and Temperance in Nineteenth Century America* (Middletown, Conn.: Wesleyan University Press, 1981), 84, 149.

10. Kathryn Kish Sklar, *Catharine Beecher: A Study in American Domesticity* (New Haven, Conn.: Yale University Press, 1973), xiv.

11. Coontz, *Social Origins of Private Life*, 252.

12. Glenda Elizabeth Gilmore, ed., *Who Were the Progressives?* (Boston: Bedford/ St. Martin's, 2002), 13.

13. Coontz, *Social Origins of Private Life*, 216.

14. Degler, *At Odds*, 283.

15. Coontz, *Social Origins of Private Life*, 218.

16. Barbara Welter, "Cult of True Womanhood, 1820–1860," *American Quarterly* 23 (Summer 1966): 152.

17. Degler, *At Odds*, 349.

18. Milton M. Klein, ed., *The Empire State: A History of New York* (Ithaca, N.Y.: Cornell University Press, 2001), 438–39.

19. Aileen S. Kraditor, *The Ideas of the Woman Suffrage Movement/1890–1920* (New York: Norton, 1981), vi.

20. Cora Maynard, "The Woman's Part," *Arena* 7 (March 1893): 476.

21. Lewis L. Gould, ed., *The Progressive Era* (Syracuse, N.Y.: Syracuse University Press, 1974), 9; Robert H. Weibe, *The Search for Order, 1877–1920* (New York: Wang and Hill, 1967), 141.

22. Gilmore, ed., *Who Were the Progressives?*, 3.

23. "The Anti-Suffragist," *New York Times,* February 6, 1909; Margaret Doane Gardiner, "The Matriarchs," *New York Times,* March 12, 1909; "The Voice of the Majority," *Anti-Suffragist* (September 1909): 3 (emphasis in the original); "One Reason Why We Oppose," *Anti-Suffragist* 3, no. 1 (September 1910): 8.

24. Coontz, *Social Origins of Private Life*, 336; Mary Ryan, *Womanhood in America: From Colonial Times to the Present*, 3rd ed. (New York: Franklin Watts, 1975), 226–27.

25. Ryan, *Womanhood in America*, 197.

26. Morton Keller, *Affairs of State: Public Life in Late Nineteenth Century America* (Cambridge: Belknap, 1977), 285; Weibe, *Search for Order*, 164–70.

27. Kraditor, ed., *Up from the Pedestal*, 12–13.

28. Paula Baker, "The Domestication of Politics: Women and American Political Society, 1780–1920," in *Women, the State, and Welfare*, ed. Linda Gordon (Madison: University of Wisconsin Press, 1990), 74.

29. Estelle B. Freedman, "Separatism Revisited: Women's Institutions, Social Reform, and the Career of Miriam Van Waters," in *U.S. History as Women's History: New Feminist Essays*, ed. Linda K. Kerber, Alice Kessler-Harris, and Kathryn Kish Sklar (Chapel Hill: University of North Carolina Press, 1995), 171.

30. Elisabeth Israels Perry, "Men Are from the Gilded Age, Women Are from the Progressive Era," *Journal of the Gilded Age and Progressive Era* 1, no. 1 (January 2002): 37.

31. On radicalism and woman suffrage, see Degler, *At Odds*, 328, 341; Ellen Carol DuBois, *Woman Suffrage & Women's Rights* (New York: New York University Press, 1998), 68–69.

32. Susan E. Marshall, *Splintered Sisterhood: Gender and Class in the Campaign against Woman Suffrage* (Madison: University of Wisconsin Press, 1997), 12.

33. See Kim E. Nielsen, *Un-American Womanhood: Antiradicalism, Antifeminism, and the First Red Scare* (Columbus: Ohio State University Press, 2001); Catherine E. Rymph, *Republican Women: Feminism and Conservatism from Suffrage through the Rise of the New Right* (Chapel Hill: University of North Carolina Press, 2006); Mary C. Brennan, *Wives, Mothers, and the Red Menace: Conservative Women and the Crusade against Communism* (Boulder: University Press of Colorado, 2008); Suzanne H. Schrems, *Who's Rocking the Cradle?: Women Pioneers of Oklahoma Politics from Socialism to the KKK, 1900–1930* (Norman: Horse Creek, 2004); and Kathleen M. Blee, *Women of the Klan: Racism and Gender in the 1920s* (Berkeley: University of California Press, 1991).

34. Carrie Chapman Catt and Nettie Rogers Shuler, *Woman Suffrage and Politics: The Inner Story of the Suffrage Movement* (New York: Scribner's, 1926), 271–72.

35. Robert F. Wesser, *Charles Evans Hughes: Politics and Reform in New York, 1905–1910* (Ithaca, N.Y.: Cornell University Press, 1967), 4–5.

36. Edgar L. Murlin, *The New York Red Book* (Albany, N.Y.: Lyons, 1907), 11, 24–25.

37. Klein, ed., *The Empire State*, 352.

38. Jacqueline Van Voris, *Carrie Chapman Catt: A Public Life* (New York: Feminist Press at the City University of New York, 1987), 117.

39. National American Woman Suffrage Association, *Victory: How Women Won It, a Centennial Symposium, 1840–1940* (New York: Wilson, 1940), 107.

40. Gerda Lerner, *The Woman in American History* (New York: Addison-Wesley, 1971), 139–40.

41. Thomas J. Jablonsky, *The Home, Heaven, and Mother Party: Female Anti-Suffragists in the United States, 1868–1920* (Brooklyn: Carlson, 1994), 72. Carrie Chapman Catt also absolved the anti-suffrage women of involvement with liquor interests and brewers in her 1926 story of woman suffrage, although she pointed out that the groups supported each other. Catt and Shuler, *Woman Suffrage and Politics*, 273.

42. Michael McGerr, "Political Style and Women's Power, 1830–1930," *Journal of American History* 77 (December 1990): 869, 870.

43. Marshall, *Splintered Sisterhood*, 194–95.

44. Elna C. Green, *Southern Strategies: Southern Women and the Woman Suffrage Question* (Chapel Hill: University of North Carolina Press, 1997), 106.

45. There have been several important studies of the anti-suffrage movement. Anne M. Benjamin wrote *A History of the Anti-Suffrage Movement in the United States From 1895 to 1920* (Lewiston, N.Y.: Mellen, 1992), a broad study of the national anti-suffrage movement that includes three chapters on New York. Jane Jerome Camhi wrote *Women against Women: American Anti-Suffragism, 1880–1920* (Brooklyn: Carlson, 1994), and Thomas J. Jablonsky wrote *The Home, Heaven, and Mother Party: Female Anti-Suffragists in the United States, 1868–1920* (Brooklyn: Carlson, 1994). Susan E. Marshall's *Splintered Sisterhood: Gender and Class in the Campaign against Woman Suffrage* (Madison: University of Wisconsin Press, 1997) is a sociological study of rhetoric and countermovement politics focusing primarily on the anti-suffrage movement in Massachusetts. Elna C. Green in *Southern Strategies: Southern Women and the Woman Suffrage Question* (Chapel Hill: University of North Carolina Press, 1997) focuses on the southern anti-suffrage movement, particularly in Virginia.

46. Elizabeth V. Burt, "The Ideology, Rhetoric, and Organizational Structure of a Countermovement Publication: The Remonstrance, 1890–1920," *Journalism & Mass Communication Quarterly* 75, no. 1 (1998): 75.

47. DuBois, *Woman Suffrage & Women's Rights*, 182.

Chapter 1. Anti-Suffragists at the 1894 New York State Constitutional Convention

1. Ida Husted Harper, *The Life and Work of Susan B. Anthony*, 2 vols., vol. II (Indianapolis: Hollenbeck, 1898), 760–61, 764, 765.

2. Ibid., 765.

3. Women's Anti-Suffrage Association of the Third Judicial District, *Pamphlets*

Printed and Distributed by the Women's Anti-Suffrage Association of the Third Judicial District of the State of New York, Headquarters at Albany, N.Y. (Littleton, Colo.: Rothman, 1990), introduction.

4. Harper, *Life and Work of Susan B. Anthony*, 766.

5. John Baker, *The Constitution of 1894* (New York: New York History, 1897–99), 171.

6. Harper, *Life and Work of Susan B. Anthony*, 758–59.

7. Kraditor, *Ideas of the Woman Suffrage Movement*, 44.

8. Eleanor Flexner and Ellen Fitzpatrick, *Century of Struggle: The Woman's Rights Movement in the United States* (Cambridge: Belknap, 1996 [1959]), 209, 211, 213.

9. Kraditor, *Ideas of the Woman Suffrage Movement*, 55–56.

10. Katherine Anthony, *Susan B. Anthony: Her Personal History and Her Era* (Garden City, N.J.: Doubleday, 1954), 405.

11. Quoted in Catt and Shuler, *Woman Suffrage and Politics*, 27.

12. Susan Fenimore Cooper, "Female Suffrage: A Letter to the Christian Women of America, Part 1," *Harper's New Monthly Magazine* 41, no. 243 (August 1870): 438, 439.

13. Ibid., 439, 440, 443.

14. Susan Fenimore Cooper, letter dated April 7, 1874. No salutation. Chicago Historical Society. Cooper, "Female Suffrage," 594–98.

15. Catharine Beecher, *Woman's Profession as Mother and Educator with Views in Opposition to Woman Suffrage* (Philadelphia: Maclean, 1872), dedication, introduction, 29, 52.

16. "Annual Report," American Woman's Educational Association, Issue 5 (New York: Bedford, 1857), 3. Emphasis in the original.

17. Catharine Beecher, "Something for Women Better Than the Ballot," *Appleton's Journal: A Magazine of General Literature* (1869): 84.

18. Sklar, *Catharine Beecher*, 134.

19. Wendy Hamand Venet, *A Strong-Minded Woman: The Life of Mary A. Livermore* (Amherst: University of Massachusetts Press, 2005), 7, 61, 88, 137–38.

20. "An Address on Female Suffrage, Delivered in the Music Hall of Boston, in December, 1870," reprinted in Beecher, *Woman's Profession*, 17.

21. Ibid., 18–19.

22. Ibid., 5–28, 55, 60, 181.

23. DuBois, *Feminism and Suffrage*, 172.

24. Helen Kendrick Johnson, *Woman and the Republic: A Survey of the Woman Suffrage Movement in the United States and a Discussion of the Claims and Arguments of Its Foremost Advocates; A New and Enlarged Edition with an Index* (New York: Guidon Club Opposed to Woman Suffrage, 1913), postscript; Elizabeth Cady Stanton, Matilda Joslyn Gage, and Susan B. Anthony, *History of Woman Suffrage*, 6 vols., vol. II (New York: Fowler & Wells, 1882), 494–95.

25. *Godey's Lady's Book and Magazine* 82 (January–June 1871): 476.

26. "Woman Suffrage," *New York Times*, February 2, 1871.

27. "Notes and Notices," (May 1871), in *Godey's Lady's Book and Magazine* 82 (January–June 1871), 476.

28. Ibid., 477; Johnson, *Woman and the Republic*, postscript; Frances Willard and Mary A. Livermore, eds., *A Woman of the Century: Fourteen Hundred-Seventy Biographical Sketches Accompanied by Portraits of Leading American Women in All Walks of Life* (Buffalo: Moulton, 1893), 225.

29. Quoted in Sally Roesch Wagner, *A Time of Protest: Suffragists Challenge the Republic: 1870–1887* (Aberdeen: Sky Carrier, 1992), 86.

30. United States Senate, "Arguments before the Committee on Privileges and Elections of the United States Senate on Behalf of a Sixteenth Amendment to the Constitution of the United States, Prohibiting the Several States from Disfranchising United States Citizens on Account of Sex" (Washington, D.C.: United States Senate, 1878), 43–45.

31. Degler, *At Odds*, 298, 302.

32. Kate Gannett Wells, "Women in Organizations," *Atlantic Monthly* 46, no. 275 (September 1880): 360.

33. Degler, *At Odds*, 306.

34. Baker, "Domestication of Politics," 65.

35. Lyman Abbott, "An Anti-Suffrage Movement," *Outlook* 49 (April 28, 1894): 738.

36. Lyman Abbott, "A Woman's Protest against Woman's Suffrage," *Outlook* 49 (April 28, 1894): 760.

37. "Women Who Would Not Vote," *New York Times,* April 22, 1894; "They Would Scorn to Vote," *New York Times,* April 24, 1894.

38. Letter, May 2, 1897, Helena de Kay Gilder to Mary Hallock Foote, box 4, folder Helena de Kay Gilder to Mary Hallock Foote, 1897, Gilder Mss.

39. "Brooklyn Society Split," *New York Sun,* April 22, 1894.

40. *Brooklyn Museum Quarterly*, vols. 2, 7. Collection of the Brooklyn Museum, Brooklyn, N.Y.

41. "Women Opposed to Woman Suffrage are Leaders in Manifold Activities," *New York Herald Magazine Section,* June 14, 1914; "Brooklyn Society," *Brooklyn Daily Eagle,* January 13, 1901.

42. "For the Child Widows," *Brooklyn Daily Eagle,* February 3, 1895; "Hampton Institute," *Brooklyn Daily Eagle,* February 10, 1900.

43. "Was in Germany with Dr. Abbott When Attacked with Pneumonia," unattributed newspaper clipping, July 21, 1907; "A Helpmeet Gone on Before," unattributed newspaper clipping, July 25, 1907. Special Collections and Archives, Bowdoin College, Brunswick, Maine.

44. See, for example, Mrs. Lyman Abbott, ed., "Just Among Ourselves," *Ladies' Home Journal* 9, no. 7 (June 1892): 26. See also "Mrs. President and Friends of the Club," Special Collections and Archives, Bowdoin College, Brunswick, Maine.

45. Helen Damon-Moore, *Magazines for the Millions: Gender and Commerce in the Ladies Home Journal and the Saturday Evening Post, 1880–1910* (Albany: State University of New York Press, 1994), 59.

46. "Abby Frances Hamlin, Wife of Dr. Lyman Abbott," *Plymouth Chimes*, October, 1907; "Religious Organizations," *Brooklyn Daily Eagle Almanac,* vol. 4 (New York: Brooklyn Daily Eagle, 1889), 103; "Twenty-Fifth Annual Report," *New York City Indian Association* (New York: New York City Indian Association, 1907): 7.

47. Ira V. Brown, *Lyman Abbott: Christian Evolutionist* (Cambridge: Harvard University Press, 1953), 208.

48. "Sighs from Weary Women," *New York Times,* May 9, 1894.

49. The Gilder Manuscript Collection holds extensive correspondence with elites such as Grover Cleveland, Theodore Roosevelt, Andrew Carnegie (who, after Richard Watson Gilder's death, sent Helena $10,000 annually to help with her living expenses), and many other prominent people of the time. Letter, April 27, 1910, Andrew Carnegie to Helena de Kay Gilder, box 4, folder Corres., Carnegie, Andrew and Louise, 1908–1916, Gilder Mss.

50. Thayer C. Tolles, "Helena de Kay Gilder: Her Role in the New Movement," (master's thesis, University of Delaware, December 1990), 5, 7–8. See also correspondence in the collection of the Gilder Mss.

51. Jennifer Martin Bienenstock, "The Career of Helena de Kay Gilder: 1874–1886," unpublished manuscript, box 15, Gilder Mss., 3–5.

52. Letter, 1873, Helena de Kay Gilder to Richard Watson Gilder, box 5, folder Helena de Kay Gilder to Richard Watson Gilder, 1873–1875, See also Rosamond Gilder, "Dialogue," unpublished manuscript, Gilder Mss.

53. "The Century's American Artist Series," *Century Illustrated Magazine* 44, no. 6 (October 1892): 959. The Art Students' League of New York continues to provide independent instruction for artists. See http://www.theartstudentsleague.org/Home.aspx (accessed June 29, 2012).

54. Tolles, "Helena de Kay Gilder," 26.

55. Letter, 1892, Helena de Kay Gilder to Mary Hallock Foote, box 4, Helena de Kay Gilder to Mary Hallock Foote, 1892, Gilder Mss.

56. Tolles, "Helena de Kay Gilder," 35.

57. Letter, June 26, 1894, Helena de Kay Gilder to Mary Hallock Foote, box 4, Helena de Kay Gilder to Mary Hallock Foote, 1894, Gilder Mss.

58. "A Letter on Woman Suffrage: From One Woman to Another" (New York: De Vinne, 1894), 5–6, box 16, Gilder Mss.

59. Rosamond Gilder, ed., *Letters of Richard Watson Gilder* (Boston: Houghton Mifflin, 1916), 258.

60. Letter, August 22, 1894, Sarah B. Shaw to Helena de Kay Gilder, box 14, Gilder Mss.

61. Herbert F. Smith, "Jeannette Leonard Gilder," in *Notable American Women, 1607–1950: A Biographical Dictionary*, vol. 1, ed. Edward T. James (Cambridge: Belknap, 1971), 33.

62. "Jeannette L. Gilder," *American Magazine Journalists, 1850–1900. Dictionary of Literary Biography,* vol. 79, ed. Sam G. Riley (Detroit: Gale, 1989). Literature Resource Center (accessed July 28, 2011); Herbert F. Smith, "Jeannette Leonard Gilder," *Notable*

American Women, 1607–1950: A Biographical Dictionary, vol. 1, ed. Edward T. James (Cambridge: Belknap, 1971): 32–34; Jeannette Leonard Gilder, "Why I Am Opposed to Woman Suffrage," *Harper's Bazar* (May 19, 1894): 399–401. *Harper's Bazar* became *Harper's Bazaar* after October 1929.

63. Gilder, "Why I Am Opposed to Women's Suffrage," 399–401.

64. Cynthia D. Kinnard, "Mariana Griswold Van Rensselaer (1851–1934): America's First Professional Woman Art Critic," in *Women as Interpreters of the Visual Arts, 1820–1979*, ed. Claire Richter Sherman and Adele M. Holcomb (Westport, Conn.: Greenwood, 1981), 187.

65. Ibid., 181, 199, 200.

66. Mariana Griswold Van Rensselaer, "Should We Ask for the Suffrage?" (New York: O'Brien, 1894), 6–57. Originally published in six installments in the *New York World*, May 12, 14, 19, 20, 27, and June 3, 1894.

67. One of the daughters, also named Lucy Parkman Scott, would die at age thirteen in July 1896. "New Rochelle," *New York Tribune*, July 30, 1896.

68. Calendars, box 25, Gilder Mss. "The Antis to Protest," *Brooklyn Daily Eagle*, April 27, 1895.

69. Edward Marshall, "A Woman Tells Why Woman Suffrage Would Be Bad," *New York Times,* May 19, 1912.

70. "Francis Markoe Scott," in *Who's Who in New York: A Biographical Dictionary of Prominent Citizens of New York City and State*. 7th ed., 1917–1918, ed. Herman W. Knox (New York: Who's Who Publications, Inc., 1918), 951; "Mrs. Francis M. Scott," *New York Times,* November 12, 1937; Mrs. Francis M. Scott, "The Legal Status of Women" (New York: New York State Association Opposed to Woman Suffrage, 1910); Edna Kenton, "The Militant Women—And Women," *Century* 87, no. 1 (November 1913): 13–20; Mrs. Francis M. Scott, "The Militant and the Child" (New York: National Association Opposed to Woman Suffrage, 1913).

71. "A Social Event," *New York Times,* October 7, 1875.

72. Josephine Jewell Dodge Papers, 1873–1874, VC; "Josephine Marshall Jewell Dodge," *Women's Who's Who of America, 1914–1915*, ed. John William Leonard (New York: American Commonwealth, 1914): 250–51; Robert Cross, "Josephine Marshall Jewell Dodge," American National Biography Online, http://www.anb.org (accessed Jun. 16, 2002); L. P. S., "The Late Mrs. Arthur M. Dodge," *New York Times,* March 16, 1928): 16; "Mrs. Arthur Murray Dodge," *New York World,* March 22, 1928, clipping in archives of the Alumnae and Alumni of Vassar College, Poughkeepsie, N.Y.; I. T. Martin, "Concerning Some of the Anti-Suffrage Leaders," *Good Housekeeping* 55 (July 1912): 80–81. The quote is from "Remember Woman Who Founded Day Nurseries," unattributed newspaper clipping, Collection of the Alumnae and Alumni of Vassar College, Poughkeepsie, N.Y.

73. "Every New Kindergarten," *New York Evangelist* 65, no. 38 (September 20, 1894): 7; "The Development of the Day Nursery Idea," *Outlook* 56, no. 1 (May 1, 1897): 60; and "Mrs. Arthur Murray Dodge," *New York World,* March 22, 1928. Both the Virginia Day Nursery and the Hope Day Nursery continue to operate.

74. "Mrs. Arthur Murray Dodge," in *Who's Who in New York City and State* 3rd ed., ed. John W. Leonard (New York: Hamersly, 1907), 418; and Mrs. Barclay Hazard, "New York State Association Opposed to Woman Suffrage," *Chautauquan* 59, 1 (June 1910): 84.

75. "The Federation of Day Nurseries, *Harper's Bazar* 32, no. 5 (February 4, 1899): 96.

76. "David Hummell Greer," *Who's Who in New York City and State,* 1st ed., ed. John W. Leonard (New York: Hamersly, 1904): 270–71.

77. "Twenty-Five Years' Good Work," *New York Times,* March 17, 1896; "Some Happenings in Good Society," *New York Times,* April 22, 1900: 19; "New Anti-Suffrage Officers," *New York Times,* December 10, 1910; "Colonial Dames' Sewing Class," *New York Times,* February 29, 1912; "Mrs. Greer Dies, Widow of Bishop," *New York Times,* June 18, 1919.

78. "Caroline McPhail Bergen," in *Who's Who in New York City and State,* 4th ed., ed. John W. Leonard (New York: Hamersly, 1908): 113; "Brooklyn Women's Club," *New York Times,* February 19, 1890; "Suffragists Ready for War," *Brooklyn Daily Eagle,* April 23, 1894; "Sighs from Weary Women," *New York Times,* May 9, 1894; "Women Who Won't Vote," *Brooklyn Daily Eagle,* March 5, 1896; "State Charities Aid," *Brooklyn Daily Eagle,* May 21, 1896; "Woman Suffrage Opposed," *Brooklyn Daily Eagle,* March 3, 1898; "The State Charities Aid," *New York Times,* December 8, 1899; "Play Merry Games on Waldorf Roof," *New York Times,* March 30, 1909.

79. "Francis Lynde Stetson," in *Who's Who in New York City and State,* 4th ed., ed. John W. Leonard (New York: Hamersly, 1908): 1233; "New Directors Chosen," *Brooklyn Daily Eagle,* April 18, 1901; *Cathedral Church of Saint John the Divine* (New York: St. Bartholomew's, 1916); "Legal Aid Convention," *New York Times,* November 8, 1912; "New-York Women's Protest," *New York Times,* April 26, 1894.

80. Sven Beckert, *The Monied Metropolis: New York City and the Consolidation of the American Bourgeoisie, 1850–1896* (Cambridge: Cambridge University Press, 1993), 7.

81. "New-York Women's Protest," *New York Times,* April 26, 1894.

82. "Women Who Would Not Vote," *New York Times,* April 22, 1894; "To the Constitutional Convention," CAKL; Abbott, "A Woman's Protest," 760.

83. Anna Howard Shaw, *The Story of a Pioneer* (New York: Harper Brothers, 1915), 245.

84. "They Would Scorn to Vote," *New York Times,* April 24, 1894; "No Compromise with Antis," *New York Times,* April 29, 1894; "To the Constitutional Convention," Committee on Protest against Woman Suffrage, box 15, folder 4, Suffrage, SSC; Mrs. Barclay Hazard, "The New York Anti-Suffrage Association," *Harper's Bazar* 43 (July 1909): 730.

85. "Following Brooklyn's Lead," *New York Times,* April 27, 1894.

86. "Why They Oppose the Ballot," *New York Times,* April 26, 1894; "New York State Association Opposed to Woman Suffrage," [1912?], CAKL.

87. "Not as a Counterfeit Man," *New York Times,* May 4, 1894.

88. Women's Anti-Suffrage Association of the Third Judicial District, *Pamphlets Printed and Distributed*, introduction.

89. "Antis Fire the Last Shot," *New York Times,* May 27, 1894.

90. "Anti-Suffrage Campaign Closed," *New York Times,* May 18, 1894; "Antis Fire the Last Shot," *New York Times,* May 27, 1894.

91. "Personal," *Harper's Bazar* (May 12, 1894): 378.

92. This very successful magazine, edited for forty-seven years by Lyman Abbott, published articles on current events, autobiographies of famous people, and criticisms of art and literature. Lyman Abbott, "Woman Suffrage," *Outlook* 49 (March 31, 1894): 577; Jean Hoornstra and Trudy Heath, eds., *American Periodicals, 1741–1900: An Index to the Microfilm Collections* (Ann Arbor: University Microfilms International, 1979), 158–59.

93. Anti-suffragists often reprinted the articles published in the *Outlook. Why Women Do Not Want the Ballot*, vol. 1, "To the Constitutional Convention," Committee on Protest against Woman Suffrage, box 16, folder 2, Suffrage Collection, Series I, United States, SSC.

94. Mary Putnam Jacobi and Maud Wilder Goodwin, "The Woman Suffrage Question: Pro and Con," *Outlook* 49 (May 12, 1894): 821.

95. Lyman Abbott, "Is the Suffrage a Duty?" *Outlook* 49 (May 19, 1894): 860.

96. Lyman Abbott, "Is Suffrage Her Right?" *Outlook* 49 (May 26, 1894): 908.

97. Huybertie Pruyn Hamlin, *An Albany Girlhood*, ed. Alice P. Kenney (Albany: Washington Park, 1990), 255.

98. Harper, *Life and Work of Susan B. Anthony*, 764, 767.

99. Root was also a "confidant" of Theodore Roosevelt. Philip C. Jessup, *Elihu Root*, 2 vols. (New York: Dodd, Mead, 1938), 166, 174; Wesser, *Charles Evans Hughes*, 51.

100. Baker, *Constitution*, 172, 174.

101. "Statement in Regard to the Suffrage. To the Constitutional Convention, May 1894," in *Why Women Do Not Want the Ballot*, bound pamphlets, 2 vols. (New York State Association Opposed to Woman Suffrage, n.d.), n.p., URSC.

102. Ibid. for quotations; Harper, *Life and Work of Susan B. Anthony*, 768–69; Women's Anti-Suffrage Association of the Third Judicial District, *Pamphlets Printed and Distributed*, introduction, n.p.

103. "A Record of the Campaign: Woman Suffrage and the Constitutional Convention, 1894," *Annual Report of the New York State Woman Suffrage Association* (Rochester: Charles Mann, 1895), 11. Suffrage Collection, Series I. United States, States, New York: New York State Woman Suffrage Party: Annual Report, 1894. SSC.

104. Harper, *Life and Work of Susan B. Anthony*, 769, 770, 771; Women's Anti-Suffrage Association of the Third Judicial District, *Pamphlets Printed and Distributed*, n.p.

105. William H. Steele, *Revised Record of the Constitutional Convention of the State of New York*, 5 vols., vol. II (Albany: Argus, 1900), 445.

106. Ibid., 222, 405–13, 417–25.

107. Ibid., 426, 427.

108. Baker, *Constitution*, 174; Steele, *Revised Record*, 451–52, 521–24.

109. Quotations are from Elihu Root, "Address Delivered Before the New York State Constitutional Convention, August 15, 1894." Issued by the New York State Association Opposed to Woman Suffrage, Clinton Political Equality Club Collection, Clinton Historical Society, Clinton, N.Y.; Steele, *Revised Record*, 521.

110. Although suffragists criticized the anti-suffrage view, they also acknowledged that for the most part "the question was treated with the dignity and seriousness it deserved." "A Record of the Campaign: Woman Suffrage and the Constitutional Convention, 1894," *Annual Report of the New York State Woman Suffrage Association* (Rochester: Charles Mann, 1895), 16. Suffrage Collection, Series I. United States, States, New York: New York State Woman Suffrage Party: Annual Report, 1894. SSC.

111. "Against Suffrage for Women," *New York Times*, February 24, 1896.

112. "Copy of Preamble and Protest," in *Why Women Do Not Want the Ballot*, vol.1 (New York: New York State Association Opposed to the Extension of Woman Suffrage, 1897), n.p. CAKL.

113. Degler, *At Odds*, 348, 350.

114. Ibid., 341–42.

115. "Antis Fire the Last Shot," *New York Times*, May 27, 1894; "Anti-Suffrage Campaign Closed," *New York Times*, May 18, 1894.

Chapter 2. Establishing New York State Anti-Suffrage Organizations, 1895–1911

1. "Now that Organized Opposition," *New York Times*, June 19, 1895.

2. "Do Women Hate Women?" *New York Times*, January 3, 1897.

3. Sara Hunter Graham, *Woman Suffrage and the New Democracy* (New Haven, Conn.: Yale University Press, 1996), 33.

4. Kraditor, *Ideas of the Woman Suffrage Movement*, 53, 55, 66; Suzanne M. Marilley, *Woman Suffrage and the Origins of Liberal Feminism in the United States, 1820–1920* (Cambridge, Mass.: Harvard University Press, 1997), 187.

5. Mari Jo Buhle and Paul Buhle, eds., *The Concise History of Woman Suffrage: Selections from the Classic Work of Stanton, Anthony, Gage, and Harper* (Urbana: University of Illinois Press, 2005), 365.

6. Marilley, *Woman Suffrage and the Origins of Liberal Feminism in the United States, 1820–1920*, 188.

7. More radical suffrage groups would form before the controversy ended. The more radical groups included Harriot Stanton Blatch's New York–based Women's Political Union, founded in 1910, and Alice Paul's National Woman's Party, founded in 1913. See Ellen Carol DuBois, *Harriot Stanton Blatch and the Winning of Woman Suffrage* (New Haven, Conn.: Yale University Press, 1997) and Christine Lunardini, *From Equal Suffrage to Equal Rights: Alice Paul and the National Woman's Party, 1910–1928* (San Jose: ToExcel, 2000).

8. "Anti-Suffragists in a National Union," *New York Times*, November 29, 1911.

9. "Women Start League against Suffragists," *New York Times,* May 14, 1908; "League for the Civic Education of Women," and "The Guidon," *Anti-Suffragist* 1, no. 2 (December 1908): 2, 6.

10. Extensive unification of anti-suffragists into formal organizations happened throughout the United States between the 1890s and the 1910s. Antis in other states followed the New York antis: Massachusetts (May 1895), Illinois (May 1897), Iowa (1897), South Dakota (1898), Oregon (1899), Rhode Island (1903), Pennsylvania (1909), New Jersey (1912), Virginia (1912), and Nebraska (1914). Caroline F. Corbin, "The Woman Movement in America," folder 11, box 14, Suffrage Collection, Series I. United States, Anti-Suffrage: Illinois, SSC.

11. Edward Ringwood Hewitt, *Ringwood Manor: The Home of the Hewitts* (Trenton, N.J.: Trenton Printing, 1946).

12. Allan Nevins, *Abram S. Hewitt, with Some Account of Peter Cooper* (New York: Harper, 1935): 76, 145–50, 279, 542–47; http://www.ringwoodmanor.com (accessed June 30, 2012).

13. Abram S. Hewitt, "Statement in Regard to the Suffrage" (New York: New York State Association Opposed to Woman Suffrage, 1894).

14. "New York State Association Opposed to Woman Suffrage" [1912?], CAKL.

15. Hazard, "New York Anti-Suffrage Association," 730.

16. "Against Suffrage for Women," *New York Times,* June 18, 1895.

17. "Oppose Women's Suffrage," *New York Times,* December 1, 1909.

18. Abby Hamlin Abbott died in 1907. "Mrs. Lyman Abbott Dead," *New York Times,* July 21, 1907; "New York State Association Opposed to Woman Suffrage," [1912?], CAKL; "Anti-Suffragists' Election," *New York Times,* December 6, 1902; "New Anti-Suffrage Officers," *New York Times,* December 7, 1909.

19. "Anti-Suffragist Head Quits," *New York Times,* December 6, 1910; "New Anti-Suffrage Officers," *New York Times,* December 7, 1910; "Anti-Suffragists Elect Mrs. Putnam," *New York Times,* December 5, 1911; "Officers N.Y. State Association," *Anti-Suffragist* 4, no. 1 (January 1912): 3.

20. *Woman's Protest* (January 1913): 2.

21. Marshall, *Splintered Sisterhood,* 189.

22. Thomas J. Jablonsky, "Duty, Nature, and Stability: Female Anti-Suffragists in the United States, 1894–1920" (PhD diss., University of Southern California, 1978), 68.

23. "Women at Odds over the Suffrage Question," *New York Times,* March 17, 1907; "New York State Association Opposed to Woman Suffrage" [1912?], CAKL.

24. Extant annual reports include the "Annual Report of the Chairman of the Executive Committee," April 1896, the Eleventh Annual Report in 1906, the Fourteenth Annual Report in 1909, the Fifteenth Annual Report in 1910, and the Sixteenth Annual Report in 1911.

25. According to the website http://www.measuringworth.com/ppowerus/result

.php (accessed June 30, 2012), in 1910 $3.00 was the equivalent of $69.90 in today's money; $5.00 would equate to $116.00 today.

26. Quote is from "New York State Association Opposed to Woman Suffrage," [1912?], CAKL.

27. "Women at Odds over Suffrage Question," *New York Times,* March 17, 1907.

28. "Women Who Do Not Want to Vote," *New York Times,* May 22, 1896.

29. "The National Anti-Suffrage League," *Anti-Suffragist* 1, no. 2 (December 1908): 10, describes the anti-suffrage movement in Britain; "Fifteenth Annual Report, December 1910," New York State Association Opposed to Woman Suffrage, 7, 11. HCH.

30. "Against Suffrage for Women," *New York Times,* June 18, 1895; McGerr, "Political Style," 871.

31. "Do Not Want Woman Suffrage," *New York Times,* April 29, 1897; "Anti-Suffragists Meet," *New York Times,* May 2, 1898; "Meeting of the Executive Committee of the Albany Branch," *Anti-Suffragist* 3, no. 2 (December 1910): 3. Local newspapers reported on anti-suffrage and suffrage activities in their communities.

32. This statistic is for 1900. Barbara Shupe, Janet Steines, and Jyoti Pandit, *New York State Population, 1790–1980: A Compilation of Federal Census Data* (New York: Neal-Schuman, 1987), 2.

33. Women's Anti-Suffrage Association of the Third Judicial District, *Pamphlets Printed and Distributed*, introduction.

34. Hamlin, *An Albany Girlhood*, 255.

35. Ellen Carol DuBois, *Harriot Stanton Blatch and the Winning of Woman Suffrage* (New Haven, Conn.: Yale University Press, 1997), 105.

36. Hamlin, *An Albany Girlhood*, 255.

37. Harper, *Life and Work of Susan B. Anthony*, 765.

38. "Mrs. Mackay Opens Campaign in Albany," *New York Times,* January 26, 1910; "Nelson Herrick Henry," *Who's Who in New York City and State* 3rd ed., ed. John W. Leonard (New York: Hamersly, 1907), 657.

39. "Against Suffrage for Women," *New York Times,* February 24, 1896. This article was submitted by "A. P. P.," Anna Parker Pruyn of the Albany organization.

40. John Alden Dix, Democrat, was governor of New York State from 1911 to 1913.

41. "The Annual Meeting," *Anti-Suffragist* 2, no. 3 (March 1910): 3; "Annual Meeting," *Anti-Suffragist* 3, no. 3 (March 1911); 2.

42. Ida Husted Harper, *History of Woman Suffrage*, 6 vols., vol. 5 (New York: Little and Ives, 1922).

43. *Anti-Suffragist* 1, no.1 (July 1908): 1.

44. The Sophia Smith Collection holds the most complete collection of these bound volumes of anti-suffrage pamphlets. There is actually little difference between the volumes, as anti-suffragists recycled most of the articles. Suffrage Collection, Series I, United States: *Why Women Do Not Want the Ballot*, SSC.

45. "Report of Third Judicial District of New York State Association Opposed to the Extension of Suffrage to Women, from May 1st 1896, to May 1st 1897," Women's

Anti-Suffrage Association of the Third Judicial District, *Pamphlets Printed and Distributed*, n.p.

46. Jablonsky, *Home, Heaven, and Mother Party*, 28.

47. "Women and the Ballot," *New York Times,* March 14, 1900.

48. *Anti-Suffragist* 2, no. 3 (March 1910): 8.

49. U.S. Congress, House, Committee on Judiciary, *Hearings on Woman Suffrage*, 63rd Cong., 2nd sess. (Washington, D.C., March 3, 1914), 75. According to Jablonsky, anti-suffragists included apathetic or inactive women in their membership counts and they counted virtually all women over the age of twenty-one who were not enrolled on the suffrage lists. Jablonsky, "Duty, Nature, and Stability," 76–77.

50. "Talked against Woman Suffrage," *New York Times,* April 17, 1896.

51. "Against Woman Suffrage," *New York Times,* April 14, 1898.

52. "Anti-Suffragists Growing," *New York Times,* January 4, 1910. These junior leagues may have been modeled after the Junior League organized by Mary Harriman in 1901 to encourage young women to work for community welfare and social betterment; Mary Harriman Rumsey was a member of the New York State Association.

53. The New York State Association, unlike the Massachusetts association, apparently did not publish membership lists.

54. Jablonsky, "Duty, Nature, and Stability," 77.

55. Form letter with New York State Association letterhead, SC 13339, box 1, NYSA.

56. Jablonsky, *Home, Heaven, and Mother Party*; Marshall, *Splintered Sisterhood*, 17–18.

57. "Association of Brewers Replies," May 19, 1913, Pamphlet in LSHS; "Antis Call Fight for Votes Sex War," *New York Times,* April 16, 1914; Mrs. Arthur M. Dodge, "It Is with Great Regret," *Woman's Protest* 7, no. 5 (September 1915): 4; "To the Speakers in the New York Campaign," Letter (October 9, 1915), box 2, folder 11, CCC Papers.

58. Jablonsky, *Home, Heaven, and Mother Party*, 75.

59. Benjamin, *History of the Anti-Suffrage Movement*, 39.

60. Mrs. Francis M. Scott, "First Legislative Address in Opposition to Woman Suffrage Delivered before the Judiciary Committee of the New York State Senate, April 10, 1895" (New York: New York State Association Opposed to Woman Suffrage, n.d.). Reprinted from *Harper's Bazar*, May 19, 1895; "Anti-Suffrage Documents to Be Had," *New York Times,* February 19, 1910; "Women at Odds over Suffrage Question," *New York Times,* March 17, 1907; "Anti-Suffrage Growing," *New York Times,* January 4, 1910.

61. Mrs. Lyman Abbott, "Mrs. Lyman Abbott on Woman Suffrage." Address Before the Anti-Woman Suffrage Society of Albany, New York, n.d. CAKL.

62. "Home, Woman's Sphere," *New York Times,* April 11, 1895.

63. "Against Suffrage for Women," *New York Times,* June 18, 1895. When Nixon died in 1905, the virulently anti-suffragist James W. Wadsworth Jr. was elected as assembly speaker. Wesser, *Charles Evans Hughes*, 54.

64. "Now That Organized Opposition . . .," *New York Times,* June 19, 1895.

65. "Women at Odds over Suffrage Question," *New York Times,* March 17, 1907.

66. Manuela Thurner, "'Better Citizens without the Ballot,'" 208.

67. Estelle Freedman, "Separatism as Strategy," 513.

68. DuBois, *Woman Suffrage & Women's Rights,* 181.

69. "Mrs. Fish an Ally of Anti-Suffragists," *New York Times,* February 5, 1909; Andrew Sinclair, *The Better Half: The Emancipation of the American Woman* (New York: Harper & Row, 1965), 89.

70. Alice Hill Chittenden, "The Counter Influence to Woman Suffrage," *Independent* 67 (July 29, 1909): 249.

71. Jane Jerome Camhi, *Women against Women,* 115.

72. E. C. S., "Woman Suffrage and Wages," reprinted from the *New York Tribune,* 1896.

73. McGerr, "Political Style," 864, 869.

74. Baker, *Moral Frameworks of Public Life,* xiv.

75. The mock referendum caused some excitement in the women's colleges of Massachusetts, as indicated by the letter a student wrote to her father and an article detailing the results. However, even in women's colleges, students opposed the vote for women. "Dear Papa," letter in Student Life, General, Political Activity Concerning Suffrage, and the *Mount Holyoke* 5, no. 3 (November 1895): 111, Mount Holyoke College, South Hadley, Mass.

76. "The Anti-Suffrage Movement," *Harper's Bazar* 43 (April 1909): 424; Stanton, Gage, and Anthony, *History of Woman Suffrage,* 738.

77. Sara Hunter Graham, "The Suffrage Renaissance: A New Image for a New Century, 1896–1910," in *One Woman, One Vote: Rediscovering the Woman Suffrage Movement,* ed. Marjorie Spruill Wheeler (Troutdale, Ore.: New Sage, 1995), 160.

78. Annie Nathan Meyer, "Ways of the Suffragists," *New York Times,* February 21, 1907; Carrie Chapman Catt, "Mrs. Catt Replies to Annie Nathan Meyer's Criticisms," *New York Times,* February 22, 1907; Robert D. Cross, "Maud Nathan," *Notable American Women, 1607–1950: A Biographical Dictionary,* vol. II, ed. Edward T. James (Cambridge, Mass.: Belknap, 1971), 609. The sisters did not have a close relationship, perhaps because of jealousy the younger Meyer felt for her elder sister. Joyce Antler, *The Journey Home: Jewish Women and the American Century* (New York: Free Press, 1997), 65–66.

79. Annie Nathan Meyer, *It's Been Fun* (New York: Schuman, 1951), 202–8.

80. DuBois, *Harriot Stanton Blatch,* 108.

81. "The English Conciliation Bill," *New York Times,* March 2, 1911.

82. Hazard, "New York Anti-Suffrage Association," 730.

83. "Seek Offices for Women," *New York Times,* January 21, 1910.

84. Annie Nathan Meyer, "Spreadhenism's Spirit," *New York Times,* March 20, 1911.

85. "For and Against Woman Suffrage," *New York Times,* March 25, 1897; "Against Woman Suffrage," *New York Times,* April 15, 1897.

86. "Female Suffrage Hearing," *New York Times,* February 23, 1899.

87. "The Legislative Hearing," *Anti-Suffragist* 2, no. 3 (March 1910): 5.

88. Helen Kendrick and Rossiter Johnson Collection, Manuscripts and Archives Division, New York Public Library, New York, N.Y. Rossiter Johnson, *Helen Kendrick Johnson: The Story of Her Varied Activities* (New York: Publisher's Printing, 1917).

89. The book went into several editions, the final one in 1913. Helen Kendrick Johnson, *Woman and the Republic: A Survey of the Woman-Suffrage Movement in the United States and a Discussion of the Claims and Arguments of Its Foremost Advocates* (New York: Appleton, 1897), 7; Rossiter Johnson, *Helen Kendrick Johnson*, 13.; "Helen Kendrick Johnson," *Who's Who in New York City and State*, 3rd ed., ed. John William Leonard (New York: Hamersly, 1907): 747; Rossiter Johnson, "The Blank Cartridge Ballot" (New York: New York State Association Opposed to Woman Suffrage, n.d.).

90. The school board in New York City was appointed, not elected. Baker, *Moral Frameworks of Public Life*, 74, 77, 141.

91. "Women Object to Voting," *New York Times,* March 10, 1904.

92. "Against Woman Suffrage," *New York Times,* February 13, 1900.

93. Susan B. Anthony and Ida Husted Harper, eds., *History of Woman Suffrage*, 6 vols., vol. 4 (Indianapolis: Hollenbeck, 1902), 382.

94. "Women Argue against Universal Suffrage," *New York Times,* February 14, 1900).

95. "Anthony Memorial Fund," *New York Times,* February 16, 1907.

96. At the 1894 convention, the constitution was amended in Article 12, section 2, to divide cities into three classes by population: first class, 250,000 or over; second class, 50,000 to 250,000; and third class, under 50,000. Robert Cushing Cumming, Owen L. Potter, and Frank Gilbert, *The Constitution of the State of New York* (Albany: James B. Lyon, 1894): 199–201.

97. E. C. S., "Woman's Demand for Suffrage," Women's Anti-Suffrage Association of the Third Judicial District, *Pamphlets Printed and Distributed,* reprinted from the *New York Tribune*, 1896.

98. "Women at Odds over Suffrage Question," *New York Times,* March 17, 1907.

99. "Women Appeal for Suffrage," *New York Times,* February 20, 1908.

100. "Suffrage Hearing before the Joint Judiciary Committee," *Anti-Suffragist* 1, no. 3 (March 1909): 1.

101. "Votes for Women Week," *New York Times,* March 7, 1910.

102. Alice Hill Chittenden, "The Counter Influence to Woman Suffrage," *Independent* 67 (July 29, 1909): 246–49.

103. Mrs. William Forse Scott, "In Opposition to Woman Suffrage: Paper Read at Albany, February 24, 1909, before the Joint Senate and Assembly Judiciary Committee by Mrs. Wm. Forse Scott, of Yonkers, N.Y." (New York: New York State Association Opposed to Woman Suffrage, 1909), 6–8.

104. "Bertha Lane Scott," *Women's Who's Who of America, 1914–1915* (New York: American Commonwealth: 1914): 723; "New Anti-Suffrage Officers," *New York Times,*

December 7, 1910; "Politics, She Says, Taints Women, Too," *New York Times,* November 16, 1911; Mrs. William Forse Scott, "Women Give Reasons against Suffrage," *New York Times, May 12, 1912; Mrs. William Forse Scott, "The Feminist View," *New York Times,* December 27, 1913; Mrs. William Forse Scott, "No Suffrage Compromise," *New York Times*, February 15, 1914; Mrs. William Forse Scott, "Suffrage a Failure," *New York Times,* January 24, 1915.

105. Mrs. William Forse Scott, "Woman's Relation to Government," (New York: New York State Association Opposed to Woman Suffrage, n.d.): 6–7, 8.

106. "Suffrage Bill Up Soon," *New York Times,* February 3, 1909; "Women to Invade Albany," *New York Times,* February 21, 1909; "Women in Albany in Ballot Battle," *New York Times,* February 25, 1909.

107. Shaw, *Story of a Pioneer*, 294. Quote is from Catt and Shuler, *Woman Suffrage and Politics*, 282.

108. Quoted in Mineke Bosch and Annemarie Kloosterman, *Politics and Friendship: Letters from the International Woman Suffrage Alliance* (Columbus: Ohio State University Press, 1990), 103.

109. "Fifteenth Annual Report, December 1910," New York State Association Opposed to Woman Suffrage, 16, HCH.

110. McGerr, "Political Style," 873.

111. "Suffrage Week in Albany," *New York Times,* February 19, 1911. "Sixteenth Annual Report, December 1911," New York State Association Opposed to Woman Suffrage, 16, HCH.

112. "To Oppose Suffrage Bills," *New York Times,* February 21, 1911; "Few Seats for Men on Suffrage Day," *New York Times,* February 23, 1911; "Hearing at Capital," *Anti-Suffragist* 3, no. 3 (March 1911): 8.

113. Helen Kendrick Johnson, "The Guidon Club Opposed to Woman Suffrage," *Reply* (May 1913), 13.

114. "Suffrage Appeals to Lawless and Hysterical Women," *New York Times,* March 30, 1913; Mari Jo Buhle, *Women and American Socialism, 1870–1920* (Urbana: University of Illinois Press, 1981), 60, 105.

115. Benjamin, *History of the Anti-Suffrage Movement*, 135.

116. "Admit Anti-Suffrage Club," *New York Times,* May 9, 1908.

117. In 1914 and 1915, Caroline M. Holmes would serve as president of the Guidon Club. "The Guidon," *Anti-Suffragist* 1, no. 2 (December 1908): 6–7.

118. "Louise Caldwell Jones," *Woman's Who's Who of America*, ed. John William Leonard (New York: American Commonwealth, 1914): 441; "Eleventh Annual Report," New York State Association Opposed to the Extension of the Suffrage to Women, New York, December 1906, 4. Miller Scrapbook #5: 16, National American Woman Suffrage Collection, Library of Congress, Washington, D.C.

119. Folder, "Addresses," box 23, Richard Watson Gilder Papers, Manuscripts and Archives Division, New York Public Library, New York, N.Y.; "Suffragists Invade Opposition Meeting," *New York Times,* December 5, 1908.

120. Members made it clear, however, that the organizations were completely separate. Ina Brevoort Roberts, ed., *Club Women of New York, 1910–1911* (New York: Club Women of New York, 1910), 63.

121. Elisabeth Israels Perry, *Belle Moskowitz: Feminine Politics and the Exercise of Power in the Age of Alfred E. Smith* (New York: Oxford University Press, 1987), 46.

122. Richard Watson Gilder died of a heart attack in November 1909; thereafter Helena de Kay Gilder was no longer involved in the anti-suffrage movement. Lucy Scott explained: "With her husband's death her own personal life died too. What was left was her children's, and outside interests, excepting always through books, & friendly talks, faded into unimportance, & dropped away." "Minutes Entered into the book of the Fortnightly Club, December 18, 1916," folder, Lucy P. Scott, box 14, Gilder Mss.

123. "Anti-Suffragists Open Offices Here," *New York Times,* October 31, 1908.

124. "Women Start League against Suffragists," *New York Times,* May 14, 1908.

125. "Rabbi against Suffragettes," *New York Times,* January 30, 1909.

126. "Civic Education Programme," *New York Times,* Nov. 2, 1910.

127. "League for the Civic Education of Women," *Anti-Suffragist* 1, no. 2 (December 1908): 2.

128. "Social Notes," *New York Times,* January 4, 1910; "Suffragette Left to Debate Alone," *New York Times,* January 10, 1910; "No Equal Suffrage Debate," *New York Times,* March 14, 1909.

129. "Corrects a 'Press Agent,'" *New York Times,* January 11, 1910.

130. "Six Lectures on Anti-Suffrage," *New York Times,* March 3, 1910.

131. "Prof. Jordan No Suffragist," *New York Times,* March 22, 1910; "Academic Costumes and Suffrage," *New York Times,* May 24, 1910.

132. Barbara Miller Solomon, *In the Company of Educated Women: A History of Women and Higher Education in America* (New Haven, Conn.: Yale University Press, 1985), 111–12.

133. Apparently Gilder and Jones planned to open branches of the league in every state in the country, a goal that was never realized. Benjamin, *History of the Anti-Suffrage Movement,* 134.

134. "Women's Suffrage a Failure," *New York Times,* July 17, 1909.

135. Richard Barry, "The Truth concerning Four Woman-Suffrage States" (New York: National League for the Civic Education of Women, 1910). Suffrage Collection, Series I., United States, Anti-Suffrage, box 14, SSC; "Richard Barry," *Who's Who in New York City and State,* 85–86.

136. Camhi, *Women against Women,* 242. Ward's sister, Ethel M. Arnold, was pro-suffrage. "Miss Arnold Decries Militant Suffrage," *New York Times,* January 4, 1910.

137. Mrs. Humphry Ward, *Delia Blanchflower* (New York: Hearst's International Library, 1914).

138. Enid Huws Jones, *Mrs. Humphry Ward* (New York: St. Martin's, 1973), 136–38.

139. In 1913 the National League for the Civic Education of Women merged with the Woman's Municipal League. Benjamin, *History of the Anti-Suffrage Movement,* 135.

140. "New Anti-Suffrage Society," *Anti-Suffragist* 3, no. 3 (March 1911): 8.

141. Jane Cunningham Croly (who used the pen name of Jennie June) was one of the first female syndicated columnists in the United States. Karen J. Blair, *The Clubwoman as Feminist: True Womanhood Redefined, 1868–1914* (New York: Holmes & Meier, 1980), 5, 16, 23.

142. Mary I. Wood, *The History of the General Federation of Woman's Clubs—for the First Twenty-Two Years of the Organization* (Farmingdale, N.Y.: Dabor Social Science, 1978), 31–32.

143. Blair, *Clubwoman as Feminist*, 111.

144. Eventually Heath would join the suffragists, who quoted her as saying, "Just as soon as I made the Housewives' League an economic factor, the woman's vote became a necessity." "Housewives' Head Good Suffragist," *Woman's Journal and Suffrage News* 46, no. 4 (January 23, 1915): 26.

145. Blair, *Clubwoman as Feminist*, 4, 5, 111.

146. "Anti-Suffrage Activity," *Remonstrance* (October 1909), 2.

147. "Women's Clubs in a Peppery Contest," *New York Times,* October 23, 1909.

148. *Anti-Suffragist* 2, no. 4 (June 1910): 4; "A Timely Opinion," *Anti-Suffragist* 3, no. 1 (September 1910): 6; Wood, *History of the General Federation*, 248, 265–66.

149. "Women at Odds over Suffrage Question," *New York Times,* March 17, 1907.

150. "Statement in Regard to the Suffrage. To the Constitutional Convention, May 1894," in *Why Women Do Not Want the Ballot*, bound pamphlets, 2 vols. (New York State Association Opposed to Woman Suffrage, n.d.), n.p. URSC.

151. "Against Woman Suffrage," *New York Times,* April 14, 1898.

152. David E. Kyvig, *Explicit & Authentic Acts: Amending the U.S. Constitution, 1776–1995* (Lawrence: University Press of Kansas, 1996), 231.

153. "Anti-Suffragists Elect Mrs. Putnam," *New York Times,* December 5, 1911.

154. "The National Association," *Woman's Protest* 1, no. 1 (May 1912): 3.

155. Hazard, "New York Anti-Suffrage Association," 730.

156. Quote is from Mrs. William Forse Scott, "Woman's Relation to Government" [1903] (New York: New York State Association Opposed to Woman Suffrage, 1904), 8.

157. Graham, "Suffrage Renaissance," 162, 172, 173.

158. "Anti-Suffragists Aroused," *New York Times,* December 10, 1911.

159. Hamlin, *An Albany Girlhood,* 256.

Chapter 3. Antis Win the New York State Campaign, 1912–1915

1. "Shipping Casualties (Loss of the Steamship, "Titanic")," British Parliamentary Papers (London: His Majesty's Stationary Office, 1912), 42; Steven Biel, *Down with the Old Canoe: A Cultural History of the Titanic Disaster* (New York: Norton, 1996), 8, 10, 23.

2. Quote is from "The Lesson That Came from the Sea—What it Means to the Suffrage Cause," *Woman's Protest* 1, no. 1 (April 1912): 8. The process of extending the reach and influence of the newly founded National Association included taking over

the publication of the Albany *Anti-Suffragist*. The women who had been publishing the *Anti-Suffragist* were relieved, citing the "continued absence" of the senior editor, Elizabeth Crannell (she traveled extensively), as the primary reason for welcoming the new publication. "The Last Issue of the Anti-Suffragist," *Anti-Suffragist* 4, no. 2 (April 1912): 4.

3. Biel, *Down with the Old Canoe*, 26, 29.

4. Ibid., 104–6.

5. Ann E. Larabee, "The American Hero and His Mechanical Bride: Gender Myths of the Titanic Disaster," *American Studies* 31 (Spring 1990): 15.

6. Biel, *Down with the Old Canoe*, 106, 107.

7. Larabee, "American Hero," 5–6.

8. "Document 5," *Documents of the Constitutional Convention of the State of New York 1915* (Albany: Lyon, 1915): 1–2; Alexander Keyssar, *The Right to Vote: The Contested History of Democracy in the United States* (New York: Basic, 2000), 207.

9. Robert F. Wesser, *A Response to Progressivism: The Democratic Party and New York Politics, 1902–1918* (New York: New York University Press, 1986), 167–68.

10. Baker, "Domestication of Politics," 73.

11. Other scholars have not attached much importance to this referendum. Ronald Schaffer ignores anti-suffragists and explains the suffrage loss in 1915 by pointing to a "breakdown" in the effectiveness of the New York City Woman Suffrage party. Although he affirms that the 1915 New York anti-suffrage campaign was "the best organized and most dynamic campaign by remonstrants against a suffrage referendum," Thomas Jablonsky does not seem to consider it particularly significant. The various reasons that New York State did not pass the woman suffrage referendum in 1915, according to Susan Marshall, include generally high voter turnout, fears that voting women would support prohibition, and concerns on the part of major parties that third parties would draw women voters. "Deep-seated aversion to woman suffrage," is the reason Jane Jerome Camhi gives, and Paula Baker argues that men, especially in upstate New York, held fast to "nineteenth-century political attitudes." Anne Benjamin does not give any particular reason for the success of the anti-suffragists in New York in 1915. Baker, *Moral Frameworks of Public Life*, 143; Benjamin, *History of the Anti-Suffrage Movement*, 241; Camhi, *Women against Women*, 123; Jablonsky, *Home, Heaven, and Mother Party*, 27; Marshall, *Splintered Sisterhood*, 160–64; Schaffer, "New York City Woman Suffrage Party," 282.

12. DuBois, *Harriot Stanton Blatch*, 147.

13. National American Woman Suffrage Association, *Victory*, 108–9, 173.

14. DuBois, *Harriot Stanton Blatch*, 138.

15. This was the Murray-Stilwell Bill. "Adverse Report on the Suffrage Bill," *New York Times,* March 14, 1912.

16. DuBois, *Harriot Stanton Blatch*, 138.

17. "Robert F. Wagner," *Dictionary of American Biography*, ed. John Arthur Garraty and Kenneth T. Jackson (New York: Scribner, 1973), 718–19.

18. "How Mr. Coffey Quiets Mt. Vernon Suffragists," *Woman's Protest* 1, no. 3 (July 1912): 13.

19. "Open Hearing on Platform," *New York Times,* September 26, 1912.

20. David Zdunczyk, *200 Years of the New York State Legislature* (Albany: Albany Institute of History and Art, 1978), 62–63.

21. Wesser, *Response to Progressivism,* 170.

22. Jessup, *Elihu Root,* 291.

23. "Antis Not to Oppose Move for Suffrage," *New York Times,* November 21, 1912.

24. DuBois, *Harriot Stanton Blatch,* 140–43.

25. "Will Do Washing before Parade," *Woman's Journal and Suffrage News* 44, no. 17 (April 26, 1913): 136; "Suffragists' Washing Bee," *New York Times,* April 18, 1913.

26. "Suffragists Offer Bombs," *New York Times,* June 21, 1913.

27. Sara M. Evans, *Born for Liberty: A History of Women in America* (New York: Simon & Schuster, 1989), 160–61.

28. Nancy F. Cott, *The Grounding of Modern Feminism* (New Haven, Conn.: Yale University Press, 1987), 15.

29. Camhi, *Women against Women,* 6.

30. Baker, *Moral Frameworks of Public Life,* 141.

31. The New York State Woman Suffrage Association became the statewide Woman Suffrage Party at this time. Harriot Stanton Blatch's suffrage organization did not join the Empire State Campaign. "Suffrage Work in the States: New York," *Woman's Journal and Suffrage News* 45, no. 50 (December 12, 1914): 334; "What We Have Done With the Money," leaflet, box 12, folder 7, Suffrage Collection, Series I, United States, States: New York: Organizations: New York State Woman Suffrage Party, printed materials, SSC; "Mary Garrett Hay," *Biographical Cyclopaedia of American Women,* ed. Mabel Ward Cameron (New York: Halvord, 1924): 110; Harper, *History of Woman Suffrage,* 450, 461, 485.

32. National American Woman Suffrage Association, *Victory,* 111.

33. Schaffer, "New York City Woman Suffrage Party," 280.

34. "Enthusiasm Marks First Open Session," *Woman's Protest* 1, no. 1 (May 1912): 10.

35. "Badges for Women Who Want No Vote," *New York Times,* December 11, 1912. English anti-suffragists also used the colors black, white, and rose.

36. "Activity in New York," *Woman's Protest* 2, no. 8 (June 1913): 4.

37. "Danger Seen in Woman Suffrage," unidentified newspaper clipping, LSHS.

38. Alice Hill Chittenden, "Anti-Suffragists Do Not Intend to Have Ballot Forced on Majority Because Minority Wants It," broadside, January 27, 1913, in Lincklaen/Ledyard Collection, LSHS; quotation is from Jablonsky, "Duty, Nature, and Stability," 91.

39. "Anti-Suffrage Cry is 'Bore the Men!'" and "Jubilee for Mrs. Catt," *New York Times,* November 20, 1912.

40. "Some Anti-Suffrage 'Nevers,'" *Woman's Protest* 2, no. 3 (January 1913): 15.

41. "New Anti-Suffrage Officers," *New York Times,* December 3, 1912.

42. Personal Ancestral File, http://homepages.rootsweb.com/~wayland/fowler/pafg173.htm (accessed June 30, 2012).

43. Anna Callender Brackett was a prolific author of books and articles on the education of girls. "Why They Demand a Vote: Prominent Women Eloquently Pres-

ent Their Reasons," *New York Times,* April 17, 1894; "Miss Anna C. Brackett Dead," *New York Times,* March 19, 1911.

44. Other students who went to Miss Porter's school include Alice Hamilton, who graduated in 1889 and founded the field of industrial medicine; Julia Lathrop, the first woman to head a government agency (the Children's Bureau); and Ruth Hanna McCormick, a suffragist who graduated in 1892 and was the first woman to run for U.S. Senate. Nancy Davis and Barbara Donahue, *Miss Porter's School: A History* (Farmington, Conn.: Miss Porter's School, 1992), 23, 25.

45. Davis and Donahue, *Miss Porter's School,* 5.

46. Email correspondence with Sheri J. Caplan, archivist, Miss Porter's School, May–June 2009.

47. Davis and Donahue, *Miss Porter's School,* 21, 26–27.

48. Anna Chittenden Thayer, "Cranbrook," *Milestones of Old Guilford,* Historical Room, Guilford Free Library, Guilford, Conn.

49. "A Reception on the Heights," *Brooklyn Eagle,* December 8, 1888.

50. Martin, "Anti-Suffrage Leaders," 81.

51. *Club Worker* (1903); *Club Worker* (October 1904): 216.

52. "Brooks Vacation School," *Brooklyn Eagle,* May 7, 1898.

53. "What Women are Doing," *Washington Post,* October 29, 1911.

54. "A Full Life," *Shore Line Times* [Guilford, Conn.], October 25, 1945, Historical Room, Guilford Free Library, Guilford, Conn.

55. "'Antis' Fire the Last Shot," *New York Times,* May 27, 1894; "Against Woman Suffrage," *Brooklyn Eagle,* March 14, 1897.

56. "Lashes California Petticoat Rule," *New York Times,* July 14, 1913.

57. "'Antis' Leading Lively Attack on Suffragists," *Syracuse Herald* [?], September 1913, LSHS.

58. "Women to Debate Suffrage," *New York Times,* April 21, 1912; "Woman vs. Woman in Suffrage Debate," *New York Times,* May 1, 1912. In August 1912 Jones announced that the league would no longer discuss the question of woman suffrage. In February 1913, Jones was reported to have been ill for about six months and was then in Europe. "Anti-Suffragists Active," *New York Times,* February 10, 1913. The *Woman's Protest* also reported that on May 17, 1912, students of Howard University in Washington, D.C., debated the issue of woman suffrage. Apparently, the "sympathies of the whole audience," made up of mostly "intelligent colored women" were with the negative, which won, and the decision was "loudly applauded." "'Antis' Win Debate," *Woman's Protest* 1, no. 2 (June 1912): 13.

59. "Suffragists Hear Arguments of Antis," *New York Times,* January 21, 1913.

60. "Women Hold Debate at Republican Club," *New York Times,* January 26, 1913.

61. It is not clear who funded Martin's tour. "Jam 'Anti' Meeting," *Washington Post,* March 1, 1913. Beatrice Forbes-Robertson [Hale] wrote *What Women Want: An Interpretation of the Feminist Movement* (New York: Stokes, 1914). Many antis held membership in the Colony Club, including Josephine Jewell Dodge, Jeannette L. Gilder, Louise Caldwell Jones, and Alice Hay Wadsworth. Camhi, *Women against Women,* 239–45.

62. "Antis Denounce the 'Noisy Minority,'" *New York Times,* February 26, 1913.

63. Blake McKelvey, "A History of the Rochester City Club," *Rochester History* 9, no. 4 (October 1947): 7.

64. *Woman's Journal and Suffrage News* 45, no. 23 (June 6, 1914): 177.

65. According to records in the registrar's office at Vassar, Price did not take a public speaking or rhetoric course to obtain her A.B. degree. The New Haven, Connecticut anti-suffrage organization paid her expenses of at least two hundred dollars in 1914. *The Hartford Diaries of Mary Dudley Vaill Talcott from 1896–1919*, vol. 3 (Avon, Conn.: Alice Talcott Enders, 1990), 666, archives at Mount Holyoke College, South Hadley, Mass. Price earned fifteen dollars plus car fare for speaking at an April 28, 1915, anti-suffrage meeting in Goshen, N.Y. (Goshen County Historian's Office). "Anti-Suffragist to Speak," unidentified newspaper clipping in collection of the Alumnae House of Vassar College (January 1, 1915); "Anti-Suffrage Address Tonight," *Glens Falls Post,* May 15, 1915; "Gives Talk for Anti Suffrage," "Miss Price Speaks Against Suffrage," *Poughkeepsie Eagle,* October 13, 1915.

66. "A School for Making Anti-Suffrage Speakers," *Woman's Protest* 6, no. 6 (April 1915): 17.

67. For examples of suffrage courses and a full series of a correspondence course, see Suffrage, Series I, States, New York State Woman Suffrage Party, box 12, folder 8, SSC.

68. Quotes are from "Suffragists Applaud Anti," *New York Times,* September 26, 1913; "Want to Heckle Miss Chittenden," Syracuse newspaper, September 1913; "Miss Chittenden Accepts Challenge," September 29, 1913, in Scrapbook, LL-R-1–3, p. 29. LSHS.

69. "Talk on Suffrage Stirs Eager Crowd," *New York Times,* January 20, 1914.

70. "Suffragists Hiss Opposing Debaters," *New York Times,* January 27, 1914.

71. Suffragists attended anti-suffrage functions to learn anti-suffrage arguments in order to refute them. They stopped attending when they realized that antis counted them as supporters. "Suffragists to Shun Gatherings of Antis," unattributed newspaper clipping [*Brooklyn Eagle*], Ethel Dreier Papers, box 7, folder 3a, SSC.

72. "Suffragists Spice Anti Mass Meeting," *New York Times,* January 9, 1914.

73. "Antis Condemn Paraders," *New York Times,* May 6, 1913.

74. "To Anti-Suffragists" (New York: New York State Association Opposed to Woman Suffrage, n.d.) broadside in LSHS.

75. See, for example, "Antis Caught in Plan with Liquor Interests," *Woman's Journal and Suffrage News* 45, no. 5 (January 31, 1914): 37. Suffragists retracted or apologized for some of their statements.

76. "To the Speakers in the New York Campaign," letter, October 9, 1915, box 2, folder 11, CCC Papers.

77. See, for example, Mrs. Gilbert F. Jones, "Some Impediments to Woman Suffrage," *North American Review* 190, no. 645 (August 1909): 158–69. Mrs. Francis M. Scott, "The Militant and the Child," *New York Times,* November 16, 1913; "Antis Call Fight for Votes Sex War," *New York Times,* April 16, 1914.

78. See, for example, Inez Milholland, "The Liberation of a Sex," *McClure's* 40, no.

4 (February 1913): 181; Charlotte Perkins Gilman, "Is Feminism Really So Dreadful? Listen to Charlotte Perkins Gilman," *Delineator* 85 (August 1914): 6; Carrie Chapman Catt, "Mrs. Catt on Feminism," *Woman's Journal* (January 9, 1915): 12.

79. Winifred Harper Cooley, "The Younger Suffragists," *Harper's Weekly* 58 (September 27, 1913): 7–8; Edna Kenton, "Feminism Will Give—Men More Fun, Women Greater Scope . . . ," *Delineator* 85 (July 1914): 17.

80. Cott, *Grounding of Modern Feminism*, 15.

81. Mr. and Mrs. John Martin, "Feminism and Her Master," chap. 12 in *Feminism: Its Fallacies and Follies* (New York: Dodd, Mead, 1916), 341.

82. Postcard, postmarked March 24, 1914, in collection of Staten Island Institute of Arts and Sciences, Staten Island, N.Y.

83. Quotes are from "Feminism Making a Tomcat of Father," *New York Times,* April 3, 1914. Some of the responses to the article include Elizabeth Newport Hepburn, "'Homes for Women!'" *New York Times,* April 6, 1914; Marjorie Dorman, "Women in the Home," *New York Times,* April 7, 1914; Edith Drescher, "Homes, Not Votes," *New York Times,* April 14, 1914.

84. "Roosevelt Prelude to Suffrage Parade," *New York Times,* May 2, 1913; "Antis Work Downtown," *New York Times,* May 27, 1913; "Activity in New York," *Woman's Protest* 3, no. 2 (June 1913): 4.

85. Harper, *History of Woman Suffrage* 5, 680.

86. "Everett P. Wheeler," *Men and Women of America* (1910) and Everett P. Wheeler, *Who's Who in New York City and State*, microfilm collection at the Library of Congress, Washington, D.C. "Everett P. Wheeler Dies in 85th Year," *New York Times,* February 10, 1925.

87. "Women in Albany in Ballot Battle," *New York Times,* February 25 1909; "Antis Elect Officers," *New York Times,* December 2, 1913; "Everett P. Wheeler Dies in 85th Year," *New York Times,* February 10, 1925.

88. "Men to Oppose Suffrage," *New York Times,* August 1, 1915.

89. "Men Oppose Suffrage," *New York Times,* September 27, 1913.

90. "Everett P. Wheeler an Anti," *New York Times,* May 2, 1913; Harper, *History of Woman Suffrage* 5, 680–82.

91. David Kevin McDonald, "Organizing Womanhood: Women's Culture and the Politics of Woman Suffrage in New York State, 1865–1917" (PhD diss., State University of New York at Stony Brook, 1987), 220.

92. Massachusetts anti-suffragist Alice George claimed that it had always been a men's organization that fought their battle. "Some Things Men Can Do Better," *Woman's Protest* 7, no. 1 (May 1915): 16.

93. Harper, *History of Woman Suffrage* 5, 680–82.

94. Jerold S. Auerbach, *Unequal Justice: Lawyers and Social Change in Modern America* (London: Oxford University Press, 1977), 65, 115.

95. "Dear Sir," letter dated May 7, 1914, box 5, folder 2, EPW Papers.

96. "Mrs. Catt Wants to Know," *New York Times,* March 16, 1914. Carrie Chapman Catt called the questionnaire an "interrogation" and asked for the results in vain. A copy of the questionnaire was included in a 1916 publication of the Man-Suffrage

Association and raised issues common to the arguments for and against woman suffrage, although its tenor is distinctly anti-suffrage. "Questions on Woman Suffrage," *Publications Issued by the Man-Suffrage Association Opposed to Political Suffrage for Women* (New York: 1916), EPW Papers.

97. Quotes are from an editorial to the *New York Times,* January 7, 1915; an editorial to the *New York Sun,* January 7, 1915; and an editorial to the *Tribune,* May 3, 1915: EPW Papers.

98. Everett P. Wheeler, "The Ballot's Burden," *New York Times,* February 10, 1914; "The Bee in Their Bonnet," *New York Times,* February 14, 1915; Everett P. Wheeler, "In Reply to Mrs. Harper," *New York Times,* September 19, 1915; Harper, *History of Woman Suffrage* 5, 683; J. Stanley Lemons, *The Woman Citizen: Social Feminism in the 1920s* (Charlottesville: University Press of Virginia, 1990), 11, 12.

99. "Anti-Suffrage River Trip," *New York Times,* April 23, 1913; "Anti-Suffragists Cruise," *New York Times,* May 31, 1913. Working people often planned an excursion for Decoration Day, today known as Memorial Day (officially set on the last Sunday of May by a statute in 1871). Mitford M. Mathews, ed. *A Dictionary of Americanisms on Historical Principles,* vol. 1 (Chicago: University of Chicago Press, 1951), 471. According to suffragists, antis found it necessary to admonish the girls who sat in the laps of young men or to discipline those guests who gambled or danced the turkey trot. Problems with discipline may explain the singularity of the event. "Notorious Dance on Anti Picnic," *Woman's Journal and Suffrage News* 44, no. 24 (June 14, 1913).

100. According to Jablonsky, antis formed the New York Wage Earners' Anti-Suffrage League in response to the work done by the New York Wage Earners' Suffrage League founded by Leonora O'Reilly in 1911. Jablonsky, *Home, Heaven, and Mother Party*, 20–21.

101. "Against Woman Suffrage," *New York Times,* April 14, 1898. In 1912 wage earning women told their audience at the Cooper Union that they did not want the "antis [to] say that the workingwoman doesn't want the vote." This episode could also have provided impetus for anti-suffragists to look for wage earners' support. "Suffrage Demanded by Working Women," *New York Times,* April 23, 1912.

102. "Adeline Knapp, "Do Working Women Need the Ballot?" An Address to the Senate and Assembly Judiciary Committees of the New York Legislature, February 19th, 1908 (New York: New York State Association Opposed to Woman Suffrage), 5.

103. Camhi, *Women against Women,* 119; Kathleen Sprows Cummings, *New Women of the Old Faith: Gender and American Catholicism in the Progressive Era* (Chapel Hill: University of North Carolina Press, 2009), 179, 184.

104. "Women Opposed to Woman Suffrage are Leaders in Manifold Activities," *New York Herald,* June 14, 1914.

105. While Edith Drescher and Marjorie Dorman ran the Wage Earners' Anti-Suffrage League, evidence suggests that they did not wholly depend on their own wages. Ethel Beyea took over the position of secretary, probably because Dorman had extensive speaking engagements. "Calls Suffrage a Menace," *New York Times,* February 21, 1915.

106. "Women's Hotel Opened," *New York Times,* April 29, 1914.

107. Jablonsky, *Home, Heaven, and Mother Party,* 20.

108. Mrs. Gilbert E. Jones, "Some Impediments to Woman Suffrage," *North American Review* 190, no. 645 (August 1909): 167.

109. "Women Must Be Protected," *New York Times,* February 14, 1915. This same argument would be used by women who opposed the equal rights amendment.

110. Marjorie Dorman, "A Lesson for Suffragists," *New York Times,* May 13, 1913.

111. Between 1900 and 1920, the number of married women who worked outside the home rose from 13 to 21 percent; the married wage earner was no longer an anomaly. Quote is from Marjorie Dorman, "A Fatal Flaw in the 'Equality' Argument," *Woman's Protest* 6, no. 4 (February 1915): 3. See also Marjorie Dorman, "The Cost of Elections," *New York Times,* April 21, 1914; "No Blessings Go to Waste," *New York Times,* July 14, 1915. Camhi points out that the most "striking" aspect to the anti-suffragists' approach to the female labor force was their "incredible naiveté." Camhi, *Women against Women,* 115, 117.

112. "Intensive Work in Campaign States: New York," *Woman's Protest* 7, no. 6 (October 1915): 13.

113. "Work the States are Doing to Educate the Voters: New York," *Woman's Protest* 6, no. 1 (November 1914): 12–13. If the league did sponsor another barge trip or hold a series of events and meetings, *New York Times* editors did not think they were newsworthy.

114. "Stimson to Head Platform Drafters," *New York Times,* July 25, 1914.

115. Alice Hill Chittenden, "Convention, Red Cross and Other Anti-Suffrage State Work: New York," *Woman's Protest* 5, no. 5 (September 1914): 12.

116. "A Woman's Referendum," *New York Times,* February 13, 1914.

117. "Antis Like Miss Davis," *New York Times,* January 1, 1914. It is possible that the anti-suffragists were initially unaware of Davis's pro-suffrage efforts.

118. "Progress of the Campaign: New York," *Woman's Protest* 7, no. 5 (September 1915): 19.

119. "Anti-Suffrage and Preparedness" (New York: New York State Association Opposed to Woman Suffrage, n.d. [but before Jan. 27, 1916]), SC 13339, box 1, NYSA.

120. "Lincoln on Suffrage," *New York Times,* February 15, 1914.

121. "Anti-Suffragists Meet," *New York Times,* December 8, 1914; "How the Campaign States of 1915 are Educating the Voters: New York," *Woman's Protest* 6, no. 3, (January 1915): 12–13.

122. Jablonsky, *Home, Heaven, and Mother Party,* 87.

123. Blair, *Clubwoman as Feminist,* 112–13; Thurner, "'Better Citizens without the Ballot?'" 211.

124. "Activities in Clubland," *New York Times,* March 9, 1913.

125. "Anti-Suffragists Active," *New York Times,* February 10, 1913; "The Following Letter was Sent," *Woman's Protest* 4, no. 2 (December 1913): 4.

126. Mrs. Arthur M. Dodge, "Only Favored Submission," *Woman's Protest* 2, no. 2 (December 1912): 13.

127. "Women's Clubs at Biennial Endorse Political Equality," *Woman's Journal and Suffrage News* 45, no. 25 (June 20, 1914): 193–94.

128. "The Federated Clubs' Misfortune," *Woman's Protest* 5, no. 3 (July 1914): 4.

129. "The Directors of the National Association Opposed to Woman Suffrage," *Woman's Protest* 6, no. 4 (February 1915): 4. Edited by Helen S. Harmon-Brown from 1913 to 1915, the *Reply* was originally published in Connecticut. Publication soon moved to New York, where it remained until its last issue, May 1915.

130. Quotes are from "Suffrage Appeals to Lawless and Hysterical Women," *New York Times,* March 30, 1913. See also "The Vote in the House," *Woman's Protest* 6, no. 4 (February 1915): 4. Chittenden corresponded with Johnson, encouraging her to distribute her writings more broadly, and Johnson was invited to New York State Association meetings. Alice Hill Chittenden to Helen Kendrick Johnson, May 26, 1915, and Eleanor Phillips to Helen Kendrick Johnson, n.d. [1915], HKRJ.

131. "Vote on Suffrage Pleases Both Sides," *New York Times,* January 14, 1915.

132. Keyssar, *Right to Vote,* 207; David Morgan, *Suffragists and Democrats: The Politics of Woman Suffrage in America* (East Lansing: Michigan State University Press, 1972), 108.

133. Wesser, *Response to Progressivism,* 161, 164.

134. Thomas Reed Powell, "Woman Suffrage," *Revision of the State Constitution* (New York: New York State Constitutional Convention Commission, 1915): 80; "Suffrage Leaders Fear Legal Tangle," *New York Times,* May 1, 1915; "Suffragists Leave for Albany Today," *New York Times,* May 5, 1915.

135. "Anti-Suffragists are Active," *New York Times,* May 23, 1915; "Important Work by State Associations: New York," *Woman's Protest* 7, no. 2 (June 1915): 21.

136. "Anti-Suffrage Rose Named Mrs. Dodge," *New York Times,* April 6, 1915; "Working and Voting against Woman Suffrage: New York," *Woman's Protest* 6, no. 6 (April 1915): 18.

137. "Important Work by State Associations: New York," *Woman's Protest* 7, no. 2 (June 1915): 21. At about the same time, suffragists had their biggest suffrage luncheon of the Empire State Campaign, raising $50,000 for their movement. "Suffrage Luncheon Wins $50,000 Fund," *New York Times,* May 9, 1915.

138. "Miss Alice Hill Chittenden Says Cataclysm Will be Consequence of Giving Vote to Women," *New York Times,* February 14, 1915; "Suffragists Leave for Albany Today," *New York Times,* May 5, 1915.

139. "Historic Women Tableaux," *New York Times,* March 28, 1915. Suffragists were more capable of raising funds than antis, although Carrie Chapman Catt alone raised most of the initial campaign fund of $20,000 for the Empire State campaign. The next year suffragists received $105,619 at a single meeting held in Carnegie Hall. National American Woman Suffrage Association, *Victory,* 112. Suffragists, by 1915, according to Anna Howard Shaw, drew pledges of $150,000 for the New York State campaign. Shaw, *Story of a Pioneer,* 335.

140. Quote is from "Accomplishments in Campaign States: New York," *Woman's Protest* 7, no. 4 (August 1915): 13; see also "Anti-Suffragists Also Busy," *New York Times,* May 10, 1915.

141. "Important Work by State Associations: New York," *Woman's Protest* 7, no. 2 (June 1915): 21.

142. "Working and Voting against Woman Suffrage: New York," *Woman's Protest* 6, no. 6 (April 1915): 18; "Vital Reports of Recent Anti-Suffrage Work: New York," *Woman's Protest* 7, no. 1 (May 1915): 21.

143. "State is against Suffrage," *New York Times,* February 14, 1915): xxi; "Plans of the Anti-Suffragists," *New York Times,* April 25, 1915.

144. The Chautauqua lecture series, founded in 1874 and organized as part of an adult-education movement, offered platforms for academics, politicians, reformers, and other speakers. Andrew C. Rieser, "Chautauqua Institution," *Encyclopedia of New York State,* ed. Peter Eisenstadt (Syracuse: Syracuse University Press, 2005): 309–10. "Anti-Suffragists Are Active," *New York Times,* May 23, 1915; "An Anti-Suffrage Garden Party," *New York Times,* June 21, 1915; "Important Work by State Associations: New York," *Woman's Protest* 7, no. 2 (June 1915): 21; "Progress of the Campaign: New York," *Woman's Protest* 7, no. 5 (September 1915): 13. Entry, dated May 8, 1915, "Minutes' Book," Cazenovia Public Library, Cazenovia, N.Y.

145. "Accomplishments in Campaign States," *Woman's Protest* 7, no. 4 (August 1915): 13; Lucy Jeanne Price, "New York Anti-Suffrage by 250,000," *Woman's Protest* 7, no. 5 (September 1915): 8; "From Miss Chittenden," *New York Times,* August 13, 1915.

146. "Anti-Suffrage Address Tonight," *Glens Falls Post,* May 15, 1915; "Miss Price Speaks against Suffrage," *Poughkeepsie Eagle,* October 13, 1915; "Gives Talk for Anti-Suffrage," *Poughkeepsie Enterprise,* October 14, 1915, Collection of Alumnae and Alumni of Vassar College, Poughkeepsie, N.Y.

147. "Working and Voting against Woman Suffrage: New York," *Woman's Protest* 6, no. 6 (April 1915): 18; "Antis Warn Fair Officer," *New York Times,* August 24, 1915. In both 1915 and 1917, Tompkins County came out in support of woman suffrage.

148. "Intensive Work in Campaign States: New York," *Woman's Protest* 7, no. 6 (October 1915): 13.

149. "An Irreparable Wrong; Not an Inalienable Right," *Woman's Protest* 7, no. 5 (September 1915): 3, 11.

150. "Accomplishments in Campaign States," *Woman's Protest* 7, no. 4 (August 1915): 13.

151. Chad Wheaton, "New York State Fair," *Encyclopedia of New York State,* 1096–97.

152. "The State Fair," *Anti-Suffragist* 1, no. 2 (December 1908): 3.

153. "People Wanted Speeches," *Syracuse Herald,* September 10, 1913, in scrapbook, LL-R-1-2, p. 26. LSHS.

154. "New York," *Woman's Protest* 3, no. 6 (October 1913): 14. "Minutes' Book," Cazenovia Public Library, Cazenovia, N.Y. Quote is from "'Antis' Leading Lively Attack on Suffragists," *Syracuse Herald* [?] (September 1913), scrapbook, LL-R-1-2, LSHS.

155. "Progress of the Campaign: New York," *Woman's Protest* 7, no. 5 (September 1915): 12–13.

156. The complete words of the song are: "Suffragists say, happen what may/They'll win the coming fight;/'Twixt you and me, I don't agree;/We're going to show them who's right!/Jonquils they wear cannot compare/With the Anti-Suffrage Rose,/Token

of love and gift from above,/Loveliest flow'r that grows." Phil Hanna, "The Anti-Suffrage Rose" (Boston: Women's Anti-Suffrage Association, 1915). Elizabeth Cady Stanton Trust Collection. Greenwich, Conn. There is some evidence of another anti-suffrage song. Helen Kendrick Johnson wrote "The Woman's Battle Song," which Mrs. Henry Seligman much admired. Apparently, Seligman had ten thousand copies of it made and organized students to sing the song during the summer of 1913. "A Battle Song for the Anti-Suffragists," *New York Times,* March 16, 1913.

157. "Progress of the Campaign: New York," *Woman's Protest* 7, no. 5 (September 1915): 17.

158. "Progress of the Campaign: New York," *Woman's Protest* 7, no. 5 (September 1915): 13; "Intensive Work in Campaign States: New York," *Woman's Protest* 7, no. 6 (October 1915): 13.

159. "Intensive Work in Campaign States: New York," *Woman's Protest* 7, no. 6 (October 1915): 13, and "How the Campaign was Carried to Success: New York," *Woman's Protest* 8, no. 1 (November 1915): 17.

160. "Anti-Suffrage Notes," *Skaneateles Free Press,* September 7, 1915, clipping in collection of the Skaneateles Historical Society, Skaneateles, N.Y.

161. "An Incident" and "An Explanation," *Skaneateles Free Press,* August 27, 1915: 1; "Old Home Week was a Glorious Success" and "Concerning Skaneateles 'Incident,'" *Skaneateles Free Press,* August 31, 1915; *Democrat,* September 2, 1915. Anna Howard Shaw called the anti-suffrage organization the "Home, Heaven, and Mother Party" in one of her speeches that year. She meant it as an insult, but anti-suffragists liked the name and often used it.

162. "5,000 Women Picked for Work at Polls," *New York Times,* November 2, 1915.

163. New York State, Department of State, *Manual for the Use of the Legislature of the State of New York* (Albany: Department of State, 1916): 854–55; "Notes and Comment," *Woman's Protest* 7, no. 1 (May 1915): 23; Baker, *Moral Frameworks of Public Life,* 142–43, 145; Jablonsky, "Duty, Nature, and Stability," 79, 92.

164. "5,000 Women Picked for Work at the Polls," *New York Times,* November 2, 1915.

165. Quotes are from "Progress of the Campaign: New York," *Woman's Protest* 7, no. 5 (September 1915).

Chapter 4. Suffragists Win the New York State Campaign, 1915–1917

1. "Two Studies in Patriotism," *Woman's Protest* 5, no. 1 (May 1914): 20.

2. Nell Irvin Painter, *Standing at Armageddon: The United States, 1877–1919* (New York: Norton, 1987), 174.

3. Quote is from "Women Denounce War with Mexico," *New York Times,* April 24, 1914. See also "Two Studies in Patriotism," *Woman's Protest* 5, no. 1 (May 1914): 20.

4. "Prominent Women Stand by Wilson," *New York Times,* May 15, 1915; Robert H. Zieger, *America's Great War: World War I and the American Experience* (Lanham, Mass.: Rowman & Littlefield, 2000): xv–xvi.

5. "Antis Aid the Red Cross," *New York Times,* September 4, 1914. See also "Appeals

to Mrs. Dodge," *New York Times,* October 11, 1913; "An Appeal for Red Cross Funds," *Woman's Protest* 5, no. 5 (September 1914): 7–8.

6. "Anti-Suffrage Response to Red Cross Appeal," *Woman's Protest* 5, no. 6 (October 1914): 9; "How Anti-Suffrage Red Cross Work Progresses," *Woman's Protest* 6, no. 1 (November 1914): 11; "Directions for Red-Cross Shipments," *Woman's Protest* 6, no. 5 (March 1915): 14.

7. Ronald Schaffer contends that the vote in 1915 had simply taken place too early, and that voters had more time to get used to the idea of women voting by 1917. Positing that the suffragists won on the basis of their well-organized and influential leadership in New York City, he argues that the declaration of war in April 1917 gave New York politicians an opportunity to reward suffragists for their wartime service. Paula Baker points out that both the Democratic and Republican parties supported woman suffrage and Tammany leaders stopped opposing it. Eleanor Flexner credited a change of heart from Tammany Hall as the critical factor, and other scholars agree with her. However, Charles Murphy, head of Tammany, agreed to support woman suffrage before the 1915 referendum, and Eileen McDonagh and Douglas Price convincingly argue that Tammany Hall's support affected only one borough of New York in the second referendum. Sara Hunter Graham considers Tammany Hall's support was an important factor, but she also attributes the victory to the "suffrage machine's new wartime publicity efforts" and to "revenge for its loss in 1915." Historian Alexander Keyssar suggests that there was a "remarkable shift" in the immigrant and working class neighborhoods in New York City, tipping the balance in the state. Anti-suffrage historians have not attached particular importance to the differences in the two campaigns, nor do they seem to see anti-suffrage war work as a particularly significant factor. Thomas Jablonsky explains the 1917 referendum by writing that the anti-suffragists were exhausted from the 1915 campaign, had lost heart, and were quarreling and suffering from internal problems. Susan Marshall argues that anti-suffragists believed their cause to be lost and were suffering a "feeling of impending doom." While Anne Benjamin argues that the war was injurious to both sides of the campaign, she also considers that "the war was simply not mentioned prominently in much of the anti-suffrage literature." Baker, *Moral Frameworks of Public Life,* 145; Benjamin, *History of the Anti-Suffrage Movement,* 261–63; Flexner and Fitzpatrick, *Century of Struggle,* 282; Graham, *New Democracy,* 112; Jablonsky, "Duty, Nature, and Stability," 93; Jablonsky, *Home, Heaven, and Mother Party,* 95–96, 112; Keyssar, *Right to Vote,* 215, 450n, 75; Marshall, *Splintered Sisterhood,* 202–3; Eileen L. McDonagh and H. Douglas Price, "Woman Suffrage in the Progressive Era: Patterns of Opposition and Support in Referenda Voting, 1910–1918," *The American Political Science Review* 79, no. 155.2 (1985); Schaffer, "New York City Woman Suffrage Party," 283.

8. Catt and Shuler, *Woman Suffrage and Politics,* 280.

9. Alice Hill Chittenden, "Woman's Service or Woman Suffrage," *Woman's Protest* 11, no. 1 (May 1917): 5; Graham, *New Democracy,* 107; Barbara J. Steinson, *American Women's Activism in World War I* (New York: Garland, 1982), 317–18.

10. Graham, *New Democracy*, 102.

11. According to Barbara Steinson, no prominent suffragist was involved in war preparedness activities in 1914 or early 1915. "Society Diversions," *New York Times,* May 24, 1914; Steinson, *American Women's Activism in World War I*, 174.

12. "Antis Aid the Red Cross," *New York Times,* September 4, 1914; "Red Cross Sends More Aid to Servia [sic]," *New York Times,* November 21, 1914.

13. "Theatrical Notes," *New York Times,* October 15, 1914.

14. "Antis and the Red Cross," *New York Times,* September 4, 1914.

15. "Annual Meeting of the National Association," *Woman's Protest* 6, no. 2 (December 1914): 3.

16. "An Appeal for Red Cross Funds," *Woman's Protest* 5, no. 5 (September 1914): 7–8; "Anti-Suffrage Response to Red Cross Appeal," *Woman's Protest* 5, no. 6 (October 1914): 9; "How Anti-Suffrage Red Cross Work Progresses," *Woman's Protest* 6, no. 1 (November 1914): 11; "Directions for Red-Cross Shipments," *Woman's Protest* 6, no. 5 (March 1915): 14.

17. "Notes From the States," *Woman's Protest* 11, no. 3 (July-August 1917): 12.

18. Marjorie Dorman, "Suffragists Traitors to Democracy," *Woman's Protest* 8, no. 2 (December 1915): 6.

19. Steinson, *American Women's Activism in World War I*, 317–18.

20. "'Will and Won't Pledge,'" *New York Times,* February 23, 1914.

21. "Antis Again Attack Suffrage Leaders," *New York Times,* October 21, 1917.

22. "Preparedness or Pacifism," *Woman's Protest* 9, no. 6 (October 1916): 19.

23. "Notes and Comment," *Woman's Protest* 10, no. 6 (April 1917): 15.

24. "Suffrage Versus Patriotic Service," *Woman's Protest* 10, no. 3 (January 1917): 9. See also "Patriotism—At a Price—Unmasked," and "Pacifism Sacrificed for Suffrage Publicity," *Woman's Protest* 10, no. 5 (March 1917): 9.

25. Steinson, *American Women's Activism in World War I*, 40, 220.

26. Annie Nathan Meyer, "To the Editor," *Detroit Free Press,* April 25, 1915, clipping in Scrapbook, folder 1, box 20, ANM Papers.

27. "Peace or Politics," *Woman's Protest* 6, no. 5 (March 1914): 4.

28. *Mabel Vernon: Speaker for Suffrage and Petitioner for Peace* (Bancroft Library, University of California/Berkeley, Suffragists Oral History Project, 1976), 70. Copy at SSC; Mary Gray Peck, *Carrie Chapman Catt* (New York: Wilson, 1944), 267–71.

29. Doris Stevens, *Jailed for Freedom: American Women Win the Vote* (Troutdale, Ore.: New Sage, 1995 [1920]), 68 (emphasis in original). See also Katherine H. Adams and Michael L. Keene, *Alice Paul and the American Suffrage Campaign* (Urbana: University of Illinois Press, 2008), 169; Christine Lunardini, *From Equal Suffrage to Equal Rights: Alice Paul and the National Woman's Party, 1910–1928* (San Jose: ToExcel, 2000), 87–90, 110.

30. Suffragist refusal to contribute to charities continued to anger antis for the duration of the war. "Suffragists Desert Philanthropy until They Can Vote," pamphlet in LSHS; "The State Campaigns: New York," *Woman's Protest* 2, no. 5 (March 1913): 12; "Suffragists Would Let Belgians Starve," *Woman's Protest* 6, no. 2 (December 1914):

13; "Suffrage First," *Woman's Protest* 8, no. 2 (December 1915): 4; "Suffrage Sabotage: Editorial," *Unpopular Review* 6 (July-September 1916): 219–20.

31. Jeannette Rankin was a committed pacifist. Catt condemned her for her negative vote in Congress, saying it would "set woman suffrage back twenty years." Alice Paul expressed her support to Rankin the night before the vote. "The Congresswoman. Act I," *Woman's Protest* 10, no. 6 (April 1917): 5; Melanie Gustafson, "Partisan Women in the Progressive Era: The Struggle for Inclusion in American Political Parties," *Journal of Women's History* 9, no. 2 (Summer 1997): 171–72; Lunardini, *From Equal Suffrage to Equal Rights*, 113–14.

32. There are many examples of criticizing suffragists as unpatriotic and traitorous during the 1915–1917 campaign. Brooklyn *Daily Eagle,* September 28, 1917, folder 4, Ida Harper Scrapbook, Manuscripts and Archives Division, New York Public Library, New York, N.Y.

33. "Suffragists Traitors to Democracy," *Woman's Protest* 8, no. 2 (December 1915): 6.

34. "Suffragists' Machine Perfected in All States under Mrs. Catt's Rule," *New York Times,* April 29, 1917.

35. They suffered this dilemma throughout 1916 and 1917. Alice Hill Chittenden, "Our Duty to the State," *Woman's Protest* 10, no. 6 (April 1917): 3.

36. "Antis Elect Officers," *New York Times,* December 7, 1915.

37. "A Call for Concentration," *Woman's Protest* 8, no. 5 (March 1916): 4.

38. "States' Evidence Against Woman Suffrage," *Woman's Protest* 8, no. 6 (April 1916): 12; "The Anti-Suffrage Campaigns: New York," *Woman's Protest* 9, no. 6 (October 1916): 15.

39. "To the Editor of the Star," SC 13339, box 1, NYSA.

40. Mrs. Arthur M. Dodge, "Anti-Suffrage Claims," *New York Times,* November 10, 1916.

41. Susan Henry, *Anonymous in Their Own Names: Doris E. Fleischman, Ruth Hale, and Jane Grant* (Nashville, Tenn.: Vanderbilt University Press, 2012), 85–8.

42. "The Anti-Suffrage Campaigns: New York," *Woman's Protest* 9, no. 6 (October 1916): 14–15.

43. "Notes From the States: New York," *Woman's Protest* 10, no 3 (January 1917): 14.

44. "Notes From the States: New York," *Woman's Protest* 10, no. 4 (February 1917): 14.

45. "States' Evidence against Woman Suffrage," *Woman's Protest* 8, no. 6 (April 1916): 12.

46. "The Progress of the Anti-Suffrage Movement: New York," *Woman's Protest* 9, no. 4 (August 1916): 13; Mrs. Nelson H[enry] to Henry F. H. Brereton, Jan. 7, 1916, SC 13339, box 1, NYSA.

47. Wesser, *Response to Progressivism*, 180.

48. Van Voris, *Carrie Chapman Catt*, 143.

49. "Suffrage Bill Goes Before Assembly," *New York Times,* February 23, 1916.

50. "Suffrage Tactics Protest," *New York Times,* March 19, 1916.

51. "States' Evidence against Woman Suffrage," *Woman's Protest* 8, no. 6 (April 1916): 12.

52. "The Progress of the Anti-Suffrage Movement: New York," *Woman's Protest* 9, no. 5 (September 1916): 14.

53. "The Anti-Suffrage Campaigns: New York," *Woman's Protest* 9 no. 6 (October 1916): 14.

54. Morgan, *Suffragists and Democrats*, 107–10.

55. "Mrs. Mackay Opens Campaign at Albany," *New York Times,* January 26, 1916. Hughes was governor of New York from 1907 to 1910.

56. Quote is from "A Visit to Mr. Hughes," *Woman's Protest* 9, no. 3 (July 1916): 9. See also Mrs. Wm. Forse Scott, "Mr. Hughes and Suffrage," *New York Times,* August 6, 1916.

57. Mrs. Wm. Forse Scott, "Mr. Hughes and Suffrage," *New York Times,* August 6, 1916.

58. Margaret Finnegan, *Selling Suffrage: Consumer Culture & Votes for Women* (New York: Columbia University Press, 1999), 47, 11.

59. "Criticizes Hughes Party," *New York Times,* September 24, 1916. Two scrapbooks compiled by Harriet Vittum in the collection of Northwestern University Archives, Evanston, Ill. provide a record of the Hughes campaign train.

60. Gustafson, "Partisan Women," 165–71.

61. Quotes are from "Our First National Convention," *Woman's Protest* 9 no. 6 (October 1916): 3. See also "Anti-Suffragists Move," *New York Times,* December 3, 1916; "Notes on the Year's Work," *Woman's Protest* 10, no. 2 (December 1916): 14.

62. Quote from "Add[endum] Anti-Suffrage Convention," box 1, file 1, Woman's Suffrage and Women's Rights Collection, VC. See also "Two Anti-Suffragists," *New York Times,* December 10, 1916; "Root and Gibbons Oppose Suffrage," *New York Times,* December 8, 1916; Elihu Root, "Federal Amendment: A Destruction of the Right of Self Government . . . read at the convention of the National Association Opposed to Woman Suffrage, Washington, D.C., December 7, 1916."

63. "Add[endum] Anti-Suffrage Convention," Woman's Suffrage, box 1, file 1, VC. General Leonard Wise was supposed to speak but was unable to attend.

64. Box 8, Mabel Thorp Boardman Papers, Manuscript Division, Library of Congress, Washington, D.C. See also Gwendolyn Shealy, *A Critical History of the American Red Cross, 1882–1945* (Lewiston: Mellen, 2003), 41.

65. "Add[endum] Anti-Suffrage Convention," box 1, file 1, Woman's Suffrage and Women's Rights Collection, VC; "Mabel Thorp Boardman," *Biographical Cyclopaedia of American Women,* vol. 1 (New York: Halvord, 1924): 104. Boardman was the "archenemy" of Clara Barton, the founder of the Red Cross; her efforts resulted in Barton's resignation from the Red Cross in 1904. Boardman exerted increasing influence over the organization. Shealy, *A Critical History of the American Red Cross, 1882–1945,* 39–48, 54–56, 62; Steinson, *American Women's Activism in World War I,* 166.

66. Steinson, *American Women's Activism in World War I,* 170.

67. Louis Frederick Huidekoper, "Women and Preparedness," *Woman's Protest* 10, no. 2 (December 1916): 5–6.

68. "The State Campaigns," *Woman's Protest* 10, no. 6 (April 1917): 14; "New York State Activities," *Woman's Protest* 11, no. 1 (May 1917): 14; "Notes From the States: New York," *Woman's Protest* 11, no. 5 (October 1917): 14.

69. "The Anti-Suffrage Campaigns: New York," *Woman's Protest* 10, no. 1 (November 1916): 14.

70. Quote is from "Notes on the Year's Work," *Woman's Protest* 10, no. 2 (December 1916): 14. See also "The Anti-Suffrage Campaigns: New York," *Woman's Protest* 10, no. 1 (November 1916): 14; "Anti-Suffragists Move," *New York Times,* December 3, 1916.

71. Alice Hill Chittenden, "Our Duty to the State," *Woman's Protest* 10, no. 6 (April 1917): 3.

72. "Notes From the States: New York," *Woman's Protest* 10, no. 4 (February 1917): 14.

73. "The State Campaigns: New York," *Woman's Protest* 10, no. 5 (March 1917): 14.

74. "New York State Activities," *Woman's Protest* 11, no. 1 (May 1917): 14.

75. "Notes From the States: New York," *Woman's Protest* 11, no. 3 (July-August 1917): 12; "Notes From the States: New York," *Woman's Protest* 11, no. 4 (September 1917): 18.

76. "The Anti-Suffrage Campaigns: New York," *Woman's Protest* 9, no. 6 (October 1916): 15. Groton is eleven miles west of Cortland; Weedsport is about twenty-six miles west of Syracuse.

77. "Debates and Woman Suffrage," *Woman's Protest* 9, no. 6 (October 1916): 9; "The Anti-Suffrage Campaigns: New York," *Woman's Protest* 9, no. 6 (October 1916): 15.

78. "Notes from the States: New York," *Woman's Protest* 10, no. 3 (January 1917): 14.

79. "The State Campaigns: New York," *Woman's Protest* 8, no. 5 (March 1916): 17; "States' Evidence against Woman Suffrage: New York," *Woman's Protest* 8, no. 6 (April 1916): 12.

80. "The Active Opposition to Woman Suffrage: New York," *Woman's Protest* 9, no.1 (May 1916): 12.

81. Quote is from "Pose as Posters at Vanity Fete," *New York Times,* February 8, 1917. See also "Notes from the States: New York," *Woman's Protest* 10, no. 4 (February 1917): 14; "Anti-Suffragists to Give Vanity Fete," *New York Times,* January 21, 1917; "Junior Anti-Suffrage League Fete," *New York Times,* January 28, 1917.

82. "New York State Activities," *Woman's Protest* 11, no. 1 (May 1917): 14.

83. "Notes from the States: New York," *Woman's Protest* 11, no. 2 (June 1917): 12.

84. "Every Calling in the Line," *New York Times,* May 14, 1916; "Notes from the States: New York," *Woman's Protest* 11, no. 2 (June 1917): 12.

85. "Anti-Suffrage—For Patriotism and Preparedness," *Woman's Protest* 9, no. 2 (June 1916): 5.

86. Quotes are from "Opposes Suffrage Parade," *New York Times,* October 4, 1917. See also "Suffragists Parade Today," *New York Times,* October 27, 1917; "20,000 March in Suffrage Line," *New York Times,* October 28, 1917; Linda J. Lumsden, *Rampant Women: Suffragists and the Right of Assembly* (Knoxville: University of Tennessee Press, 1997), 86. Alice Hill Chittenden used the parade as another opportunity to criticize suffragists for refusing to debate. Alice Hill Chittenden, "Suffrage Claims," *New York Times,* November 5, 1917; Steinson, *American Women's Activism in World War I,* 214–15.

87. National American Woman Suffrage Association, *Victory,* 117.

88. Alice Hill Chittenden, "The Fat Suffrage Purse," *New York Times,* June 27, 1916.

89. "The State Campaigns," *Woman's Protest* 10, no. 6 (April 1917): 14.

90. Marshall, *Splintered Sisterhood,* 200.

91. "Notes from the States: New York," *Woman's Protest* 10, no. 3 (January 1917): 14; "Notes from the States: New York," *Woman's Protest* 10, no. 4 (February 1917): 14; "Junior Anti-Suffrage League Fete," *New York Times,* January 28, 1917; "Pose as Posters at Vanity Fete," *New York Times,* February 8, 1917.

92. "The Progress of the Anti-Suffrage Movement: New York," *Woman's Protest* 9, no. 4 (August 1916): 13; "The Anti-Suffrage Campaigns: New York," *Woman's Protest* 9, no. 6 (October 1916): 15.

93. "The Anti-Suffrage Campaigns: New York," *Woman's Protest* 9, no. 6 (October 1916): 15. Warrensburg is sixty-seven miles north of Albany.

94. For example, suffragists took out a quarter-page advertisement in the 1916 program of the Paris Hill Fair, held annually in September from 1905 to 1937 in the "remote country hamlet" near Utica. Miss Jennie Jones, whom locals called the "mayor" of Paris Hill, and the one responsible for organizing the fair, wrote to the suffragists the following year, explaining that anti-suffragists were taking a full-page advertisement in the program, shrewdly suggesting that suffragists would also want to buy an advertisement, which they ultimately did. "Presidential Candidates Declare for Woman Suffrage," *Souvenir Programme, Eleventh Annual Paris Hill Fair and Institute* (Utica: Purvis, 1916): n.p.; "As a War Measure" and "Anti-Suffrage Notes," *Souvenir Programme, Twelfth Annual Paris Hill Fair and Institute* (Utica: Purvis, 1917): n.p.; Newspaper clippings, n.d. [1914] and "Miss Jennie C. Jones Dies in Home," newspaper clipping, June 25, 1943 collection of Lincoln Davis Museum, Paris Station, N.Y. Jennie C. Jones to Mrs. Samuel J. Bens, July 26, 1917, New York State Woman Suffrage Party Collection, Manuscripts and Archives Division, New York Public Library, New York, N.Y. Edna Townsend, a local historian, assisted the author with this research.

95. "Notes From the States: New York," *Woman's Protest* 11, no. 3 (July-August 1917): 12; "Notes from the States: New York," *Woman's Protest* 11, no. 4 (September 1917): 18.

96. Steinson, *American Women's Activism in World War I,* 210–11.

97. "Anti-Suffrage and Preparedness," n.d., LSHS. See also "'America First'—For Home and Humanity," *Woman's Protest* 9, no. 3 (July 1916): 3.

98. "Anti-Suffrage Aid to Preparedness: New York," *Woman's Protest* 9, no. 3 (July 1916): 13–14; "The Progress of the Anti-Suffrage Movement: New York," *Woman's Protest* 9, no. 4 (August 1916): 13.

99. "The State Campaigns: New York," *Woman's Protest* 8, no. 4 (February 1916): 17; "Anti-Suffragist in War Relief Work," *Woman's Protest* 11, no. 2 (June 1917): 8.

100. Meyer's dilemma regarding war is apparent in several articles in the collection of scrapbooks she kept. ANM Papers.

101. Newspaper clippings in scrapbook in folder 1 (1913–1918), box 20, ANM Papers.

102. "Women Organize Canteen," *New York Times,* March 31, 1917; "The National League for Woman's Service," *Woman's Protest* 10 no. 4 (February 1917): 3; "The National League for Woman's Service," *Woman's Protest* 10 no. 6 (April 1917): 3.

103. By November 1917, the Motor Corps separated from the league to form the Motor Corps of America. Apparently, under the league, the women were too often asked to perform taxi service, not necessarily official governmental business. "Women Motorists at Government's Call," *New York Times,* September 16, 1917; "War Motorists Scorn Taxi Work," *New York Times,* November 19, 1917.

104. Steinson, *American Women's Activism in World War I*, 305.

105. "The National League for Woman's Service," *Woman Patriot* 1, no. 1 (April 27, 1918): 6.

106. Dorothy Schneider and Carl J. Schneider, *American Women in the Progressive Era, 1900–1920* (New York: Anchor, 1994), 243.

107. Anna Howard Shaw, "NAWSA Convention, Washington, D.C., December 12–15, 1917," document 80 in *The Concise History of Woman Suffrage: Selections from the Classic Work of Stanton, Anthony, Gage, and Harper,* ed. Mari Jo Buhle and Paul Buhle, eds. (Urbana: University of Illinois Press, 1978), 140. Quoted in Schneider and Schneider, *American Women in the Progressive Era*, 214.

108. Graham, *New Democracy*, 103; David M. Kennedy, *Over Here: The First World War and American Society* (New York: Oxford University Press, 2004), 286; Schneider and Schneider, *American Women in the Progressive Era*, 213–16, 220, 243; Steinson, *American Women's Activism in World War I*, 309.

109. According to her biographer, the decision to dedicate the services of the National American Woman Suffrage Association was one of the most difficult ones Catt, a fervent pacifist, had ever made, and one for which she received the most criticism. Catt and Shuler, *Woman Suffrage and Politics*, 294; Steinson, *American Women's Activism in World War I*, 237–38; Van Voris, *Carrie Chapman Catt*, 136–39. "14 Points," leaflet, box 5, folder 9, Suffrage Collection, Series I, United States, Organizations, National American Woman Suffrage Association: Publications: Leaflets, 1913–19, SSC. Harriot Stanton Blatch remarked in her autobiography that Wilson was an anti-suffragist, "but sufficient of a politician to wish to hide the fact." Harriot Stanton Blatch and Alma Lutz, *Challenging Years: The Memoirs of Harriot Stanton Blatch* (New York: Putnam's, 1940), 249–50.

110. Suffragists also worked with the Red Cross, even including "contingents of Red Cross women, office workers, and 'farmerettes'" in their suffrage parades. "Pilgrims for

Peace to Visit Congress," *New York Times,* February 9, 1917; Graham, *New Democracy,* 105; Steinson, *American Women's Activism in World War I,* 236–37.

111. James P. Louis, "Josephine Marshall Jewell Dodge," *Notable American Women, 1607–1950: A Biographical Dictionary,* vol. 1, ed. Edward T. James (Cambridge: Belknap, 1971): 492–93; Benjamin, *History of the Anti-Suffrage Movement,* 266.

112. "Our New Headquarters in Washington," *Woman's Protest* 11, no. 3 (July–August 1917): 3.

113. Dodge continued as vice president of the New York State Association Opposed to Woman Suffrage until January 1918. *Woman's Protest* 11, no. 7 (January 1918): 2.

114. "Alice Hay Wadsworth," *Biographical Cyclopaedia of American Women,* ed. Mabel Ward Cameron (New York: Halvord: 1924): 32; "Alice Hay Wadsworth," *Woman's Who's Who of America, 1914–1915,* ed. John William Leonard (New York: American Commonwealth, 1914): 843.

115. Kenton J. Clymer, "Hay, John Milton," http://www.anb.org/articles/05/05-00888.html; *American National Biography Online* (accessed June 30, 2012).

116. Mrs. James W. Wadsworth Jr. "Case Against Suffrage," *New York Times,* September 9, 1917: 55.

117. "Off for Suffrage Battle," *New York Times,* March 2, 1917; "New Head for the Antis," *New York Times,* July 1, 1917.

118. "Anti-Suffrage Work to Go On," *New York Times,* February 18, 1917. Many of the men who belonged to the men's anti-suffrage association were also on the executive committee of the Mayor's Committee on National Defense. "To the Citizens of New York," *New York Times,* March 13, 1917.

119. Henry A. Wise Wood, "Government a Man's Job," *Woman's Protest* 11, no. 1 (May 1917): 3.

120. "Anti-Suffrage—For Positive Patriotism," *Woman's Protest* 11, no. 1 (May 1917): 5. For more on the jingoism of the period, see the conclusion of Kristin L. Hoganson, *Fighting for American Manhood: How Gender Politics Provoked the Spanish-American and Philippine-American Wars* (New Haven, Conn.: Yale University Press, 1998): 200–208. For more on male fears of effeminacy, see Adam Rome, "'Political Hermaphrodites': Gender and Environmental Reform in Progressive America, *Environmental History* 11, no. 3 (July 2006): 440–63.

121. Marshall, *Splintered Sisterhood,* 203.

122. *Philadelphia Inquirer,* April 27, 1915; *Philadelphia Inquirer,* October 29, 1915; *Oregonian,* January 31, 1917; "Organized Manufacturers vs. Organized Women," *Life and Labor Bulletin* 3, no. 9 (May 1925): 1; Kathryn Kish Sklar and Beverly Wilson Palmer, eds., *The Selected Letters of Florence Kelley, 1869–1931* (Urbana: University of Illinois Press, 2009), 288.

123. Quotes are from Eichelberger to Everett P. Wheeler, letter fragment, n.d. [1916?], folder 2, box 8, EPW Papers.

124. "Anti-Suffrage Men Unite," *New York Times,* September 28, 1917.

125. "Notes from the States," *Woman's Protest* 11, no. 3 (July–August 1917): 12.

126. Alice Hill Chittenden, "Our Duty to the State," *Woman's Protest* 10, no. 6 (April 1917): 3.

127. "Notes From the States: New York," *Woman's Protest* 11, no. 5 (October 1917): 14–15.

128. Graham, *New Democracy*, 111.

129. Woodrow Wilson to Carrie Chapman Catt, copy of letter dated October 13, 1917, Carrie Chapman Catt Papers, Series II, Correspondence, Incoming, Woodrow Wilson, 1917–20, SSC; C. K. McFarland and Nevin E. Neal, "The Reluctant Reformer: Woodrow Wilson and Woman Suffrage, 1913–1920," *Rocky Mountain Social Science Journal* 11 (April 1974): 33, 41–42; Morgan, *Suffragists and Democrats*, 112–14; Steinson, *American Women's Activism in World War I*, 315–16.

130. Alice Hill Chittenden, "Woman's Service or Woman Suffrage," *Woman's Protest* 11, no. 1 (May 1917): 5; Mrs. Barclay Hazard, "Penalizing Patriotism," *Woman's Protest* 11, no. 2 (June 1917): 5; "Anti-Suffragist in War Relief Work," *Woman's Protest* 11, no. 2 (June 1917): 8; "A Letter to the Governor of New York," *Woman's Protest* 11, no. 4 (September 1917): 17.

131. "Suffragists Calm in Face of Defeat," *New York Times,* September 12, 1917.

132. National American Woman Suffrage Association, *Victory*, 118.

133. "Suffrage Outlook Dark Up the State," *New York Times,* November 4, 1917; "Antis Again Attack Suffrage Leaders," *New York Times,* October 21, 1917; "'Antis' Give Benefit for Army Christmas" and "Gerard Tells Why Women Should Vote," *New York Times,* November 4, 1917.

134. National American Woman Suffrage Association, *Victory*, 119–20.

135. James Malcolm, ed. *New York Red Book* (Albany: Lyon, 1918): 649; New York (State) Department of State, *Manual for the Use of the Legislature of the State of New York* (Albany: Department of State, 1918): 819–20.

136. Baker, *Moral Frameworks of Public Life*, 146.

137. The counties included Bronx, Kings, Nassau, New York, Putnam, Queens, Richmond, Rockland, Suffolk, and Westchester.

138. Doris Daniels, "Building a Winning Coalition: The Suffrage Fight in New York State," *New York History* 60 (January 1979): 79; Jablonsky, "Duty, Nature, and Stability," 94.

139. The copy and proofs for the *Woman's Protest* for December 1917 were apparently lost in the mail from Washington to New York; that issue probably published the results. "Diagram of Official New York Vote," *Woman's Protest* (February 1918): 8–9.

140. "Suffrage Fight Won in Cities," *New York Times,* November 8, 1917.

141. Rochester had apparently forgotten Susan B. Anthony, who lived in the city most of her life. "Suffrage Made Gains Up-State," *New York Times,* November 7, 1917; "Suffrage Fight Won in the Cities," *New York Times,* November 8, 1917; "Women Win Vote in New York State by 100,000," *Binghamton Press*, November 7, 1917; "Local Suffragists Overjoyed at Victory in City and State," *Buffalo Evening News,* November 7, 1917; *Niagara Falls Gazette*, November 7, 1917; "Republicans Elect City and

County Ticket," *Times Union,* November 7, 1917; "Suffragists Lose County, but Gain Substantially over Vote Cast in 1915," *Rochester Herald,* November 7, 1917; "State and County Election Results," *Troy Record,* November 7, 1917; "Tuesday's Election Results," *Skaneateles Free Press,* November 9, 1917.

142. New York (State), Department of State, *Manual for the Use of the Legislature of the State of New York* (Albany: Department of State, 1918): 819–20; Barbara Shupe, Janet Steins, and Jyoti Pandit, *New York State Population: A Compilation of Federal Census Data* (New York: Neal-Schuman, 1987); "Suffrage Made Gains Up-State," *New York Times,* November 7, 1917; "Suffrage Fight in the Cities," *New York Times,* November 8, 1917; Baker, *Moral Frameworks of Public Life,* 146.

143. "New Suffrage Drive Planned By Women," *New York Times,* November 7, 1917.

144. Graham, *New Democracy,* 112.

145. National American Woman Suffrage Association, *Victory,* 120.

146. John D. Buenker, "The Urban Political Machine and Woman Suffrage: A Study in Political Adaptability," *Historian* 33 (February 1971): 264.

147. Ibid., 277.

148. McDonagh and Price, "Woman Suffrage in the Progressive Era," 430n36.

149. NAWSA eventually received almost $1,000,000 from the Leslie Estate, a sum far less than that bequeathed by Mrs. Frank Leslie. In spite of Leslie's great care in drawing up her will, clearly leaving the bulk of her estate to Carrie Chapman Catt for the suffrage campaign, the "legal welter" related to the Leslie fortune was settled only at a great cost to the suffragists. Half a million dollars went to the "settlement of claims not recognized by Mrs. Leslie in her will," the executors got $20,000, the lawyers of the executors got $190,000, and it was two and a half years before Catt received the first installment of the inheritance. Van Voris, *Carrie Chapman Catt,* 144–45; Rose Young, *The Record of the Leslie Woman Suffrage Commission, Inc., 1917–1929* (New York: Leslie Woman Suffrage Commission, 1929), 59–62, 91.

150. "Woman Suffrage," *New York Times,* November 7, 1917.

151. Michael E. McGerr, *The Decline of Popular Politics: The American North, 1865–1928* (New York: Oxford University Press, 1986), 185–86.

152. Quotes are from "Declares Pacifists Helped Women to Win," *New York Times,* November 8, 1917. See also "Sees Suffragists All Turning Anti," *New York Times,* November 16, 1917.

153. "Anti-Suffragists Not Ashamed" *Woman's Protest* 11, no. 6 (November 1917): 4.

154. "How Pro-Germans and Pacifists Carried Suffrage in New York," *Woman's Protest* 11, no. 6 (November 1917): 4.

155. Daniels, "Building a Winning Coalition," 80.

156. Wesser, *Response to Progressivism,* 201.

157. New York (State), Department of State, *Manual for the Use of the Legislature of the State of New York* (Albany: Department of State, 1918): 819–20; McDonagh and Price, "Woman Suffrage in the Progressive Era," 430.

158. Maud Wood Park, *Front Door Lobby* (Boston: Beacon, 1960), 120–21.

159. Graham, *New Democracy,* 114.

160. National American Woman Suffrage Association, *Victory*, 120.

161. Marshall, *Splintered Sisterhood*, 203.

162. Quote is from "For and Against Equal Suffrage," *New York Times*, May 11, 1912.

Chapter 5. Using Enfranchisement to Fight Woman Suffrage, 1917–1932

1. Lyman Abbott, "Anti-Suffragists and Suffragists in New York," *Outlook* 117 (November 28, 1917): 487.

2. "New Suffrage Drive Planned by Women," *New York Times*, November 7, 1917; "Declares Pacifists Helped Women to Win," *New York Times*, November 8, 1917; "Sees Suffragists All Turning Anti," *New York Times*, November 16, 1917; "New York's Antis Go Out of Business," *New York [Sun?]*, November 16, 1917, Scrapbook, p. 51, box 20, folder 1, ANM Papers.

3. Alice Hill Chittenden to Mrs. E. Remington, December 5, 1917, LSHS. See also "No Peace Prospect in Suffrage Victory," *New York Times*, November 24, 1917.

4. Abbott, "Anti-Suffragists and Suffragists," 487.

5. "Antis Renew War on Suffragists," *New York Times*, March 24, 1918; "Repeal of Suffrage Sought by Women," *New York Times*, April 3, 1918.

6. "Their Golden Wedding," *New York Times*, May 23, 1918; "War Hostesses," *Chicago Daily Tribune*, August 25, 1918; "Alice Chittenden of the Red Cross Dead," *New York Times*, October 3, 1945.

7. "Miss Mary Kilbreth," *New York Times*, June 28, 1957.

8. "Notes on the Year's Work," *Woman's Protest* 10, no. 2 (December 1916): 14; "Notes from the States: New York," *Woman's Protest* 11, no. 4 (September 1917): 18; "A New National President," *Woman Patriot* 3, no. 13 (July 12, 1919): 2; "Island News Notes," *Suffolk County [Sayville] News* (September 13, 1918): 6.

9. Mary G. Kilbreth, "A Distinct Political Issue," *Woman's Protest* 10, no. 1 (November 1916): 10; "Sex War Threatened by Suffrage Action," *Woman Patriot* 1, no. 8 (June 15, 1918): 3; "Childless Women Politicians," *Woman Patriot* 1, no. 17 (August 17, 1918): 4.

10. "No Peace Prospect in Suffrage Victory," *New York Times*, November 24, 1917.

11. "Antis to Continue Fight on Suffrage," *New York Times*, September 18, 1919.

12. "Open Letter to Chairman Will H. Hays," *New York Times*, January 18, 1919.

13. "New York Suffrage Accepted by Antis," *New York Times*, May 9, 1918.

14. Quote is from "Anti Sees Danger in Woman Autocracy," *New York Times*, January 12, 1918. See also "The Repeal of Suffrage Sought by Women," *New York Times*, April 3, 1918; "A Vision of the Last March," *New York Times*, September 14, 1919; "Women Boost War League," *New York Times*, July 3, 1921; "Honor Roll of Representatives," *Woman's Protest* 11, no. 7 (January 1918): 2; "A Symposium of Fundamental Principles," *Woman's Protest* (February 1918): 1–3; "The Repeal of Suffrage in New York," *Woman's Protest* (February 1918): 11; "Anti-Suffragists to Wage Unceasing War against Feminism and Socialism," *Woman Patriot* 1, no. 1 (April 27, 1918): 2; "Fair

Play," *Woman Patriot* 1, no. 6 (June 1, 1918): 3; "Petition from the Women Voters Anti-Suffrage Party of New York to the United States Senate," [1918], available at http://www.archives.gov/education/lessons/woman-suffrage/ny-petition.html (accessed June 30, 2012); Mrs. Benjamin Aymar Sands, Secretary, to members of Women Voters' Anti-Suffrage Party, SC 13339, box 1, NYSA.

   15. "Antis Renew War on Suffragists," *New York Times,* March 24, 1918.

   16. "New York Suffrage Accepted by Antis," *New York Times,* May 9, 1918; "Topics of the Times: Wise Action Taken By the 'Antis,'" *New York Times,* May 10, 1918; "Suffragist Camouflage," *Woman Patriot* 3, no. 5 (May 17, 1919): 4.

   17. "Anti-Suffrage Women Voters May Swing New York Elections: 'Cazenovia Idea' Is Latest Move," *Woman Patriot* 1, no. 12 (July 13, 1918): 1–2. It was called the "Cazenovia Idea" because Helen Fairchild lived in Cazenovia.

   18. Mary Kilbreth headed the Democratic section. Quote is from "New York State Women Enroll," *Woman Patriot* 1, no. 5 (May 25, 1918): 1. See also "Women Voters' Anti-Suffrage Party," *Woman Patriot* 1, no. 3 (May 11, 1918): 6; "Mrs. Henry Wise Wood Scores Suffragists for National Delay," *Woman Patriot* 1, no. 4 (May 18, 1918): 5.

   19. Quote is from "Appeal to United States Senate from Anti-Suffrage Women Voters," *Woman Patriot* 1, no. 10 (June 29, 1918): 3. See also "Antis Send Protest to the President," *New York Times,* August 12, 1918; "War and Woman Suffrage," *New York Times,* August 13, 1918; "Time Worn Statements," *New York Times,* August 14, 1918.

   20. "Suffrage Federal Amendment: Open Letter to the President of the United States from the Women Voters' Anti-Suffrage Party," *New York Times,* August 12, 1918; "Another Open Letter to Will Hays From Republican 'Antis,'" *Woman Patriot* 2, no. 12 (March 22, 1919): 3; "Anti-Suffrage Women Voters," *Woman Patriot* 3, no. 2 (April 26, 1919): 2; *Woman Patriot* (May 11, 1918), 6.

   21. Jablonsky conjectures that the membership never exceeded two hundred thousand, and that the seven hundred thousand membership declared was the result of the tendency of the organization to include the "silent majority" of women who did not publicly state their views on suffrage. Jablonsky, *Home, Heaven, and Mother Party,* 84–85.

   22. "Suffrage and Women's Ideals," *New York Times,* May 13, 1913.

   23. "Anti-Suffragists in a National Union," *New York Times,* November 29, 1911; "Protecting the Needy against Tragedies of the Law," *New York Times,* November 10, 1912; "Women's Bitter Wail," *New York Times,* November 10, 1912. There seems also to have been a short-lived National Anti-Suffrage Association using the address PO Box 2617, Boston, Mass. At least one letter, September 21, 1916, used the letterhead (SC 13339, box 1, NYSA).

   24. "Anti-Suffragists in a National Union," *New York Times,* November 29, 1911; Jablonsky, *Home, Heaven, and Mother Party,* 60, 84–85.

   25. Harper, *History of Woman Suffrage 5,* 679.

   26. Mrs. Arthur M. Dodge, letter (October 7, 1916) in the collection of the Maine Historical Society, Portland, Maine, announced that "on Wednesday, December 6th,

this association will hold its first national convention at Washington, D.C." The first convention of the National Association Opposed to Woman Suffrage," *Woman's Protest* (December 1916): 4. Copies of some of the speeches are in box 1, file 1, Woman's Suffrage and Women's Rights Collection, Special Collections, VC.

27. Julia T. Waterman, "Why the Suffragists Argue Their Case before Congressional Committees, *Woman's Protest* 1, no. 1 (May 1912): 11; Harper, *History of Woman Suffrage* 5, 355, 363.

28. "This is Anti-Suffrage Day," *New York Times,* April 19, 1913.

29. Quote is from "Congressional Hearing," *Woman's Protest* 3, no. 1 (May 1913): 4. See also "Senate Hears from Foes of Suffrage," *New York Times,* April 20, 1913.

30. Jablonsky, *Home, Heaven, and Mother Party*, 35.

31. Eleanor Foster Lansing attended Smith College from 1885 to 1886. Robert Lansing served as Wilson's Secretary of State from 1915 to 1920. Smith College Archives, Smith College, Northampton, Mass.; "Off for Suffrage Battle," *New York Times,* March 2, 1917.

32. "Federal Amendment Hearings," *Woman's Protest* 11, no. 1 (May 1917): 8.

33. Jablonsky contends that Wadsworth was a "relative neophyte" for the office, which she was, but he apparently attached little significance to the influence of her husband on the national anti-suffrage organization. Jablonsky, *Home, Heaven, and Mother Party*, 97.

34. "Our Second Annual Convention," *Woman's Protest* 11, no. 7 (January 1918): 5.

35. *Woman's Protest* 11, no. 3 (July-August 1917): 1. Until Wadsworth was no longer editor, photographs of prominent anti-suffragists graced the front cover of each issue.

36. "To Uphold and Defend the Constitution of the United States Against all Foreign and Domestic Enemies," *Woman's Protest* 11, no. 6 (November 1917): 3 (emphasis in the original).

37. Quotes are from "Our New National Newspaper," *Woman's Protest* (February 1918): 17. It appears that in spite of the announcement, the *Remonstrance* did not actually merge with the *Woman's Protest*, as they continued publishing until 1920. Apparently there were a number of complaints about the newspaper format, for by April 1919, the editors announced another format, as well as a price increase. The new format was remarkably like that of the *Woman's Protest*. "Notice to Subscribers," *Woman Patriot* 2, no. 15 (April 12, 1919): 4 (emphasis in the original).

38. Kristy Maddux, "When Patriots Protest: The Anti-Suffrage Discursive Transformation of 1917," *Rhetoric & Public Affairs* 7, no. 3 (2004): 295.

39. Anti-suffragists were proud of their contributing editors, for most of them were very well known. For example, in 1918, Watterson, an important Southern journalist, won a Pulitzer Prize for his two editorials supporting entry into World War I. Anna Katharine Green was a popular novelist. Octave Thanet, the pseudonym of Alice French (1850–1934), was a popular magazine contributor. According to Jill Gage, the reference librarian at the Newberry Library in Chicago, nothing in French's papers indicates any affiliation with the Woman Patriot Publishing Company or Mary G. Kilbreth. Elizabeth Ogden Wood was married to Henry A. Wise Wood of the Na-

tional Security League. Annie Nathan Meyer stepped down as a contributing editor by May 1919. The business manager was J. S. Eichelberger, whose name first appeared in the January 1917 *Woman's Protest*. "Statement of the Ownership, Management, Circulation, Etc., Required by the Act of Congress of August 24, 1912, of The Woman Patriot," *Woman Patriot* 1, no. 24 (October 5, 1918): 2. Margaret C. Robinson was a Massachusetts anti-suffrage leader and longtime president of the Massachusetts Public Interests League. It is not clear how closely connected the contributors were to anti-suffrage activities and ideals, and few articles in the journal are signed unless they were reprinted from other sources. Kim E. Nielsen, *Un-American Womanhood: Antiradicalism, Antifeminism, and the First Red Scare* (Columbus: Ohio State University Press, 2001), 61–72.

40. "Political Embroilment Means Degradation of Womanhood," *Woman Patriot* 3, no. 21 (September 6, 1919): 2. Carter Glass was vice president from April 1918 until May 1919, when his name was removed from the masthead. He was a newspaper editor from Lynchburg, Virginia, the prominent head of a major Democratic faction, and he succeeded McAdoo as Secretary of the Treasury. He does not seem to have done much more than lend his name to the anti-suffrage organization. He apparently switched sides on woman suffrage, prompting the *Woman Patriot* to condemn him as "the Benedict Arnold of the anti-suffragists." "Carter Glass and Benedict Arnold," *Woman Patriot* 4, no. 33 (August 14, 1920): 4–5; "To the Manhood of the Democratic Party," *Woman Patriot* 5, nos. 8 and 9 (February 26, 1921): 3. James Callaway, editor of the Macon, GA *Telegraph*, became vice-president in October 1919, according to the masthead of the *Woman Patriot* 3, no. 25 (October 4, 1919): 4. His name last appeared on the masthead in the April 10 issue. He died on April 10, 1920. *Woman Patriot* 4, no. 15 (April 10, 1920): 4; "James Callaway, Southern Martyr," *Woman Patriot* 4, no. 16 (April 17, 1920): 8.

41. "Wanted: Correspondents and Local Representatives," *Woman Patriot* 1, no. 8 (June 15 1918): 2.

42. "Anti-Suffragists to Wage Unceasing War against Feminism and Socialism," *Woman Patriot* 1, no. 1 (April 27, 1918): 2 (emphasis in the original).

43. This was one of only two articles Meyer signed while she was a contributing editor for the *Woman Patriot*. "The Moment for Self-Defense," *Woman Patriot* 1, no. 1 (April 27, 1918): 4.

44. "Women to Register First in New York," *Woman Patriot* 1, no. 2 (May 4, 1918): 7; "Anti-Suffrage Women Lead in Enrollment," and "Women Enroll to Defeat Suffragists," *Woman Patriot* 1, no. 7 (June 8, 1918): 6.

45. "Red Cross to Use Anti Headquarters," *Woman Patriot* 1, no. 4 (May 18, 1918): 1.

46. See, for example, "Red Cross Asks for More Kits and Socks," *Woman Patriot* 1, no. 2 (May 4, 1918): 2.

47. "The National League for Woman's Service," *Woman Patriot* 1, no. 2 (May 4, 1918): 6.

48. Mrs. James W. Wadsworth Jr., "The Wane of Feminism," *Woman's Protest* 11, no. 5 (October 1917): 3. See also Mrs. James W. Wadsworth Jr., "For Home and Na-

tional Defense, Against Woman Suffrage, Feminism and Socialism," *Woman's Protest* (February 1918): 7.

49. "'Wadsworthians' Should Worry: There Being as Good Fish in the Sea and As Good Words in the Dictionary as Mrs. Catt Ever Caught," *Woman Patriot* 1, no. 1 (April 27, 1918): 3.

50. Martin L. Fausold, *James W. Wadsworth, Jr.* (Syracuse: Syracuse University Press, 1975), 106.

51. Mrs. James W. Wadsworth Jr. "Case against Suffrage," *New York Times,* September 9, 1917.

52. Quote is from "Foes of America: Questions for Mrs. Catt to Answer," *Woman's Protest* 11, no. 4 (September 1917): 16. See also "The Wane of Feminism," *Woman's Protest* 11, no. 5 (October 1917): 3; "Mrs. Catt and the Schwimmer Peace Plan, *Woman's Protest* 11, no. 5 (October 1917): 10–11; "Will Mrs. Catt Answer These Questions?" *Woman's Protest* 11, no. 6 (November 1917): 10–11; "A Public Challenge to Mrs. Catt," *Woman's Protest* (February 1918): 6; and "Absolutely False," and "But What are the Facts?" *Woman Patriot* 1, no. 3 (May 11, 1918): 7; Jablonsky, *Home, Heaven, and Mother Party*, 99.

53. "A Public Challenge to Mrs. Catt," *Woman's Protest* (February 1918): 6.

54. In May 1918, both Catt and Alice Wadsworth were named to a League for National Unity committee to assure that all candidates to the U.S. Congress were loyal citizens. "Strive for Congress 100 Per Cent. Loyal," *New York Times,* May 13, 1918.

55. Clement E. Vose, *Constitutional Change: Amendment Politics and Supreme Court Litigation since 1900* (Lexington: Lexington Books, 1972), 52.

56. Lemons, *The Woman Citizen: Social Feminism in the 1920s*, 210.

57. Jablonsky, *Home, Heaven, and Mother Party*, 95–99.

58. "Representing New York in the Senate," *Woman's Protest* (February 1918): 14.

59. "Some Information for Suffragists," and "Senator Wadsworth Explains Attitude," *Woman Patriot* 1, no. 4 (May 18, 1918): 7; "On Suffrage, Wadsworth Is No One-State Senator," *Woman Patriot* 1, no. 14 (July 27, 1918): 1.

60. "Our Second Annual Convention," *Woman's Protest* 11, no. 7 (January 1918): 5.

61. "A Letter to Members of Congress," *Woman's Protest* 11, no. 7 (January 1918): 6.

62. "Miss Boardman Says Best Type of Women Needed 'Over There,'" *Woman Patriot* 1, no. 10 (June 29, 1918): 5.

63. Quote is from "Some Simplified Statistics of Interest to All Patriots," *Woman Patriot* 1, no. 11 (July 6, 1918): 2. See also "Massachusetts 'Antis' Ask Referendum to Women," *Woman Patriot* 1, no. 9 (June 22, 1918): 6; Annie Nathan Meyer, "Interfering with the War," *Woman Patriot* 1, no. 12 (July 13, 1918): 4. An argument antis often used against suffrage was the increased cost of democracy—more voting booths, counting more votes, and other costs of doubling the electorate. See, for example, "Will You Help Save the United States Seventy Thousand Dollars A Day?" *Woman Patriot* 2, no. 13 (March 29, 1919): 8.

64. Anna Katherine Green, "Make This Your War," *Woman Patriot* 1, no. 1 (April 27, 1918): 1. See also "Washington News and Notes," *Woman's Protest* 11, no. 7 (January

1918): 9; "Anti-Suffragists to Wage Unceasing War against Feminism and Socialism," *Woman Patriot* 1, no. 1 (April 27, 1918): 2, 5; "The National League for Women's Service," *Woman Patriot* 1, no. 1 (April 27, 1918): 6.

65. "Anti-Suffragists in Convention Plan Dual Fight against Federal Suffrage Amendment and Red Flag," *Woman Patriot* 2, no. 2 (January 11, 1919): 1.

66. "Maintain American Morale," *Woman's Protest* (February 1918): 12; Keyssar, *Right to Vote*, 216.

67. "The Honor Roll of Representatives," *Woman's Protest* 11, no. 7 (January 1918): 3. Representatives Daniel J. Riordon of New York County, Norman J. Gould of Seneca County, and Archie D. Sanders of Genesee County voted against the woman suffrage amendment. Of these counties, only Seneca County came out against woman suffrage in 1917.

68. Wilson agreed to the idea of woman suffrage as a war measure the previous October. Morgan, *Suffragists and Democrats*, 112–14; Steinson, *American Women's Activism in World War I*, 315–16.

69. Jablonsky, *Home, Heaven, and Mother Party*, 92.

70. Graham, *New Democracy*, 101, 105.

71. Quote is from "The President and Woman Suffrage Policy," *Woman's Protest* (February 1918): 4. In spite of the president's support, in September 1918 the Senate voted the measure down. "Senate Defeats Woman Suffrage: Refuses to Jump on 'Band Wagon' Newly Painted as Chariot of War," *Woman Patriot* 1, no. 23 (September 28, 1918): 1.

72. "The President's Views on Suffrage," *Woman Patriot* 1, no. 9 (June 22, 1918): 4; "Women Voters' Anti-Suffrage Party Appeals to the President against Intolerable Distraction during War," *Woman Patriot* 1, no. 17 (August 17, 1918): 1; "Decries Women Delegates: Mrs. Wadsworth Wants None at Peace Table If for Suffrage," *New York Times*, November 17, 1918; "Wants Men to Make Peace," *New York Times*, November 23, 1918.

73. Wilson's speech is quoted in Flexner and Fitzpatrick, *Century of Struggle*, 302–3. See also "Not Cast Down by Suffrage Defeat," *New York Times*, October 6, 1918.

74. Fausold, *James W. Wadsworth*, 94.

75. "Annual Meeting of National Association Opposed to Woman Suffrage To Be Held in Washington January 9," *Woman Patriot* 1, no. 35 (December 21, 1918): 1, 2; "Anti-Suffragists in Convention Plan Dual Fight against Federal Suffrage Amendment and Red Flag," *Woman Patriot* 2, no. 2 (January 11, 1919): 1.

76. "The Women's Republican Suffrage Committee," *Woman Patriot* 2, no. 2 (January 11, 1919): 2; "Women Voters' Anti-Suffrage Party Asks Will Hays If Republicans Have Been 'Roped, Thrown and Tied by Suffs'" and "Resolutions Passed at Annual Meeting of Women Voters' Anti-Suffrage Party January 15, 1919," *Woman Patriot* 2, no. 3 (January 18, 1919): 1–2, 5; "Open Letter to Will H. Hays," *New York Times*, January 18, 1919; "Protest to New York State Republican Committee from Women Voters' Anti-Suffrage Party," *New York Times*, February 15, 1919.

77. "Harding Promises Hearing to Antis," *Woman Patriot* 4, no. 29 (July 17, 1920): 3.

"To the Manhood of the Democratic Party," *Woman Patriot* 5, nos. 8 and 9 (February 26, 1921): 3.

78. "Suffrage Force Bill Defeated for Fourth Time in U.S. Senate," *Woman Patriot* 3, no. 7 (February 15, 1919): 1–2; "The following is a list of men who voted no . . ." Request attached to an invitation to a March 6, 1919, meeting for members of the Women Voters' Anti-Suffrage Party and their men and women friends, Nassau County Red Cross Collection, Special Collections, Hofstra University Library, West Campus, Hempstead, N.Y.

79. "A Petition to the Senate of the United States," *Woman Patriot* 2, no. 7 (February 15, 1919): 2.

80. Keyssar, *Right to Vote*, 217.

81. "Suffragists Break Through Senate," *Woman Patriot* 3, no. 8 (June 7, 1919): 2; Flexner and Fitzpatrick, *Century of Struggle*, 307–8.

82. Keyssar, *Right to Vote*, 217.

83. "Suffragists Turn to Legislatures," *New York Times,* June 6, 1919; "Antis to Continue Fight on Suffrage," *New York Times,* September 18, 1919; "Mrs. Wadsworth No Longer Member Anti-Suffragists," *Ogdensburg News,* September 19, 1919; Fausold, *James W. Wadsworth*, 106, 123–25.

84. "An All-American Responsibility," "National Association to Meet June 26," and "Anthony Amendment Can be Rejected," *Woman Patriot* 3, no. 9 (June 14, 1919): 4, 5.

85. Giberta S. Whittle, "A Letter from Virginia," *Woman Patriot* 3, no. 12 (July 5, 1919): 2.

86. "A New National President," *Woman Patriot*, 3, no. 13 (July 12, 1919): 2. Kilbreth may have feared losing the support of the Wadsworths, for James Wadsworth responded to her letter assuring her of their continuing support of anti-suffragism. "I Have Not Surrendered My Convictions," *Woman Patriot* 3, no. 24 (September 27, 1919): 1; "National Association Opposed to Woman Suffrage," *Woman Patriot* 3, no. 25 (October 4, 1919): 5. It is not clear whether or not Alice Wadsworth actually suffered from ill health. Apparently she did not even write articles for the *Woman Patriot* after she stepped down. She seems to have continued her financial backing, but her name rarely appears in connection with anti-suffrage after 1919. She was designated as president of the Woman Patriot Publishing Company in the January 1, 1923, issue, but by February 1, 1923 Kilbreth was named as its president. "Mrs. Wadsworth Not Responsible," *Woman Patriot* 4 no. 30 (July 24, 1920): 4.

87. "A New National President," *Woman Patriot*, 3, no. 13 (July 12, 1919): 2.

88. "Housewarming," *Woman Patriot* 3, no. 22 (September 13, 1919): 3.

89. "Antis to Continue Fight on Suffrage," *New York Times,* September 18, 1919.

90. Quotes are from "A Petition for National Security," *Woman Patriot* 3, no. 24 (September 27, 1919): 3. The specific article to which anti-suffragists referred is Article X: "The powers not delegated to the United States by the Constitution, nor prohibited by it to the States, are reserved to the States respectively, or to the people."

91. For example, she was at the meeting arranged by the Delaware Association

Opposed to Woman Suffrage in March 1920, arguing that passing a federal amendment without the consent of the people was "dishonest." "The Public Triumph of Anti-Federalism in Delaware," *Woman Patriot* 4, no. 13 (March 27, 1920): 2.

92. Kilbreth may have been responsible for Rossiter Johnson's becoming a contributing editor for the *Woman Patriot*. They had a fairly extensive correspondence from at least December 1918 to July 1923. HKRJ Papers. "Contributing Editors," *Woman Patriot* 3, no. 25 (October 4, 1919): 1. The antis published some of the letters criticizing the *Patriot* for "nagging tell tales" and "personal abuse." "As Others See Us," *Woman Patriot* 3, no. 29 (November 1, 1919): 4.

93. "Woman Suffrage Amendment Wins in Legislature," *New York Times,* June 17, 1919; Colby to Proclaim Suffrage Promptly," *New York Times,* August 19, 1920.

94. "The Amendment Situation," *Woman Patriot* 4, no. 1 (January 3, 1920): 7. "Suffrage Situation at a Glance," *Woman Patriot* 3, no. 16 (August 2, 1919): 2; "Two Heroic Governors" and "Suffragists Defy Majority Rule," *Woman Patriot* 4, no. 14 (April 3, 1920): 3, 4–5; "How Delaware and Mississippi Defeated Federalism," *Woman Patriot* 4, no. 15 (April 10, 1920): 2.

95. "Will Open Headquarters," *Woman Patriot* 4, no. 22 (May 29, 1920): 7.

96. "National Anti-Suffragists Hold Greatest Meeting," *Woman Patriot* 4, no. 18 (May 1, 1920), 1.

97. "The Opening of the New National Campaign," *Woman Patriot* 4, no. 19 (May 8, 1920): 3.

98. "The New National Campaign," "Where We Stand," and "Election of Officers," *Woman Patriot* 4, no. 19 (May 8, 1920): 3–4.

99. Alabama, Georgia, Virginia, Mississippi, South Carolina, Maryland, Delaware, and Louisiana all rejected the amendment. "The Amendment Situation," *Woman Patriot* 4, no. 33 (August 14, 1920): 8.

100. Rowe also represented the American Constitutional League. The anti-suffragists in Tennessee considered the national anti-suffrage organization to be too dominant. "Anti-Suffrage Leader Resents 'Mail Order' Vote," *Woman Patriot* 4, no. 32 (August 7, 1920): 5; "Miss Rowe Challenges Suffrage Threat," *Woman Patriot* 4, no. 34 (August 21, 1920) 2; "The Truth about the Tennessee Campaign," *Woman Patriot* 4, no. 37 (September 11, 1920): 6–7; Green, *Southern Strategies,* 115.

101. "Vote in Tennessee to Clinch Suffrage Despite Big Bolt," *New York Times,* August 22, 1920; "Women Spent $80,000 to Get 36th State," *New York Times,* August 22, 1920.

102. Mary G. Kilbreth to Harry T. Burn, telegrams (2), August 19, 1920, Harry T. Burn Papers, C. M. McClung Historical Collection, Knox County Public Library, Knoxville, Tenn.; "The Case of Harry T. Burn," *Nashville Tennessean,* August 21, 1920; "Word from Mother Won for Suffrage," *Nashville Tennessean,* August 20, 1920; "Burn Changed Vote on Advice of His Mother," *Commercial Appeal,* August 20, 1920; Catt and Shuler, *Woman Suffrage and Politics,* 449; Flexner and Fitzpatrick, *Century of Struggle,* 316; Graham, *New Democracy,* 144.

103. "Colby Proclaims Woman Suffrage," *New York Times,* August 26, 1920.

104. "Charges of Fraud in Suffrage Fight Made in Tennessee," *New York Times,* August 20, 1920.

105. "Ratification Wins by Narrow Margin in Tennessee," *Woman Patriot* 4, no. 34 (August 21, 1920): 1; "The Truth about the Tennessee Campaign," *Woman Patriot* 4, no. 37 (September 11, 1920): 6–7.

106. The anti-suffragists claimed that Missouri and West Virginia had not conducted their ratification process according to the procedures outlined in their own state constitutions, and they claimed other illegal actions. "To Fight Suffrage on Tennessee Note," *New York Times,* September 6, 1920; "Suffrage Lawyers Confirm Our Legal Arguments," *Woman Patriot* 4, no 20 (May 15, 1920): 3; "The Indictment of the Proposed Nineteenth Amendment," *Woman Patriot* 4, no. 30 (July 24, 1920): 8.

107. "Supreme Court to Hear Anti-Suffrage Cases January 20th," *Woman Patriot* 6, no. 2 (January 15, 1922): 1.

108. Anti-suffragists contested ratification in Missouri, Rhode Island, West Virginia, Texas, and Tennessee. "Was the Nineteenth Amendment Ever Legally Ratified?" *Woman Patriot* 6, no. 1 (January 1, 1922): 4.

109. Quote is from Lemons, *The Woman Citizen*, 14. See also Vose, *Constitutional Change*, 58.

110. "National Association Moves to Washington," *Woman Patriot* 4, no. 41 (October 9, 1920): 2.

111. "The Need of Further Organization," *Woman Patriot* 4, no. 43 (October 23, 1920): 4; "Separate Ballot Boxes for Women!" *Woman Patriot* 4, no. 44 (October 30, 1920): 1–2.

112. "Child Labor Amendment Means Federal Control of Schools," *Woman Patriot* 8, no. 6 (March 15, 1924): 1–2; Molly Ladd-Taylor, *Mother-Work: Women, Child Welfare, and the State, 1890–1930* (Urbana: University of Illinois Press, 1994), 91, 96, 169.

113. Vose, *Constitutional Change*, 243.

114. Nielsen, *Un-American Womanhood*, 1, 3; Suzanne H. Schrems, *Who's Rocking the Cradle? Women Pioneers of Oklahoma Politics from Socialism to the KKK, 1900–1930* (Norman: Horse Creek, 2004), 35.

115. "The New Anti-Feminist Campaign," *Woman Patriot* 5, no. 20 (June 15, 1921): 2–3.

116. "We Have Just Begun to Fight," *Woman Patriot* 5, nos. 8 and 9 (February 26, 1921): 5.

117. Grace Abbott of the Children's Bureau and the editor of the *Woman Patriot* corresponded in 1927. "Salaried Idealists of the Women's Bureau," *Woman Patriot* 5, nos. 8 and 9 (February 26, 1921): 10–12; "Double-Barrelled Feminism," *Woman Patriot* 5, no. 10 (March 5, 1921): 3, 6; "The Case against the League of Women Voters," *Woman Patriot* 6, no. 4 (February 15, 1922): 4; "Our Refutation of Miss Abbott's Charges," *Woman Patriot* 11, no. 1 (January 1, 1927): 1; Robyn Muncy, *Creating a Female Dominion in American Reform, 1890–1935* (New York: Oxford University Press, 1991), 128.

118. "Constitutional Case Appealed to High Court," *Woman Patriot* 4, no. 29 (July 17, 1920): 6.

119. "The Indictment of the Proposed Nineteenth Amendment," *Woman Patriot* 4, no. 30 (July 24, 1920): 8; *Woman Patriot* 4, no. 31 (July 31, 1920): 8; *Woman Patriot* 4, no. 34 (August 21, 1920): 8; *Woman Patriot* 4, no. 35 (August 28, 1920): 8; *Woman Patriot* 4, no. 38 (September 18, 1920): 6–7; "Great Legal Cases against Alleged Amendment," *Woman Patriot* 4, no. 40 (October 2, 1920): 1.

120. "Motion to Advance Filed in Supreme Court," *Woman Patriot* 4, no. 42 (October 16, 1920): 8; "Fairchild-Colby Case to Come Up after Election," *Woman Patriot* 4, no. 43 (October 23, 1920): 3.

121. "Supplemental Brief against Nineteenth Amendment," *Woman Patriot* 6, no. 1 (January 1, 1922): 1; "Supreme Court Hears 19th Amendment Cases," *Woman Patriot* 6, no. 3 (February 1, 1922): 4; Fairchild *v.* Hughes, as Secretary of the United States, et. al. U.S. 148 (1922), argued January 23, 1922, decided February 27, 1922.

122. "Nineteenth Amendment Held Constitutional," *Woman Patriot* 6, no 5 (March 1, 1922): 3. See also Kyvig, *Explicit & Authentic Acts*, 248–49; Vose, *Constitutional Change*, 60–63.

123. "Oral Argument on Nineteenth Amendment," *Woman Patriot* 6, no. 6 (March 15, 1922): 3.

124. "Anti-Suffrage Meetings," *Woman Patriot* 5, no. 10 (March 5, 1921): 7; "Regular Monthly Meeting," *Woman Patriot* 6, no. 1 (January 1, 1922): 3; "National Anti-Suffrage Meeting," *Woman Patriot* 5, no. 27 (October 1, 1921): 2.

125. If there were any forthcoming ideas for a new organization, the journal did not publish them. "Notice of National Meeting," *Woman Patriot* 6, no. 5 (March 1, 1922): 2; "Reorganization Meetings," *Woman Patriot* 6, no. 7 (April 1, 1922): 2.

126. See, for example, "Seeks Prosecution of Senator France," *New York Times,* April 15, 1922; "Senator France Given 'Benefit of Doubt," *Woman Patriot* 6, no. 10 (May 15, 1922): 5–6.

127. "N.E.A. Bloc Dictatorship, Not Federal Control, Aim of Education Bill: Extracts from Statement of Mary G. Kilbreth, Representing the Woman Patriot Publishing Company, Board of Directors," *Woman Patriot* 12, no. 10 (May 15, 1928): 73; Fausold, *James W. Wadsworth*, 125.

128. "The Federal Octopus," *Woman Patriot* 6, no. 8 (April 15, 1922): 1; "The Gossip of a Lifetime," vol. 2, Rossiter Johnson Papers, Manuscript Memoirs, URSC.

129. "Why the Patriot Supports Reed," *Woman Patriot* 6, no. 15 (August 1, 1922): 5.

130. "Our New National Newspaper," *Woman's Protest* (February 1918): 17; "The Woman Patriot" and "The Woman Patriot Publishing Company," *Woman Patriot* 1, no. 1 (April 27, 1918): 4.

131. "Twice a Month Hereafter," *Woman Patriot* 5, no. 16 (April 16, 1921): 4. The publication became a monthly again in April 1931, but there were several issues prior to that which were delayed or not printed.

132. An announcement in the *Woman Patriot* claimed that there was "*no organic connection*" between the Woman Patriot Publishing Company and the Sentinels of the Republic or any other organization. "Sentinels to Hold Convention at Washington January 12th and 13th," *Woman Patriot* 10, no. 1 (January 1, 1926): 8 (emphasis in the original).

133. Quotes are from "Sentinels of the Republic!" *Woman Patriot* 6, no. 16 (August 15, 1922): 8. See also "Sentinels of the Republic: Every Citizen a Sentinel! Every Home a Sentry Box!" *Woman Patriot* 6, nos. 17 and 18 (September 1 and 15, 1922): 2.

134. "Sentinels of the Republic Announce Organization Plans," *Woman Patriot* 7, no. 13 (July 1, 1923): 1.

135. Lemons, *The Woman Citizen*, 241–42.

136. Quote is from Kyvig, *Explicit & Authentic Acts*, 252. See also Mary G. Kilbreth to Rossiter Johnson, letter, July 2, [1921], HKRJ. "An Amendment to Restore the Rights of the People," *Woman Patriot* 4, no. 46 (November 13, 1920): 1–2; "The Second 'Bill of Rights' or 'Back-to-the-People' Amendment," *Woman Patriot* 5, no. 1 (January 1, 1921): 1–2.

137. "President Receives Anti-Suffrage Delegation," *Woman Patriot* 5, no. 19 (June 1, 1921): 1.

138. Kyvig, *Explicit & Authentic Acts*, 251.

139. "People's Amendment Favorably Reported," *Woman Patriot* 7, no. 2 (January 15, 1923): 1–2. It is probable that the editor was J. S. Eichelberger, for Minnie Bronson had already severed her ties with the organization. Rossiter Johnson, author of the "Story of the Constitution," must have been quite a character. In 1924, at age 84, he married Mary Agnes Keys. "Author, 84 Years Old, Married to Nurse, 40; Laughs over His Age as He Gets License," *New York Times,* May 23, 1924.

140. Wadsworth persisted in promoting the Wadsworth-Garrett amendment, discussing it at a meeting of the Women's National Republican Club on January 17, 1925. Ultimately, no version of the amendment was "brought to a determinative vote." Kyvig, *Explicit & Authentic Acts*, 252–53.

141. Lemons, *The Woman Citizen*, 159, 170.

142. In its 1920 *Eighth Annual Report*, the Children's Bureau published graphic representations that clearly showed maternal deaths in the U.S. to be higher than those in any industrialized country, while ranking eleventh in infant deaths for 1918. Theda Skocpol, *Protecting Soldiers and Mothers: The Political Origins of Social Policy in the United States* (Cambridge: Belknap, 1992), 489–500.

143. Quote is from Ladd-Taylor, *Mother-Work*, 167–69. See also Kriste Lindenmeyer, *"A Right to Childhood": The U.S. Children's Bureau and Child Welfare, 1912–1946* (Urbana: University of Illinois Press, 1997), 89.

144. Lemons, *The Woman Citizen*, 155; Lindenmeyer, *A Right to Childhood*, 81.

145. Mary G. Kilbreth to Rossiter Johnson, November 30, 1921, HKRJ.

146. Skocpol, *Protecting Soldiers and Mothers*, 501–3.

147. Allan M. Brandt, *No Magic Bullet: A Social History of Venereal Disease in the United States since 1880* (New York: Oxford University Press, 1987), 123; Ladd-Taylor, *Mother-Work*, 169; Lemons, *The Woman Citizen*, 160; Vose, *Constitutional Change*, 66.

148. Carroll Smith-Rosenberg, *Disorderly Conduct: Visions of Gender in Victorian America* (New York: Oxford University Press, 1985).

149. Mary G. Kilbreth, "Investigating Motherhood—As a Political Business," *Woman Patriot* 5, no. 2 (January 8, 1921): 5–6 (emphasis in the original).

150. Sklar, ed., *The Selected Letters of Florence Kelley, 1869–1931*, 386, 288, 467.

151. Quote is from "Supreme Court Declines to Pass on Maternity Act," *Woman Patriot* 7, no. 11 (June 1, 1923): 1. See also "The Towner Twins," *Woman Patriot* 5, no. 10 (March 5, 1921): 2; "The Spontaneous Opposition to the Sheppard-Towner Bill," *Woman Patriot* 6, no. 1 (January 1, 1922): 7; "Sheppard-Towner Act Held Unconstitutional," *Woman Patriot* 6, no. 10 (May 15, 1922): 1; "State Rights and 'Back to the Constitution,'" *Woman Patriot* 6, no. 12 (June 15, 1922): 2; "Maternity Case Argued in District Supreme Court," *Woman Patriot* 7, no. 4 (February 15, 1923): 1, 6; "Supreme Court Hearing on Maternity Act Cases," *Woman Patriot* 7, no. 10 (May 15, 1923): 1–5.

152. Rosika Schwimmer, "Einstein and the American Amazons," unpublished writing [1933?], Schwimmer-Lloyd Collection, box 1, folder 5, p. 31–32, SSC. See also Ladd-Taylor, *Mother-Work*, 175, 184–90; Lemons, *The Woman Citizen*, 174–75.

153. Kyvig, *Explicit & Authentic Acts*, 258.

154. The *Woman Patriot* printed its petition and memorandum against the child labor amendment in three issues: "Petition against Child Labor Amendment," *Woman Patriot* 8, no. 10 (May 15, 1924): 1–8; "Petition against Child Labor Amendment, Part II," *Woman Patriot* 8, no. 11 (June 1, 1924): 1–8; and "Petition against Child Labor Amendment, Part III," *Woman Patriot* 8, no. 12 (June 15, 1924): 1–6. See also Kyvig, *Explicit & Authentic Acts*, 259, 309.

155. "We Have Won a Battle, Not a War!" *Woman Patriot* 9, no. 14 (July 15, 1925): 112 (emphasis in the original).

156. "The Alice Paul Amendment," *Woman Patriot* 6, no. 6 (March 15, 1922): 5–6; "Analysis of Radical Congressional Program," *Woman Patriot* 7, no. 19 (December 1, 1923): 6–13.

157. "A Parasite Political Party," *Woman Patriot* 10, no. 2 (January 15, 1926): 13.

158. "The Interlocking Lobby Dictatorship," *Woman Patriot* 6, no. 23 (December 1, 1922): 1; "Equal Rights, or 'Lucretia Mott' Amendment," *Woman Patriot* 7, no. 19 (December 1, 1923): 12; "Legislative Policies Recommended . . .," *Woman Patriot* 13, no. 4 (February 15, 1929): 1. Quote is from "Bills and Amendments Pending," *Woman Patriot* 13, no. 1 (January 1, 1929): 7.

159. "Communists Charged with Crimes Under Federal Statutes," *Woman Patriot* 7, no. 6 (March 15, 1923): 2–6. "An Appeal to President Coolidge," *Woman Patriot* 7, no. 17 (October 15, 1923): 1–2.

160. See, for example, "Women Patriots Rout Aliens," *Woman Patriot* 9, no. 10 (May 15, 1925): 75.

161. "Mrs. Catt and the Schwimmer Peace Plan," *Woman's Protest* 11, no. 5 (October 1917): 10–11; "United States of America *v.* Rosika Schwimmer," *Woman Patriot* 13, no. 4 (February 15, 1929): 1; "A Wise Exclusion," *Woman Patriot* 13, no. 11 (June 1, 1929): 85; "Government Considering Plea for Frau Schwimmer's Exclusion," *Woman Patriot* 13, no. 15 (August 1, 1929): 113–15.

162. "Enforce the Alien Exclusion Laws!" *Woman Patriot* 13, no. 23 (December 1, 1929): 177–81, 184; "The Einstein Incident (Part I)," *Woman Patriot* 16, no. 12 (Decem-

ber 1932): 1–3. According to Rosika Schwimmer, Hitler congratulated the "American women for demanding Einstein's exclusion" in an article in the *Völkischer Beobachter*. Rosika Schwimmer, "Einstein and the American Amazons," unpublished writing [1933?], Schwimmer-Lloyd Collection, box 1, folder 5, p. 18–19. SSC; "Headline Footnotes," *New York Times,* December 11, 1932.

Chapter 6. Antis Adjust to Enfranchisement, 1917–1932

1. Annie Nathan Meyer, "Test of Women's Votes," *New York Times,* November 12, 1917. Meyer's sister, Maud Nathan, wrote an editorial criticizing anti-suffragists for believing that Tammany controlled New York for the same column. Maud Nathan, "From a Suffragist," *New York Times,* November 12, 1917.

2. Meyer employed a clipping service and collected every article published by any newspaper or magazine that mentioned her name, no matter how it reflected on her. ANM Papers.

3. "Rubbing New York's Nose in It," *Chicago Herald,* November 20, 1917, scrapbook, p. 33, box 20, folder 1 (1913–1918), ANM Papers.

4. "The Permanent Anti," *New York Call,* n.d., scrapbook, p. 34–35, box 20, folder 1 (1913–1918), ANM Papers.

5. Annie Nathan Meyer, "The Anti-Suffragist Responds," *New Republic* (December 1, 1917): n.p., scrapbook, p. 36, box 20, folder 1 (1913–1918), ANM Papers.

6. Meyer, *It's Been Fun,* 205.

7. Lucy Jeanne Price, "Lessons Learned from the Campaign," *Woman's Protest* 8, no. 1 (November 1915): 5.

8. Jablonsky, *Home, Heaven, and Mother Party,* 116.

9. Morgan, *Suffragists and Democrats,* 179.

10. Benjamin, *History of the Anti-Suffrage Movement;* Camhi, *Women against Women;* Green, *Southern Strategies;* Jablonsky, *Home, Heaven, and Mother Party;* Marshall, *Splintered Sisterhood.*

11. Ryan, *Womanhood in America,* 248.

12. "Suffragists Lift Ban on Old Parties," *New York Times,* April 2, 1918; Elisabeth Israels Perry, "Defying the Party Whip: Mary Garrett Hay and the Republican Party, 1917–1920," in *We Have Come to Stay: American Women and Political Parties, 1880–1960,* ed. Melanie Gustafson, Kristie Miller, and Elisabeth Israels Perry (Albuquerque: University of New Mexico Press, 1999), 101.

13. Lyman Abbott, "Woman Suffrage," *Outlook* 126 (September 8, 1920): 52–53.

14. Kristi Andersen, *After Suffrage: Women in Partisan and Electoral Politics before the New Deal* (Chicago: University of Chicago Press, 1996), 51–52.

15. Sarah Schuyler Butler, "Women Who Do Not Vote: A Motor Tour of 2800 Miles to Find Out Why," *Scribner's Magazine* 76 (November 1924): 529–30.

16. Butler's father was Nicholas Murray Butler, president of Columbia University, a man deeply involved in Republican Party politics and peace activism. Sarah Butler was politically very active during the 1920s, writing many articles for the *Woman Republican* and traveling and speaking all over the state; ibid., 532.

17. Ibid, 533. See also Sarah Schuyler Butler, "A Tour of the Upstate Counties," *Woman Republican* 5, no. 6 (June 1927): 3, 8.

18. George Madden Martin, "American Women and Public Affairs," *Atlantic Monthly* (February 1924): 170.

19. Russell won a Pulitzer Prize in 1927 for his biography of Theodore Thomas. Charles Edward Russell, "Is Woman Suffrage a Failure?" *Century* 107 (March 1924): 725, 726.

20. Carrie Chapman Catt quoted in "Woman Suffrage Declared a Failure," *Literary Digest* (April 12, 1924): 13.

21. Vira B. Whitehouse, "Is Woman Suffrage Failing?" *Woman Citizen* (April 5, 1924): 8.

22. Camhi, *Women against Women*, 234; Ida M. Tarbell, "Is Woman's Suffrage a Failure?" *Good Housekeeping* 79 (October 1924): 242.

23. Tarbell, "Woman's Suffrage a Failure," 19, 239, 240.

24. John Tracy Ellis, *The Life of James Cardinal Gibbons, Archbishop of Baltimore, 1834–1921*, 2 vols., vol. II (Milwaukee: Bruce, 1952), 542.

25. "Why 'Antis' are First to Register Where Women Vote," *Woman's Protest* 6, no. 4 (February 1915): 18; Alice Hill Chittenden, "Woman Suffrage a Mistaken Theory of Progress," *The Woman's Protest* 1, no. 5 (September 1912): 7; Cooper, "Female Suffrage," 442; Mrs. Gilbert E. Jones, "The Position of the Anti-Suffragists," in *Annals of the American Academy of Political and Social Science 35, Supplement* (Philadelphia: 1910), 22; Alice Foote MacDougall, *The Autobiography of a Business Woman* (Boston: Little, Brown, 1928), 25; Annie Nathan Meyer, "The Anti-Suffragist Replies," *New Republic* 13 (December 1, 1917): 124–25.

26. Andersen, *After Suffrage*, 40; McGerr, *Decline of Popular Politics*, 12.

27. "Shall Women Practice Party Regularity?" *New York Times,* March 7, 1920.

28. See, for example, Baker, *Moral Frameworks of Public Life;* Rebecca B. Edwards, *Angels in the Machinery: Gender in American Party Politics from the Civil War to the Progressive Era* (London: Oxford University Press, 1997); Jo Freeman, *A Room at a Time: How Women Entered Party Politics* (Lanham, Md.: Rowman & Littlefield, 2000), ix; Melanie Susan Gustafson, *Women and the Republican Party, 1854–1924* (Urbana: University of Illinois Press, 2001); McGerr, "Political Style."

29. See, for example, Gustafson, "Partisan Women," 8.

30. Mary G. Kilbreth may have been one of the few former anti-suffragists who joined the Democratic Party. "To the Manhood of the Democratic Party," *Woman Patriot* 5, nos. 8 and 9 (February 26, 1921): 3.

31. Andersen, *After Suffrage*, 46–47.

32. "Mrs. Jerome B. Moore Dies Suddenly after Illness of One Week," [*Syracuse Herald?*] (January 24, 1919), Suffrage Collection, Onondaga Historical Association, Syracuse, N.Y.; "Women and Voting," *Woman Patriot* 1, no. 25 (October 12, 1918): 7.

33. Andersen, *After Suffrage*, 2.

34. Cott, *Grounding of Modern Feminism*, 85.

35. According to McGerr, this trend ended by the early 1930s. Andersen, *After Suffrage*, 5, 10–12, 19; McGerr, *Decline of Popular Politics*, 209, 211.

36. Robert J. Dinkin, *Before Equal Suffrage: Women in Partisan Politics from Colonial Times, to 1920* (Westport, Conn.: Greenwood, 1995), 135.

37. See, for example, McGerr, *Decline of Popular Politics*, 208; Elisabeth Israels Perry, *Women in Action: Rebels and Reformers, 1920–1980* (Washington, D.C.: League of Women Voters Education Fund, 1995), 6.

38. Lemons, *The Woman Citizen*, 87.

39. Louise Young, historian of the League of Women Voters, explains that while there were women who joined the Democratic Party, they were "fewer and less well organized." Kristi Andersen writes of the "more generous spirit" with which the Democrats welcomed women to the party; apparently, Republicans did not have to cultivate women's interest. Cott observes that Emily Newell Blair, vice chair of the Democratic National Committee, 1922–28, actually promoted women's separate organizations. Cott also wrote that the decade was "Republican dominated." Andersen, *After Suffrage*, 85–86; Cott, *Grounding of Modern Feminism*, 111; Freedman, "Separatism," 522–23; Louise M. Young, *In the Public Interest: The League of Women Voters, 1920–1970* (New York: Greenwood, 1989), 34.

40. Dinkin, *Before Equal Suffrage*, 129.

41. Gustafson, "Partisan Women," 12.

42. "Women in Politics," *New York Times,* November 28, 1920.

43. Perry, "Defying the Party Whip," 97.

44. Andersen, *After Suffrage*, 13, 19, 80; Ryan, *Womanhood in America*, 255.

45. "Daily Suffrage Meetings," *New York Times,* December 14, 1914; "National Woman Suffrage Publishing Co., Inc.," American Memory, Library of Congress, Washington, D.C.; "NAWSA Convention, Washington, D.C., December 12–15, 1917," *History of Woman Suffrage* 5, 514, 541; "Mrs. A. L. Livermore is Dead in Yonkers," *New York Times,* October 16, 1933; Young, *Leslie Woman Suffrage Commission*, 62.

46. "State of New York Delegates and Alternates, Republican National Convention, Chicago, June 8, 1920," (New York: Republican State Committee, 1919), 12, Subseries 4, M.E. Grenander Department of Special Collections and Archives, University at Albany, Albany, N.Y.

47. In May 1919, nineteen women formed the Republican Women's State Executive Committee, changing the name in 1929 to the Republican Educational League, and in 1937 it became the New York State Federation of Republican Women, overseeing more than fifty clubs. The Federation today offers a Henrietta Wells Livermore Award. Available at http://www.republicanwomen.net/cgi-shl/TWServer.exe?Run:stateinfo_1:PASSPOSTS:State=ny (accessed June 30, 2012). "Parties Planning to Get Women's Votes," *New York Times,* August 20, 1920. By the 1950s Livermore was listed as the sole founder of the Women's National Republican Club. The organization commemorates her with the Henrietta Wells Livermore School of Politics. "Women's National Republican Club," folder, box I: D 285, Reid Family Papers, Manuscript Division, Library of Congress, Washington, D.C.

48. Catherine E. Rymph, *Republican Women: Feminism and Conservatism from Suffrage through the Rise of the New Right* (Chapel Hill: University of North Carolina

Press, 2006), 47. Louise Young, historian of the League of Women Voters, contends that the Republican Party was also the "natural home of many active suffragists." John D. Hicks, *Republican Ascendancy, 1921–1933* (New York: Harper & Row, 1960), 91; Young, *In the Public Interest*, 34.

49. Freeman, *A Room at a Time*, 23.

50. Rymph, *Republican Women*, 47.

51. Freeman, *A Room at a Time*, 23; Jablonsky, *Home, Heaven, and Mother Party*, 53–57.

52. Quote is from Perry, "Defying the Party Whip," 100. "Suffragists Defeated at Albany in Attempt to Boycott Wadsworth Speech at Women Voters' Dinner," *Woman Patriot* 2, no. 8 (February 22, 1919): 1–2. In addition to his opposition to suffrage, Wadsworth had a high rate of absenteeism, and, as Theodore Roosevelt put it, publicly championed "the right of big business to do wrong." Freeman, *A Room at a Time;* Lemons, *The Woman Citizen*, 95.

53. Grace Vanamee and Rosalie Loew Whitney, members of the Republican Women's State Executive Committee and soon to be members of the Women's National Republican Club, both supported Wadsworth. "Republican Women Laud Wadsworth," *New York Times,* February 13, 1920; "Shall Women Practice Party Regularity?" *New York Times,* March 7, 1920; "Mrs. Catt Renews Wadsworth Attack," *New York Times,* September 24, 1920. The Women Voters' Anti-Suffrage Party issued a flyer, "Watch the Woman Boss in Action," in Mary Garrett Hay Scrapbook, "Some Incidents in the Life of Mary Garrett Hay, A Wonderful Boss and a Gallant Fighter," Rare Books and Manuscripts Division, New York Public Library, New York, N.Y. Andersen, *After Suffrage*, 43; Lemons, *The Woman Citizen*, 94; Perry, "Defying the Party Whip," 102, 105n5.

54. Dinkin, *Before Equal Suffrage*, 134; Fausold, *James W. Wadsworth*, 127–28.

55. Perry, "Defying the Party Whip," 97.

56. Sabin founded the Women's Organization for National Prohibition Reform in 1929. Marilyn Elizabeth Perry, "Sabin, Pauline Morton," *American National Biography Online*, http://www.anb.org/articles/06/06–00142.html (accessed June 30, 2012).

57. Rosalie Loew Whitney, "Outline of the History of the Women's National Republican Club," *Guidon* 2, no. 1 (January 1928): 1; "Alice Chittenden of the Red Cross Dead," *New York Times,* October 3, 1945.

58. "Number Six and Eight East Thirty-Seventh," *Woman Republican* 2, no. 3 (February 9, 1924): 2. In 1934 the Club moved to its present address at 3 West 51st Street (http://www.wnrc.org/index.html, accessed June 30, 2012).

59. See, for example, "Luncheon of Republicans," *New York Times,* May 10, 1926; "Legislature's Acts Defended by Nicoll," *New York Times,* October 15, 1926; "Tribute to Mrs. Willard," *New York Times,* March 30, 1927; "In the Current Week," *New York Times,* October 7, 1928; "Notes of Social Activities in New York and Elsewhere," *New York Times,* December 8, 1930; "Republican Women to Hear Talks," *New York Times,* April 19, 1931; "Republican Women Map Speaking Drive," *New York Times,* September 5, 1932.

60. See, for example, "Wood Will Debate with Poindexter," *New York Times,* February 15, 1920; "Many Women in Campaign," *New York Times,* October 19, 1924; "Republicans Plan for Hylan's Defeat," *New York Times,* February 2, 1925; "Women Delegates at Wadsworth Tea," *New York Times,* September 27, 1926; "Republican Women to Wage Campaign," *New York Times,* October 2, 1926; "Women Pick Leaders for Republican Drive," *New York Times,* August 26, 1928; "Women Plan Hoover Tour," *New York Times,* October 21, 1928; "Baumes Shuns Stand of Tuttle on Repeal," *New York Times,* October 4, 1930.

61. "Trend to Hoover by Women is Seen," *New York Times,* September 16, 1928; "Mrs. Robinson Head of Women Orators," *New York Times,* September 23, 1928; "Women Plan Hoover Tour," *New York Times,* October 21, 1928; "Hoover to Win State Women Here Predict," *New York Times,* November 4, 1928.

62. See, for example, "Coleman Willing to Oppose Koenig," *New York Times,* March 11, 1924; "Women to Talk Politics," *New York Times,* April 25, 1926; "Women to Hear Roosevelt," *New York Times,* April 26, 1926; "Luncheon of Republicans," *New York Times,* May 10, 1926; "Mrs. Robinson Head of Women Orators," *New York Times,* September 23, 1928; "Plan Club Celebration," *New York Times,* January 4, 1931; "Wood Sees Swing to Better Times," *New York Times,* January 11, 1931; "To Address Women on Parks," *New York Times,* February 15, 1931; "Republican Women to Hear Talks," *New York Times,* April 19, 1931; "Republican Women Map Speaking Drive," *New York Times,* September 5, 1932; *Woman Republican* 1, no. 2 (January 27, 1923): 3.

63. "Mrs. Pratt to Speak at Republican Luncheon," *New York Times,* April 25, 1926; "Republicans Name 175 Advisors Here," *New York Times,* March 28, 1930.

64. "Alice Chittenden Heads Republican Women; Long Foe of Suffrage; Said Men Would Rue It," *New York Times,* January 15, 1926; "Call for the Republican National Committee," pamphlet (1928); *Woman Republican* 6, no. 9 (September 1928): 7; "Ninth Anniversary Luncheon," *Guidon* 4, no. 2 (December 1929): 2; "Republican Women Elect," *New York Times,* May 1, 1931; "Annual Reports," *Guidon: A Political Review* 6, no. 4 (April 1932): 8; "Heads Women's Republican Club," *New York Times,* April 29, 1932; "Republican Women Seek Members," *New York Times,* June 6, 1932; "Mrs. Roosevelt Named," *New York Times,* August 24, 1932.

65. "Candidates on Suffrage," *New York Times,* July 18, 1920.

66. "Republicans Hold Rally," *Meriden* [Connecticut] *Journal* (October 26, 1920): n.p., Collection of the Alumnae and Alumni of Vassar College, Poughkeepsie, N.Y.

67. "Coolidge Keynote Here by Hughes," *New York Times,* October 13, 1924; "Many Women in Campaign," *New York Times,* October 19, 1924.

68. "County News," *Woman Republican* 1, no. 14 (October 6, 1923): 4.

69. "County News," *Woman Republican* 1, no. 15 (November 3, 1923): 2.

70. *Woman Republican* 2, no. 6 (March 22, 1924): 6.

71. Another woman argued in favor of mandatory jury duty for women, and another argued for permissive jury duty. In an informal vote, the view on permissive jury duty won. "Shall Women Serve on Juries?" *Woman Republican* 5, no. 2 (February 1927): 12.

72. Andersen, *After Suffrage,* 111–14.

73. In 1928, Lucy Jeanne Price moved to Los Angeles, probably to be nearer to her sister. She became the editor of the *East Los Angeles Gazette* and remained so until her death April 20, 1943. "'Gazette' Editor Taken by Death," *Los Angeles Times,* April 21, 1943, Collection of the Alumnae and Alumni of Vassar College, Poughkeepsie, N.Y.

74. The obituary of Josephine Jewell Dodge mentions her service as president of the National Association Opposed to Woman Suffrage but no other political involvement. In the last years of her life she lived in Cannes, France. "Other Society Events," *New York Times,* April 25, 1926; "Mrs. Arthur M. Dodge," *New York Times,* March 7, 1928. "Mrs. Arthur Murray Dodge," *New York World*, March 22, 1928, newspaper clipping in collection of Alumnae and Alumni of Vassar College, Poughkeepsie, N.Y.

75. "Urge More Activity by Woman Voters," *New York Times,* September 30, 1927.

76. MacDougall was interviewed in the Women's National Republican Club offices just after she had signed a million-dollar lease. "Concerning Coffee and Candidates," *Woman Republican* 5, no. 5 (May 1927): 24–25.

77. While research on the political affiliation of former anti-suffrage women in up-state cities is beyond the scope of this study, clearly some of them joined the Republican Party, as did Gertrude Curran and Mrs. Henry J. Cookinham, former anti-suffragists of Utica. "County News," *Woman Republican* 4, no. 1 (January 1926): 11.

78. "Do Women Who Work in Factories and Mercantile Establishments in New York State Want a Law Limiting Their Week to 48 Hours?" Report of an Investigation under the Direction of the State Affairs Committee of the Women's National Republican Club, New York [1926], Collection Development Department, Widener Library, Harvard University, Cambridge, Mass. Chittenden was probably a member of this committee.

79. "The New York City Conference," *Woman Republican* 4, no. 2 (February 1926): 4.

80. Andrew W. Mellon, "A Balanced System of Taxation," National Affairs Committee of the Women's National Republican Club (1928) and John Q. Tilson, "The Protective Tariff," National Affairs Committee of the Women's National Republican Club (1928). Research Library, New York Public Library, New York, N.Y.

81. *Woman Republican* 1, no. 2 (January 27, 1923): 3.

82. "Women to Talk Politics," *New York Times,* April 25, 1926; "Calls Her Own Sex Inferior Mentally," *New York Times,* April 28, 1926.

83. "Mrs. J. W. Wadsworth, Jr." *Woman Republican* 4, no. 9 (September 1926): 4.

84. "Club Calendar, February 1931," *Guidon* 5, no. 3 (February 1931): 6; "The Eleventh Annual Luncheon," *Guidon* 6, no. 3 (February 1932): 11.

85. "To the Members of the Women's National Republican Club, Inc.," letter dated December 28, 1927, box 49, folder 6, Women's National Republican Club, LHH Papers.

86. In 1929, Emanuel Hertz spoke on "His Kindness and Mercy—Let Women Testify." New York Public Library, New York, N.Y.; "Fifth Annual Luncheon," *Woman Republican* 1, no. 3 (February 10, 1923): 2; "Reports of Committees," *Guidon* 6, no. 2 (December 1931): 10.

87. "Luncheon of Republican Women," *New York Times,* January 10, 1930; "Urges Women's Aid of Hoover Policies," *New York Times,* January 12, 1930.

88. Chittenden also joined the Republican Business Club. "Bridge Parties to Aid Charities," *New York Times,* August 24, 1932.

89. Alice Hill Chittenden, "Greeting from the Club President," *Guidon* 1, no. 1 (January 1927): 2; "Reports of Committees," *Guidon* 5, no. 2 (December 1930): 11; "Annual Reports," *Guidon* 6, no. 4 (April 1932): 8. In the beginning, the publication was filled with political news; by late 1931 it was less so, and the magazine would note that the monthly luncheon speaker had spoken on art, literature, travel, or drama rather than politics. In 1931, the magazine included interior design and fashion news, even making a shopping service available to its members. Thereafter political news again dominated the magazine. After 1932, although the club reported on the annual garden meeting, the journal itself became less personal and more political.

90. "Alice Chittenden Heads Republican Women; Long Foe of Suffrage; Said Men Would Rue It," *New York Times,* January 15, 1926; "President Coolidge Appoints Miss Chittenden," *Woman Republican* 3, no. 16 (December 1925): 2.

91. *Woman Republican* 2, no. 12 (July 1924): 5.

92. Kyvig, *Explicit & Authentic Acts,* 240.

93. Alice Hill Chittenden, "Amendments to the Constitution," *Woman Republican* 2, no. 6 (March 22, 1924): 3, 6. On January 17, 1925, Wadsworth addressed the Women's National Republican Club to promote his proposed amendment. "The Wadsworth-Garrett Amendment," address at the Women's National Republican Club, microfilm, Columbia University Libraries, New York, N.Y. Quote is from Kyvig, *Explicit & Authentic Acts,* 251.

94. "School Orators Enter Semi-Finals," *New York Times,* April 27, 1930; "Campbell to Name Champion Orator," *New York Times,* May 4, 1930; "'Constitution Bee' Held," *New York Times,* March 1, 1932.

95. See, for example, "G.O.P. Plans Hard Campaign in Maine," *New York Times,* August 21, 1924; "World Court Fight Will Open Today," *New York Times,* December 17, 1925; "Republican Leaders to Meet Women Today," *New York Times,* March 2, 1926; "Calls Hoover Sacrificial," *New York Times,* September 20, 1932; "Women to Study Politics," *New York Times,* November 13, 1932.

96. "Will Teach Politics to Republican Women," *New York Times,* September 13, 1927.

97. *Woman Republican* 5, no. 7 (July 1927): 7.

98. "Urge More Activity by Woman Voters," *New York Times,* September 30, 1927.

99. "Mrs. Arthur L. Livermore's Report on the School of Politics Held at the Women's National Republican Club," *Guidon* 2, no. 4 (April 1928): 4.

100. Rosalie Loew Whitney, "Outline of the History of the Women's National Republican Club," *Guidon* 2, no. 1 (January 1928): 1.

101. "School of Politics, Season 1929–1930," program, box 49, folder 7, Women's National Republican Club, LHH Papers.

102. *Woman Republican* 6, no. 3 (March 1928): 8; "School of Politics—Mrs. Arthur L. Livermore, Director, Miss Alice Hill Chittenden and Mrs. Rosalie Loew Whitney, Assistant Directors," *Guidon* 4, no. 1 (October 1929): 5.

103. "Educational Programs," *Woman Republican* 5, no. 5 (May 1927): 25.

104. The *United States Daily,* published from March 4, 1926, to March 6, 1933, offered reports on the official acts of the legislative, executive, and judicial branches of the government.

105. "Committee on Political Education," *Guidon* 4, no. 3 (January 1930): 12.

106. "Annie Matthews Shocked," *New York Times,* February 3, 1926.

107. After Chittenden's death, the Women's National Republican Club donated a treatment room in the Tower Building of Memorial Center for Cancer and Allied Diseases in New York City in her memory. "Hospital Room Memorial to Alice Hill Chittenden," *Shoreline Times,* November 22, 1951, in collection of Guilford Free Library, Guilford, Conn.

108. "A Woman Attacks a Racket," *New York Times,* May 11, 1930.

109. Perry, *Women in Action*, 7.

110. Young, *In the Public Interest*, 33.

111. Cott, *Grounding of Modern Feminism*, 86.

112. Andersen, *After Suffrage*, 44–46; William H. Chafe, *The American Woman: Her Changing Social, Economic, and Political Roles, 1920–1970* (New York: Oxford University Press, 1972), 35; Freeman, *A Room at a Time*, 125.

113. Lemons, *The Woman Citizen*, 50–51.

114. Andersen, *After Suffrage*, 36, 45.

115. Lemons, *The Woman Citizen*, 53; Young, *In the Public Interest*, 34.

116. "The Party System," *Woman Republican* 4, no. 2 (February 1926): 9; Young, *In the Public Interest*, 34.

117. Chafe, *American Woman*, 35; Cott, *Grounding of Modern Feminism*, 107; Lemons, *The Woman Citizen*, 98–100.

118. McCormick was a representative from Illinois (1924–1928) and chair of the first woman's executive committee of the Republican National Committee. She had an unsuccessful campaign for the Senate in 1928. http://bioguide.congress.gov/scripts/biodisplay.pl?index=M000372 (accessed June 30, 2012).

119. Cott, *Grounding of Modern Feminism*, 86.

120. "Suffrage League is Un-American and a Menace to National Life," *Woman's Protest* 2, no. 15 (April 12, 1919): 1; "They Want to Be Courted," *Woman's Protest* 3, no. 2 (April 26, 1919): 4. As was increasingly typical of articles published by the National Association Opposed to Woman Suffrage after 1917, it suggested that the league would support the Socialist Party. Young, *In the Public Interest*, 34.

121. Ibid.

122. Ibid., 89.

123. "League of Women Voters Plans to Co-Operate with Party Officials," *Woman Republican* 2, no. 9 (May 3, 1924): 2, 6.

124. Young, *In the Public Interest*, 82.

125. "The League of Women Voters Encourages 'New Voters' in State and Nation," *Woman Republican* 4, no. 12 (December 1926): 4.

126. Meyer, *It's Been Fun*, 205, 207.

127. McGerr, "Political Style," 883.

128. Eunice Fuller Barnard, "When New York Gave Woman the Vote," *New York Times,* November 6, 1927.

129. Jablonsky, *Home, Heaven, and Mother Party*, 115.

130. Joseph Lash, *Eleanor and Franklin: The Story of the Relationship, Based on Eleanor Roosevelt's Private Papers* (New York: W.W. Norton, 1971), 385–86. Albert Z. Guttenberg, "The Nation as Family: The Winning Plan of Prestonia Mann Martin," in *The Language of Planning: Essays on the Origins and Ends of American Planning Thought* (Urbana: University of Illinois Press, 1993).

131. Andersen, *After Suffrage*, 93.

132. Cott, *Grounding of Modern Feminism*, 109.

133. Andersen, *After Suffrage*, 55–57.

Conclusion

1. Women's National Republican Club, *Proceedings of the Mock Convention Held at the Waldorf-Astoria Hotel, New York City* (New York: Women's National Republican Club, 1928), 5.

2. "Mock National Convention," *Guidon* 2, no. 4 (April 1928): 4.

3. Women's National Republican Club, *Proceedings of the Mock Convention*, 6.

4. "The Women's National Republican Club States Successful Convention for Three Hundred Guests," *Woman Republican* 6, no. 5 (May 1928): 3.

5. Women's National Republican Club, *Proceedings of the Mock Convention*, 17, 22–23.

6. Ibid., 26–27, 33, 34.

7. Pinkham's popular tonic was about 19 percent alcohol. Sarah Stage, "Lydia Estes Pinkham," *American National Biography Online,* available at http://www.anb.org/articles/12/12-00725.html (accessed June 30, 2012). Ibid., 31.

8. Dr. Mary E. Walker (1835–1919) won a Congressional Medal of Honor for her services as a surgeon during the Civil War. Congress passed special legislation to allow her to wear trousers. Because she insisted on wearing trousers even after the war was over, she consistently aroused controversy. Elizabeth D. Leonard, *Yankee Women: Gender Battles in the Civil War* (New York: Norton, 1994), 105–57. "The Women's National Republican Club States Successful Convention for Three Hundred Guests," *Woman Republican* 6, no. 5 (May 1928): 4; Women's National Republican Club, *Proceedings of the Mock Convention*, 17.

9. This character was meant to represent Dorothea Lynde Dix, famous for her advocacy of the humane treatment of the mentally ill. Andrew G. Wood, "Dorothea Lynde Dix," *American National Biography Online,* available at http://www.anb.org/

articles/15/12–00181.html (accessed June 30, 2012). Women's National Republican Club, *Proceedings of the Mock Convention*, 41.

10. Luckett V. Davis, "Gene Tunney" *American National Biography Online,* available at http://www.anb.org/articles/19/12–00479.html (accessed June 30, 2012); Women's National Republican Club, *Proceedings of the Mock Convention*, 42, 44.

11. Ibid., 44–45.

12. Kraditor, *Ideas of the Woman Suffrage Movement*, 41.

13. See, for example, Emily Newell Blair, "Women in Political Parties," *Annals of the American Academy of Political and Social Science* 143, Women in the Modern World (May 1929): 229.

14. Women's National Republican Club, *Proceedings of the Mock Convention*, 7.

15. Degler, *At Odds*, 359.

16. Quoted in Graham, *New Democracy*, 113.

17. Ibid., 114.

18. Keyssar, *Right to Vote*, 220; McGerr, *Decline of Popular Politics*, 184–85.

19. National American Woman Suffrage Association, *Victory*, 110–11.

20. Dinkin, *Before Equal Suffrage*, 135.

21. Lerner, *Women in American History*, 152–53.

22. Quoted in Andersen, *After Suffrage*, 89.

23. As Keyssar points out, however, reforms and women's issues were "injected into the political arena" in the 1930s. Chafe, *American Woman*, 25; Keyssar, *Right to Vote*, 218; McGerr, "Political Style," 882; Kathryn Kish Sklar, "The Historical Foundations of Women's Power in the Creation of the American Welfare State, 1830–1930," in *Mothers of a New World*, ed. Seth Koven and Sonya Michel (New York: Routledge, 1993), 75–77.

24. Keyssar, *Right to Vote*, 219.

25. Cott, *Grounding of Modern Feminism*, 112–13.

26. Meyer wrote that she always had the conviction that women would never vote as a sex. Meyer, *It's Been Fun*, 207.

27. Chafe, *American Woman*, 37.

28. See, for example, Edwards, *Angels in the Machinery*, 167; Keyssar, *Right to Vote*, 219.

29. Perry, *Women in Action*, 19.

30. Sinclair, *Better Half*, 91.

31. This is the first version, written and submitted by Alice Paul at a meeting in Seneca Falls in 1923. Version 2, written and submitted by Alice Paul to the Senate Judiciary Committee in 1943, read: "Equality of rights under the law shall not be denied or abridged by the United States or by any State on account of sex." Lunardini, *From Equal Suffrage to Equal Rights*, 172.

32. "The Woman's War," *New York Times,* January 14, 1922; Kathryn Kish Sklar, "Why Were Most Politically Active Women Opposed to the ERA in the 1920s?," in *Women and Power in American History*, eds. Kathryn Kish Sklar and Thomas Dublin (Upper Saddle River, N.J.: Prentice Hall, 2002), 160.

33. Perry, *Women in Action*, 26–27.

34. Rymph, *Republican Women*, 187, 214–15.

35. Mary Frances Berry, *Why ERA Failed: Politics, Women's Rights, and the Amending Process of the Constitution* (Bloomington: Indiana University Press, 1986), 83.

36. See Amrita Basu, ed., *The Challenge of Local Feminisms: Women's Movements in Global Perspective* (Boulder: Westview, 1995), introduction.

37. Meyer refers to the many articles she collected in her scrapbooks that are full of the "most fantastic claims" of suffragists. Meyer, *It's Been Fun*, 202.

References

A Note on Sources

There are no major archival collections for the New York State Association Opposed to Woman Suffrage or the National Association Opposed to Woman Suffrage. Papers are scattered in woman suffrage collections, historical societies, and libraries. Among the best collections of anti-suffrage pamphlets, broadsides, and other materials are those in the Lincklaen/Ledyard Collection, Lorenzo State Historic Site, Cazenovia, New York, and in the Suffrage Collection of the Sophia Smith Collection, Smith College, Northampton, Massachusetts. Other highly useful collections include the Jon A. Lindseth Collection of American Woman Suffrage at the Carl A. Kroch Library of Cornell University, the National American Woman Suffrage Association Collection at the Library of Congress, the Man-Suffrage Association Opposed to Political Suffrage for Women at the New York Public Library, and the Clinton Political Equality Club collection at the Clinton, New York, Historical Society. Collections with some material specific to the New York antis are in the New York State Association Opposed to Woman Suffrage Collection in Manuscripts and Special Collections, New York State Library, Albany; the Anti-Suffrage Collection at Historic Cherry Hill also in Albany; and the small anti-suffrage collection at the Schlesinger Library in Cambridge, Massachusetts. Burke Library of Hamilton College, in Clinton, New York, has the entire collection of anti-suffrage journals on microfilm, and its shelves still hold copies of many of the books, pamphlets, and broadsides the antis published. Elihu Root, whose home and gardens are on the college grounds, donated several anti-suffrage books to the library.

Anti-suffragists generally did not collect their papers or write autobiographies; once women won the right to vote, most anti-suffragists fell silent on the topic. One notable exception is Annie Nathan Meyer, although she may not truly represent the quintessential anti-suffragist. The Annie Nathan Meyer Collection at the Jacob Rader

Marcus Center of the American Jewish Archives in Cincinnati, Ohio, holds extensive materials related to anti-suffrage. Meyer kept scrapbooks, journals, letters, and other papers, and wrote her autobiography; together these sources justify her aversion to suffrage claims. The Gilder Manuscript Collection at the Lilly Library of Indiana University in Bloomington holds an extensive collection of Helena de Kay Gilder's letters and writings, but few address her anti-suffrage perspective. Together, these collections provided the basic resources; suffrage memoirs often suggested the events and directions explored for this study.

Archival Sources

Albany Institute of History and Art, Albany, New York
  Huybertie Lansing Pruyn Hamlin Papers, Boxes 25, 26

Burke Library, Hamilton College, Clinton, New York
  Elihu Root Papers, Special Collections
  History of Women Microfilm Collection
  Periodicals on Women and Women's Rights Microfilm Collection
  A full run of the *Reply* and other publications of the period

Cazenovia Public Library, Cazenovia, New York
  Cazenovia Branch of the New York State Organization
    Opposed to Woman Suffrage Folder
  Minutes Book, Organization of Women of Cazenovia
    Opposed to the Extension of Woman Suffrage

Clinton Historical Society, Clinton, New York
  Clinton Political Equality Club Collection

Cornell University, Ithaca, New York
  Carl A. Kroch Library, Rare and Manuscript Collections,
    Jon A. Lindseth Collection of American Woman Suffrage
  Woman Suffrage Miscellany, #1576

Elizabeth Cady Stanton Trust, Greenwich, Connecticut

Guilford Free Library, Guilford, Connecticut
  Chittenden Papers

Herkimer County Historical Society, Herkimer, New York
  Woman Suffrage Collection

Historic Cherry Hill, Albany, New York
  Anti-Suffrage Collection

Hofstra University Library, Long Island Studies Institute, Hempstead, New York
  Nassau County Red Cross Collection, Special Collections

Jacob Rader Marcus Center of the American Jewish Archives, Hebrew Union
  College, Cincinnati, Ohio
  Annie Nathan Meyer Collection

Library of Congress, Washington, D.C.
  Mabel Thorp Boardman Papers
  Microfilm Collection on Biography
  National American Woman Suffrage Association Collection
  Prints and Photographs Division
  Reid Family Papers

Lilly Library, Indiana University, Bloomington
  Gilder Manuscript Collection

Lorenzo State Historic Site, Cazenovia, New York
  Lincklaen/Ledyard Collection

Madison County Historical Society, Oneida, New York
  Higinbotham Collection

Maine Historical Society, Portland
  Maine Association Opposed to Suffrage of Women Records

New York Public Library, New York City
  Anti-Woman Suffrage Scrapbooks
  Carrie Chapman Catt Papers
  Everett P. Wheeler Papers
  Guidon
  Helen Kendrick and Rossiter Johnson Papers
  Ida Husted Harper Papers
  Man-Suffrage Association Opposed to Political Suffrage for Women
  Mary Garrett Hay Scrapbook
  New York State Woman Suffrage Party Record, 1915–1919
  Richard Watson Gilder Papers
  Woman Republican

New York State Library, Manuscripts and Special Collections, Albany
  New York Association Opposed to Woman Suffrage Records

Oneida County Historical Society, Utica, New York

Onondaga Historical Society, Syracuse, New York
  Suffrage Collection

Rensselear Historical Society, Troy, New York
  Suffrage Exhibit

Rye Historical Society, Rye, New York
  Anti-Suffrage Collection

Schlesinger Library, Radcliffe College, Cambridge, Massachusetts
  New York Association Opposed to Woman Suffrage

Skaneateles Historical Society, Skaneateles, New York
  Anti-Suffrage Folder

Sophia Smith Collection, Smith College, Northampton, Massachusetts
Suffrage Collection

University at Albany Grenander Department of Special Collections and Archives,
Albany, New York

University of Rochester River Campus Libraries, Rochester, New York
Women's Rights Collection, Box 2

Vassar College Library, Poughkeepsie, New York
Alma Lutz Collection
National American Woman Suffrage Collection
Woman Suffrage and Women's Rights Collection, 1866–1974

Select Bibliography

Abbott, Lyman. "An Anti-Suffrage Movement." *Outlook* (April 28, 1894): 738–39.
———. "Anti-Suffragists and Suffragists in New York." *Outlook* 117 (November 28, 1917): 487.
———. "Is Suffrage Her Right?" *Outlook* 49 (May 26, 1894): 908–9.
———. "Is the Suffrage a Duty?" *Outlook* 49 (May 19, 1894): 860–61.
———. "A Woman's Protest against Woman's Suffrage." *Outlook* 49 (April 28, 1894): 760.
———. "Woman Suffrage." *Outlook* 49 (March 31, 1894): 577–78.
———. "Woman Suffrage." *Outlook* 126 (September 8, 1920): 52–53.
Adams, Katherine H., and Michael L. Keene. *Alice Paul and the American Suffrage Campaign*. Urbana: University of Illinois Press, 2008.
Andersen, Kristi. *After Suffrage: Women in Partisan and Electoral Politics before the New Deal*. Chicago: University of Chicago Press, 1996.
Anthony, Katherine. *Susan B. Anthony: Her Personal History and Her Era*. Garden City, N.J.: Doubleday, 1954.
Anthony, Susan B., and Ida Husted Harper, eds. *History of Woman Suffrage*. 6 vols. Vol. IV. Indianapolis: Hollenbeck, 1902.
Antler, Joyce. *The Journey Home: Jewish Women and the American Century*. New York: Free Press, 1997.
Auerbach, Jerold S. *Unequal Justice: Lawyers and Social Change in Modern America*. London: Oxford University Press, 1977.
Baker, John. *The Constitution of 1894*. New York: New York History, 1897–99.
Baker, Paula. "The Domestication of Politics: Women and American Political Society, 1780–1920." In *Women, the State, and Welfare*, edited by Linda Gordon, 55–91. Madison: University of Wisconsin Press, 1990.
———. *The Moral Frameworks of Public Life: Gender, Politics, and the State in Rural New York, 1870–1930*. New York: Oxford University Press, 1991.
Basu, Amrita, ed. *The Challenge of Local Feminisms: Women's Movements in Global Perspective*. Boulder: Westview, 1995.

Beckert, Sven. *The Monied Metropolis: New York City and the Consolidation of the American Bourgeoisie, 1850–1896*. Cambridge: Cambridge University Press, 1993.

Beecher, Catharine. "Something for Women Better Than the Ballot." *Appleton's Journal: A Magazine of General Literature* (1869).

———. *Woman's Profession as Mother and Educator with Views in Opposition to Woman Suffrage*. Philadelphia: Maclean, 1872.

Benjamin, Anne M. *A History of the Anti-Suffrage Movement in the United States from 1895 to 1920*. Lewiston: Mellen, 1992.

Berry, Mary Frances. *Why ERA Failed: Politics, Women's Rights, and the Amending Process of the Constitution*. Bloomington: Indiana University Press, 1986.

Biel, Steven. *Down with the Old Canoe: A Cultural History of the Titanic Disaster*. New York: Norton, 1996.

Blair, Karen J. *The Clubwoman as Feminist: True Womanhood Redefined, 1868–1914*. New York: Holmes & Meier, 1980.

Blatch, Harriot Stanton, and Alma Lutz. *Challenging Years: The Memoirs of Harriot Stanton Blatch*. New York: Putnam's, 1940.

Blee, Kathleen M. *Women of the Klan: Racism and Gender in the 1920s*. Berkeley: University of California Press, 1991.

Bosch, Mineke, and Annemarie Kloosterman. *Politics and Friendship: Letters from the International Woman Suffrage Alliance*. Columbus: Ohio State University Press, 1990.

Brandt, Allan M. *No Magic Bullet: A Social History of Venereal Disease in the United States since 1880*. New York: Oxford University Press, 1987.

Brennan, Mary C. *Wives Mothers, and the Red Menace: Conservative Women and the Crusade against Communism*. Boulder: University Press of Colorado, 2008.

Brown, Ira V. *Lyman Abbott: Christian Evolutionist*. Cambridge: Harvard University Press, 1953.

Buenker, John D. "The Urban Political Machine and Woman Suffrage: A Study in Political Adaptability." *Historian* 33 (February 1971): 264–79.

Buhle, Mari Jo. *Women and American Socialism, 1870–1920*. Urbana: University of Illinois Press, 1981.

Buhle, Mari Jo, and Paul Buhle, eds. *The Concise History of Woman Suffrage: Selections from the Classic Work of Stanton, Anthony, Gage, and Harper*. Urbana: University of Illinois Press, 2005.

Burt, Elizabeth V. "The Ideology, Rhetoric, and Organizational Structure of a Countermovement Publication: The Remonstrance, 1890–1920." *Journalism & Mass Communication Quarterly* 75, no. 1 (1998): 69–83.

Butler, Sarah Schuyler. "Women Who Do Not Vote: A Motor Tour of 2800 Miles to Find Out Why." *Scribner's* 76 (November 1924): 529–33.

Camhi, Jane Jerome. *Women against Women: American Anti-Suffragism, 1880–1920*. Brooklyn: Carlson, 1994.

Catt, Carrie Chapman, and Nettie Rogers Shuler. *Woman Suffrage and Politics: The Inner Story of the Suffrage Movement*. New York: Scribner's, 1926.

Chafe, William H. *The American Woman: Her Changing Social, Economic, and Political Roles, 1920–1970*. New York: Oxford University Press, 1972.

Chittenden, Alice Hill. "The Counter Influence to Woman Suffrage." *Independent* 67 (July 29, 1909): 246–49.

———. "Woman Suffrage a Mistaken Theory of Progress." *Woman's Protest* 1, no. 5 (September 1912): 7–8.

Coontz, Stephanie. *The Social Origins of Private Life: A History of American Families*. London: Verso, 1988.

Cooper, Susan Fenimore. "Female Suffrage: A Letter to the Christian Women of America, Part 1." *Harper's New Monthly* 41, no. 243 (August 1870): 438–46, and "Female Suffrage: A Letter to the Christian Women of America, Part 2." *Harper's New Monthly* 41, no. 244 (September 1870): 594–600.

Cott, Nancy F. *The Grounding of Modern Feminism*. New Haven, Conn.: Yale University Press, 1987.

Cummings, Kathleen Sprows. *New Women of the Old Faith: Gender and American Catholicism in the Progressive Era*. Chapel Hill: University of North Carolina Press, 2009.

Damon-Moore, Helen. *Magazines for the Millions: Gender and Commerce in the Ladies Home Journal and the Saturday Evening Post, 1880–1910*. Albany: State University of New York Press, 1994.

Daniels, Doris. "Building a Winning Coalition: The Suffrage Fight in New York State." *New York History* 60 (January 1979): 58–80.

Degler, Carl N. *At Odds: Women and Family in America from the Revolution to the Present*. New York: Oxford University Press, 1980.

Dinkin, Robert J. *Before Equal Suffrage: Women in Partisan Politics from Colonial Times to 1920*. Westport: Greenwood, 1995.

DuBois, Ellen Carol. *Feminism and Suffrage: The Emergence of an Independent Women's Movement in America, 1848–1869*. Ithaca, N.Y.: Cornell University Press, 1978.

———. *Harriot Stanton Blatch and the Winning of Woman Suffrage*. New Haven, Conn.: Yale University Press, 1997.

———. *Woman Suffrage & Women's Rights*. New York: New York University Press, 1998.

Edwards, Rebecca B. *Angels in the Machinery: Gender in American Party Politics from the Civil War to the Progressive Era*. London: Oxford University Press, 1997.

Ellis, John Tracy. *The Life of James Cardinal Gibbons, Archbishop of Baltimore, 1834–1921*. 2 vols. Vol. II. Milwaukee: Bruce, 1952.

Epstein, Barbara Leslie. *The Politics of Domesticity: Women, Evangelism, and Temperance in Nineteenth Century America*. Middletown, Conn.: Wesleyan University Press, 1981.

Evans, Sara M. *Born for Liberty: A History of Women in America*. New York: Simon & Schuster, 1989.

Fausold, Martin L. *James W. Wadsworth, Jr.* Syracuse, N.Y.: Syracuse University Press, 1975.

Finnegan, Margaret. *Selling Suffrage: Consumer Culture & Votes for Women*. New York: Columbia University Press, 1999.

Flexner, Eleanor, and Ellen Fitzpatrick. *Century of Struggle: The Woman's Rights Movement in the United States*. Cambridge: Belknap, 1996 [1959].

Freedman, Estelle. "Separatism as Strategy: Female Institution Building and American Feminism, 1870–1930." *Feminist Studies* 5, no. 3 (Fall 1979): 512–29.

Freedman, Estelle B. "Separatism Revisited: Women's Institutions, Social Reform, and the Career of Miriam Van Waters." In *U.S. History as Women's History: New Feminist Essays*, edited by Linda K. Kerber, Alice Kessler-Harris, and Kathryn Kish Sklar, 170–88. Chapel Hill: University of North Carolina Press, 1995.

Freeman, Jo. *A Room at a Time: How Women Entered Party Politics*. Lanham, Md.: Rowman & Littlefield, 2000.

Gilder, Rosamond, ed. *Letters of Richard Watson Gilder*. Boston: Houghton Mifflin, 1916.

Gilmore, Glenda Elizabeth, ed. *Who Were the Progressives?* Boston: Bedford/St. Martin's, 2002.

Gould, Lewis L., ed. *The Progressive Era*. Syracuse, N.Y.: Syracuse University Press, 1974.

Graham, Sara Hunter. "The Suffrage Renaissance: A New Image for a New Century, 1896–1910." In *One Woman, One Vote: Rediscovering the Woman Suffrage Movement*, edited by Marjorie Spruill Wheeler, 157–78. Troutdale, Ore.: New Sage, 1995.

———. *Woman Suffrage and the New Democracy*. New Haven, Conn.: Yale University Press, 1996.

Green, Elna C. *Southern Strategies: Southern Women and the Woman Suffrage Question*. Chapel Hill: University of North Carolina Press, 1997.

Gustafson, Melanie. "Partisan Women in the Progressive Era: The Struggle for Inclusion in American Political Parties." *Journal of Women's History* 9, no. 2 (Summer 1997): 8–30.

Gustafson, Melanie Susan. *Women and the Republican Party, 1854–1924*. Urbana: University of Illinois Press, 2001.

Guttenberg, Albert Z. "The Nation as Family: The Winning Plan of Prestonia Mann Martin." In *The Language of Planning: Essays on the Origins and Ends of American Planning Thought*. Urbana: University of Illinois Press, 1993.

Hamlin, Huybertie Pruyn. *An Albany Girlhood*. Edited by Alice P. Kenney. Albany, N.Y.: Washington Park, 1990.

Harper, Ida Husted. *History of Woman Suffrage*. 6 vols. Vol. 5. New York: Little and Ives, 1922.

———. *History of Woman Suffrage*. 6 vols. Vol. 6. New York: Little and Ives, 1922.

———. *The Life and Work of Susan B. Anthony*. 2 vols. Vol. II. Indianapolis: Hollenbeck, 1898.

Hazard, Mrs. Barclay. "The New York Anti-Suffrage Association." *Harper's Bazar* [after 1929 *Harper's Bazaar*] 43 (July 1909): 730.

Hicks, John D. *Republican Ascendancy, 1921–1933*. New York: Harper & Row, 1960.

Hoornstra, Jean, and Trudy Heath, eds. *American Periodicals, 1741–1900: An Index to the Microfilm Collections*. Ann Arbor: University Microfilms International, 1979.

Jablonsky, Thomas J. "Duty, Nature, and Stability: Female Anti-Suffragists in the United States, 1894–1920." PhD diss., University of Southern California, 1978.

———. *The Home, Heaven, and Mother Party: Female Anti-Suffragists in the United States, 1868–1920*. Brooklyn: Carlson, 1994.

Jacobi, Mary Putnam, and Maud Wilder Goodwin. "The Woman Suffrage Question: Pro and Con." *Outlook* 49 (May 12, 1894): 820–22.

Jessup, Philip C. *Elihu Root*. 2 vols. New York: Dodd, Mead, 1938.

Johnson, Helen Kendrick. *Woman and the Republic: A Survey of the Woman-Suffrage Movement in the United States and a Discussion of the Claims and Arguments of Its Foremost Advocates*. New York: Appleton, 1897.

———. *Woman and the Republic: A Survey of the Woman Suffrage Movement in the United States and a Discussion of the Claims and Arguments of Its Foremost Advocates. A New and Enlarged Edition*. New York: Guidon Club Opposed to Woman Suffrage, 1913.

Johnson, Rossiter. *Helen Kendrick Johnson: The Story of Her Varied Activities*. New York: Publisher's Printing, 1917.

Jones, Enid Huws. *Mrs. Humphry Ward*. New York: St. Martin's, 1973.

Jones, Mrs. Gilbert E. "The Position of the Anti-Suffragists." In *Annals of the American Academy of Political and Social Science 35, Supplement*, 16–22. Philadelphia, 1910.

Keller, Morton. *Affairs of State: Public Life in Late Nineteenth Century America*. Cambridge: Belknap, 1977.

Kennedy, David M. *Over Here: The First World War and American Society*. New York: Oxford University Press, 2004.

Keyssar, Alexander. *The Right to Vote: The Contested History of Democracy in the United States*. New York: Basic, 2000.

Kinnard, Cynthia D. "Mariana Griswold Van Rensselaer (1851–1934): America's First Professional Woman Art Critic." In *Women as Interpreters of the Visual Arts, 1820–1979*, edited by Claire Richter Sherman and Adele M. Holcomb. Westport, Conn.: Greenwood, 1981.

Klein, Milton M., ed. *The Empire State: A History of New York*. Ithaca, N.Y.: Cornell University Press, 2001.

Kraditor, Aileen S. *The Ideas of the Woman Suffrage Movement/1890–1920*. New York: Norton, 1981.

———, ed. *Up from the Pedestal: Selected Writings in the History of American Feminism*. Chicago: Quadrangle, 1968.

Kyvig, David E. *Explicit & Authentic Acts: Amending the U.S. Constitution, 1776–1995*. Lawrence: University Press of Kansas, 1996.

Ladd-Taylor, Molly. *Mother-Work: Women, Child Welfare, and the State, 1890–1930*. Urbana: University of Illinois Press, 1994.

Larabee, Ann E. "The American Hero and His Mechanical Bride: Gender Myths of the Titanic Disaster." *American Studies* 31 (Spring 1990): 5–23.

Lemons, J. Stanley. *The Woman Citizen: Social Feminism in the 1920s.* Charlottesville: University Press of Virginia, 1990.

Leonard, Elizabeth D. *Yankee Women: Gender Battles in the Civil War.* New York: Norton, 1994.

Lerner, Gerda. *The Woman in American History.* New York: Addison-Wesley, 1971.

Lindenmeyer, Kriste. *"A Right to Childhood": The U.S. Children's Bureau and Child Welfare, 1912–1946.* Urbana: University of Illinois Press, 1997.

Lumsden, Linda J. *Rampant Women: Suffragists and the Right of Assembly.* Knoxville: University of Tennessee Press, 1997.

Lunardini, Christine. *From Equal Suffrage to Equal Rights: Alice Paul and the National Woman's Party, 1910–1928.* San Jose: ToExcel, 2000.

MacDougall, Alice Foot. *The Autobiography of a Business Woman.* Boston: Little, Brown, 1928.

Maddux, Kristy. "When Patriots Protest: The Anti-Suffrage Discursive Transformation of 1917." *Rhetoric & Public Affairs* 7, no. 3 (2004): 283–310.

Marilley, Suzanne M. *Woman Suffrage and the Origins of Liberal Feminism in the United States, 1820–1920.* Cambridge, Mass.: Harvard University Press, 1997.

Marshall, Susan E. *Splintered Sisterhood: Gender and Class in the Campaign against Woman Suffrage.* Madison: University of Wisconsin Press, 1997.

Martin, I. T. "Concerning Some of the Anti-Suffrage Leaders." *Good Housekeeping* 55 (July 1912): 80–82.

Maynard, Cora. "The Woman's Part." *Arena* 7 (March 1893): 476–86.

McDonagh, Eileen L., and H. Douglas Price. "Woman Suffrage in the Progressive Era: Patterns of Opposition and Support in Referenda Voting, 1910–1918." *The American Political Science Review* 79, no. 155.2 (1985): 415–35.

McDonald, David Kevin. "Organizing Womanhood: Women's Culture and the Politics of Woman Suffrage in New York State, 1865–1917." PhD diss., State University of New York at Stony Brook, 1987.

McFarland, C. K., and Nevin E. Neal. "The Reluctant Reformer: Woodrow Wilson and Woman Suffrage, 1913–1920." *Rocky Mountain Social Science Journal* 11 (April 1974): 33–43.

McGerr, Michael. "Political Style and Women's Power, 1830–1930." *Journal of American History* 77 (December 1990): 864–85.

McGerr, Michael E. *The Decline of Popular Politics: The American North, 1865–1928.* New York: Oxford University Press, 1986.

Meyer, Annie Nathan. "The Anti-Suffragist Replies." *New Republic* 13 (December 1, 1917): 124–25.

———. *It's Been Fun.* New York: Schuman, 1951.

Morgan, David. *Suffragists and Democrats: The Politics of Woman Suffrage in America.* East Lansing: Michigan State University Press, 1972.

Muncy, Robyn. *Creating a Female Dominion in American Reform, 1890–1935.* New York: Oxford University Press, 1991.

Murlin, Edgar L. *The New York Red Book.* Albany: Lyons, 1907.

National American Woman Suffrage Association. *Victory: How Women Won It, a Centennial Symposium, 1840–1940.* New York: Wilson, 1940.

Nielsen, Kim E. *Un-American Womanhood: Antiradicalism, Antifeminism, and the First Red Scare.* Columbus: Ohio State University Press, 2001.

Painter, Nell Irvin. *Standing at Armageddon: The United States, 1877–1919.* New York: Norton, 1987.

Park, Maud Wood. *Front Door Lobby.* Boston: Beacon, 1960.

Peck, Mary Gray. *Carrie Chapman Catt.* New York: Wilson, 1944.

Perry, Elisabeth Israels. *Belle Moskowitz: Feminine Politics and the Exercise of Power in the Age of Alfred E. Smith.* New York: Oxford University Press, 1987.

———. "Defying the Party Whip: Mary Garrett Hay and the Republican Party, 1917–1920." In *We Have Come to Stay: American Women and Political Parties, 1880–1960,* edited by Melanie Gustafson, Kristie Miller, and Elisabeth Israels Perry, 97–107. Albuquerque: University of New Mexico Press, 1999.

———. "Men Are from the Gilded Age, Women Are from the Progressive Era." *Journal of the Gilded Age and Progressive Era* 1, no. 1 (January 2002): 25–48.

———. *Women in Action: Rebels and Reformers, 1920–1980.* Washington, D.C.: League of Women Voters Education Fund, 1995.

Ryan, Mary. *Womanhood in America: From Colonial Times to the Present.* 3rd ed. New York: Franklin Watts, 1975.

Rymph, Catherine E. *Republican Women: Feminism and Conservatism from Suffrage through the Rise of the New Right.* Chapel Hill: University of North Carolina Press, 2006.

Schaffer, Ronald. "The New York City Woman Suffrage Party, 1909–1919." *New York History* (July 1962): 269–87.

Schneider, Dorothy, and Carl J. Schneider. *American Women in the Progressive Era, 1900–1920.* New York: Anchor, 1994.

Schrems, Suzanne H. *Who's Rocking the Cradle?: Women Pioneers of Oklahoma Politics from Socialism to the KKK, 1900–1930.* Norman: Horse Creek, 2004.

Scott, Anne Firor, and Andrew MacKay Scott. *One Half the People: The Fight for Woman Suffrage.* Urbana: University of Illinois Press, 1982.

Scott, Mrs. William Forse. *In Opposition to Woman Suffrage: Paper Read at Albany, February 24, 1909 before the Joint Senate and Assembly Judiciary Committee by Mrs. Wm. Forse Scott, of Yonkers, N.Y.* New York: New York State Association Opposed to Woman Suffrage, 1909.

Shaw, Anna Howard. *The Story of a Pioneer.* New York: Harper, 1915.

Shealy, Gwendolyn. *A Critical History of the American Red Cross, 1882–1945.* Lewiston: Mellen, 2003.

Shupe, Barbara, Janet Steines, and Jyoti Pandit. *New York State Population, 1790–1980: A Compilation of Federal Census Data.* New York: Neal-Schuman, 1987.

Sinclair, Andrew. *The Better Half: The Emancipation of the American Woman.* New York: Harper & Row, 1965.

Sklar, Kathryn Kish. *Catharine Beecher: A Study in American Domesticity.* New Haven, Conn.: Yale University Press, 1973.

———. "The Historical Foundations of Women's Power in the Creation of the American Welfare State, 1830–1930." In *Mothers of a New World*, edited by Seth Koven and Sonya Michel. New York: Routledge, 1993.

———. "Why Were Most Politically Active Women Opposed to the ERA in the 1920s?" In *Women and Power in American History*, edited by Kathryn Kish Sklar and Thomas Dublin, 154–61. Upper Saddle River, N.J.: Prentice Hall, 2002.

Sklar, Kathryn Kish and Beverly Wilson Palmer, ed. *The Selected Letters of Florence Kelley, 1869–1931*. Urbana: University of Illinois Press, 2009.

Skocpol, Theda. *Protecting Soldiers and Mothers: The Political Origins of Social Policy in the United States*. Cambridge, Mass.: Belknap, 1992.

Smith-Rosenberg, Carroll. *Disorderly Conduct: Visions of Gender in Victorian America*. New York: Oxford University Press, 1985.

Solomon, Barbara Miller. *In the Company of Educated Women: A History of Women and Higher Education in America*. New Haven, Conn.: Yale University Press, 1985.

Stanton, Elizabeth Cady, Matilda Joslyn Gage, and Susan B. Anthony. *History of Woman Suffrage*. 6 vols. Vol. II. New York: Fowler & Wells, 1882.

Steele, William H. *Revised Record of the Constitutional Convention of the State of New York*. 5 vols. Vol. II. Albany: Argus, 1900.

Steinson, Barbara J. *American Women's Activism in World War I*. New York: Garland, 1982.

Stevens, Doris. *Jailed for Freedom: American Women Win the Vote*. Troutdale, Ore.: New Sage, 1995 [1920].

Tarbell, Ida M. "Is Woman's Suffrage a Failure?" *Good Housekeeping* 79 (October 1924): 18–19.

Thurner, Manuela. "'Better Citizens without the Ballot': American Anti-Suffrage Women and Their Rationale During the Progressive Era." In *One Woman, One Vote: Rediscovering the Woman Suffrage Movement*, edited by Marjorie Spruill Wheeler, 203–20. Troutdale, Ore.: New Sage, 1995.

United States Senate. "Arguments before the Committee on Privileges and Elections of the United States Senate on Behalf of a Sixteenth Amendment to the Constitution of the United States, Prohibiting the Several States from Disfranchising United States Citizens on Account of Sex." Washington, D.C.: United States Senate, 1878.

Van Voris, Jacqueline. *Carrie Chapman Catt: A Public Life*. New York: Feminist Press at the City University of New York, 1987.

Venet, Wendy Hamand. *A Strong-Minded Woman: The Life of Mary A. Livermore*. Amherst: University of Massachusetts Press, 2005.

Vose, Clement E. *Constitutional Change: Amendment Politics and Supreme Court Litigation since 1900*. Lexington, Ky.: Lexington, 1972.

Wagner, Sally Roesch. *A Time of Protest: Suffragists Challenge the Republic: 1870–1887*. Aberdeen: Sky Carrier, 1992.

Weibe, Robert H. *The Search for Order, 1877–1920*. New York: Wang and Hill, 1967.

Wellman, Judith. "Women's Rights, Republicanism, and Revolutionary Rhetoric in Antebellum New York State." *New York History* 69 (July 1988): 353–84.

Wells, Kate Gannett. "Women in Organizations." *Atlantic Monthly* 46, no. 275 (September 1880): 360–67.

Welter, Barbara. "Cult of True Womanhood, 1820–1860." *American Quarterly* 23 (Summer 1966): 151–74.

Wesser, Robert F. *Charles Evans Hughes: Politics and Reform in New York, 1905–1910.* Ithaca, N.Y.: Cornell University Press, 1967.

———. *A Response to Progressivism: The Democratic Party and New York Politics, 1902–1918.* New York: New York University Press, 1986.

Willard, Frances, and Mary A. Livermore, eds. *A Woman of the Century: Fourteen Hundred-Seventy Biographical Sketches Accompanied by Portraits of Leading American Women in All Walks of Life.* Buffalo, N.Y.: Moulton, 1893.

Women's Anti-Suffrage Association of the Third Judicial District. *Pamphlets Printed and Distributed by the Women's Anti-Suffrage Association of the Third Judicial District of the State of New York, Headquarters at Albany, N.Y.* Littleton, Colo.: Rothman, 1990.

Women's National Republican Club. *Proceedings of the Mock Convention Held at the Waldorf-Astoria Hotel, New York City.* New York: Women's National Republican Club, 1928.

Wood, Mary I. *The History of the General Federation of Woman's Clubs—for the First Twenty-Two Years of the Organization.* Farmingdale, N.Y.: Dabor Social Science, 1978.

Young, Louise M. *In the Public Interest: The League of Women Voters, 1920–1970.* New York: Greenwood, 1989.

Young, Rose. *The Record of the Leslie Woman Suffrage Commission, Inc., 1917–1929.* New York: Leslie Woman Suffrage Commission, 1929.

Zdunczyk, David. *200 Years of the New York State Legislature.* Albany: Albany Institute of History and Art, 1978.

Index

SUSAN GOODIER is scholar-in-residence at Hamilton College and museum consultant at the Matilda Joslyn Gage Foundation in Fayetteville, New York.

Women in American History

The University of Illinois Press
is a founding member of the
Association of American University Presses.

Composed in 11/14 Garamond Premier Pro
by Jim Proefrock
at the University of Illinois Press
Manufactured by Thomson-Shore, Inc.

University of Illinois Press
1325 South Oak Street
Champaign, IL 61820-6903
www.press.uillinois.edu